Daphne

Mizoguchi and Japan

With lo..., ,

Mark

Mizoguchi and Japan

Mark Le Fanu

 Publishing

For Sally and Sylvia.

First published in 2005 by the
BRITISH FILM INSTITUTE
21 Stephen Street, London W1T 1LN

The British Film Institute's purpose is to champion moving image culture in all its richness and
diversity across the UK, for the benefit of as wide an audience as possible, and to create and
encourage debate.

 The publisher gratefully acknowledges the support of the
Japan Foundation in the publication of this book.

Set by Fakenham Photosetting Ltd, Fakenham, Norfolk
Printed in the UK by Cromwell Press, Trowbridge, Wiltshire

Cover design: Ketchup/couch
Cover illustration: *The Life of Oharu* (*Saikaku Ichidai Onna*, 1952), Shintoho Eiga/Koi

British Library Cataloguing-in-Publication Data
A catalogue record for this book is available from the British Library

ISBN 1–84457–057–6 (pbk)
ISBN 1–84457–056–8 (hbk)

Contents

Preface and Acknowledgments

The book you are about to read (or to browse in) is a work of criticism rather than a full-scale biography. It aims to give an interpretative reading of Mizoguchi's thirty-one extant films, on the assumption that they are worth finding out about. Such biographical and historical material as the book contains, therefore, is subordinate to this hermeneutic endeavour. My study is an essay in appreciation, with all the subjectivity that this implies – although it is of course based on extensive research, and I hope will prove informative. I should say up front that I am not a Japanese speaker – but this is no excuse for ignorance, and I hope does not diminish the authority of whatever tentative conclusions I arrive at. The only reason for a writer to pick up his pen in the first place is because he feels an affinity with the matter in hand. Justifiably or not, I feel I understand Mizoguchi. The reader will have to judge for himself or herself whether my confidence is warranted.

It is an interesting but separate question whether film books, in general, are needed any more. With so many calls being made on everyone's time, it could be argued that the essential aid to get hold of is the DVD or set of DVDs; for with them comes access to the wealth of supplementary material (commentaries, extracts, documentaries) which are currently transforming film studies, and making them – for those bitten by the enthusiasm – such an enjoyable contemporary pastime. Actually, Mizoguchi is not well served in the DVD market as yet; but even if he were, there is still, I believe, a place for concentrated literary commentary on cinema. I am only too well aware, however, that to read a whole book is to invest twelve hours (at least) in an author's company. So he, or she, had better be friendly and entertaining!

My reasons for writing about this director are explained in Chapter 1. Just now the continent of Asia is one of the most vibrant film-producing regions in the world, and Mizoguchi forms part of the ancestry of this amazing contemporary efflorescence. I have often wondered whether directors like Hou Hsiao-hsien or Tian Zhuangzhuang or Chen Kaige or Edward Yang have 'studied' Mizoguchi. It is not possible to tell without asking them; but I would maintain that there are spiritual correspondences well worth exploring between their kind of cinema (in all its different varieties) and the sort of engaged aesthetic seriousness that Mizoguchi stands for.

Yet it is not, after all, only Asian films that are relevant. Many times I have had the feeling in watching contemporary films which appeal to me that their essence, too, is Mizoguchian in mysterious but definite ways. I think, for example, of a whole strand of British cinema: the best strand, in my opinion – the corner of culture that is represented by movies like Ken Loach's *Sweet 16* (2002), or Gary Oldman's *Nil by Mouth* (1997), or Tim Roth's *The War Zone* (1999), or Peter Mullan's *Orphans* (1999), works in which there is still an appeal to the seriousness of life, and to the ability of cinema to reflect upon it in a way that is sober and compassionate, and uncorrupted by contemporary sentimentality.

The opinions expressed in this book are my own, of course, but many people have been generous with their time in helping me in my research. I welcome the opportunity to thank them here. An earlier version of 'The Great Triptych' chapter appeared in the *Cambridge Quarterly*; I would like to thank the editor and trustees of that journal for permission to reprint it here (in slightly altered form). More generally, my book owes much, I hope, to the spirit of the late John Gillett who programmed marvellous seasons of Japanese movies at the NFT throughout the 1970s and 80s, including the first Mizoguchi retrospective (spring 1978) I attended (absent without leave from duties in Cambridge) with my friend Eric Griffiths. Subsequently, in Japan itself on short visits in the 1990s, I was lucky enough to come into contact with Donald Richie, doyen of Japanese cinema studies, who provided me with the kind of encouragement and access that every researcher needs. Another doyen of Mizoguchi studies, Tadao Sato, lent me a French translation of his excellent book on the director. I have benefited from reading it, and thank him for it.

The second of my visits to Japan was sponsored by a grant from the Japan Foundation, among whose staff I remember Tomozo Yano and Marie Suzuki with especial fondness for the friendly aid they provided. Hideo Fujita of the Japanese embassy in Copenhagen helped to arrange this bursary. Phillida Purvis of the Daiwa Anglo–Japanese Foundation was most helpful in setting up contacts. Mark Schilling, in Tokyo, was a font of useful local knowledge, generously put at my disposal. Acknowledgment, too, should be extended to the manager, librarian and staff of the International House of Japan in Roppongi who combined to make my stay in Japan an extremely pleasant one. In Tokyo, on the same trip, I re-forged an acquaintance made a few years earlier with Hisashi Okajima, curator of film at the National Film Center who (together with his staff) was helpful to me in arranging Mizoguchi screenings. Those films I could not find *there*, I found through the kind offices of Kanako Hayashi at the always cooperative Kawakita Memorial Film Institute. As a non-speaker of Japanese, I was greatly aided by the interpretive skills of Chiharu Uda and Masumichi Kanaya, and above all by my friend Mayumi Shimizu. (Further literary translations, back in Denmark and England, were provided by the kind assistance of Keiichi Ishibori of the University of Århus, and by Shoku Noguchi.) Masao Yamauchi, magician and astrologist, gave me contacts in Kyoto, including those that led me to surviving members of Mizoguchi's family. Back in Europe once again, my trawl for videos and DVDs of the films I had just seen – and others – was aided by Peter von Bagh in Finland, Tag Gallagher and Dan Talbot in America, Hubert Niogret and Marie Chené in Paris, and Nick Wrigley in the United Kingdom: I would like to thank them all for this eminently practical assistance.

During the first part of 2003, the European Film College gave me time off to complete a draft of this book, leave that was funded by Denmark's Undervisnings Ministeriet, and made memorable for me by the generosity of Jens and Marianne Engberg who lent me their house in the Aveyron to write in. Rick Senat encouraged me to get on with the task, and was immensely helpful behind the scenes. Later, at manuscript stage, Lesley Downer and Christopher Silvester read sections of the book and provided many helpful suggestions. Errors of fact that remain, needless to say, are mine not theirs. The completed text was read by Sally Laird, a rigorous copy editor. The assembling of a book like this takes time and care. I would like to thank my editor and designer Sophia Contento for the courteous efficiency with which she handled all aspects of preparation of the manuscript. Stephen McEnally, Tomozo Yano's successor at the London office of the Japan Foundation, was incredibly supportive: the few but necessary colour images in the text are due to his efforts.

The greatest debt of all (besides that unrepayable debt which I owe my family) I owe to Kimitoshi Sato, art critic and music lover, whose knowledge of Japanese life and culture have allowed me to navigate certain corners of the argument that follows with a confidence that I would otherwise have been hard put to mount. Every writer needs a friend such as this: someone he can test his ideas upon – an 'interlocutor' whose calm intelligence assuages fears and injects the project with energy.

Chronology

1898 16 May: Born in the Hongo district of Tokyo to Zentaro and Maso Mizoguchi; father a carpenter and roofer by profession (possibly of samurai ancestry).

1905 Birth of younger brother Yoshio.

Family moves to Asakusa district in downtown Tokyo in the wake of a failed business venture by Zentaro to supply raincoats to troops in the Russo–Japanese War. Kenji's older sister Suzu (born in 1891) is put up for adoption.

1906 Enrols in Ishihama primary school where his later colleague Matsutaro Kawaguchi is a fellow pupil.

1909 14 April: Yoshikata Yoda (scriptwriter) born. 29 December: Kinuyo Tanaka (actress) born.

1911 Formal schooling ends. Spends a year with pharmacist relative in Morioka (Iwate prefecture, northern Japan).

1912 Back in Tokyo. Year of illness.

Suzu becomes Nihonbashi geisha.

1913 Apprenticed to a company that designs *yukata* (light summer kimonos).

Suzu becomes mistress of Viscount Madsudaira.

1914 Moves out of family home to Nihonbashi, near to Suzu. New design apprenticeship.

1915 Mother dies. Together with Yoshio, moves into Suzu's house.

1916 Supported by Suzu, enrols in Aoibashi Yoga Kenkyujo (academy of Western-style painting) in Akasaka, central Tokyo. Through the academy becomes involved in set design for the Royal Theatre, Akasaka.

1917 Moves to Kobe to work in the publicity and sales department of the Kobe Yuishin Nippo newspaper; contributes poetry and articles to its 'Arts and performance' pages.

5 February: Birth of Isuzu Yamada (actress).

1918 Returns to Tokyo; begins to study the *biwa* with Tomioka Takashi, who works at the Nikkatsu film studio in Mukojima, eastern Tokyo.

1919 Year of study: libraries, museums, galleries, opera.

1920 First employment in the film industry: enters Nikkatsu as a protégé of director Osamu Wakayama.

1921 Becomes assistant to Tadashi Oguchi ('my first real master').

1922 Becomes assistant to Eiji Tanaka. Strike in the studio by *onnagata* (male actors specialising in female roles) gives Mizoguchi first shot at directing.

1923 February: release of first film, *The Resurrection of Love/Ai ni Yomigaeru Hi*.

May: his fifth film, *The Sad Song of Failure/Haizan no Uta Wa Kanashi*, is an immediate hit with the public.

July: good critical reception for his seventh film, *Foggy Harbour/Kiri no Minato*, adapted from Eugene O'Neill's *Anna Christie*.

1 September: great Kanto earthquake devastates Tokyo. Kenji rescues his father and his sister's child and takes them to safety at Mukojima. With cameraman Kige Seigo, he tours Tokyo recording the destruction. This documentary footage is spliced into his next film, *In the Ruins/Haikyo no Naka*, released in October and sold abroad.

1924 Directs nine films for Nikkatsu at their new studios in Taishogun (Kyoto), none of which survive.

1925 Mizoguchi makes his first surviving film, *The Song of Home/Furusato no Uta*.

During the shooting of another (lost) film, *Shining in the Red Sunset/Akai Yuhi ni Terasarete*, Mizoguchi is attacked by his then-lover Yuriko Ichijo, who slashes him across the back with a razor. In the ensuing scandal, Mizoguchi is cashiered by Nikkatsu for six months.

1926 Six films by Mizoguchi released, among them *A Paper Doll's Whisper of Spring/Kaminingyo Haru no Sasayaki* and *The Passion of a Woman Teacher/Kyoren no Onna Shisho* (neither survives).

1927 Marries Osakan dancer and bar hostess Chieko Saga.

1929 High point of proletarian movement in the arts. Four films by Mizoguchi released, among them a (now lost) 'tendency film', *Metropolitan Symphony/Tokai Kokyagaku*, and *Tokyo March/Tokyo Koshinkyoku*, which survives in a fragment. Yoda, at that time employed at a bank, is imprisoned and tortured for left-wing activities.

1930 Mizoguchi's first sound film, *Home Town/Furusato*, released.

1931 September: Manchurian Incident.

1932 Leaves Nikkatsu for Shinko. Works there for Takako Irie's production company.

1934 Sound films finally become the universal norm in Japan.

1935 Death of Zentaro (father).

Moves to newly formed production company Daiichi Eiga. First collaboration with Isuzu Yamada (*The Downfall of Osen/Orizuru Osen*).

1936 Becomes secretary of the newly formed Japan Screen Directors' Association.

Shoots two landmark films, *Osaka Elegy/Naniwa Erejii* and *Sisters of the Gion/Gion no Shimai*, both scripted by Yoda.

1937 Moves back to Shinko after Daiichi Eiga goes bankrupt.

Becomes chairman of the Japan Screen Directors' Association after the death of incumbent Minoru Murata.

Japan goes to war with China (July).

1938 Invited by old Nikkatsu colleague Iwao Mori to join a newly founded studio, Toho, but declines.

Death of Yoshio (brother).

1939 Leaves Shinko for Shochiku. Moves his official residence from Kyoto back to Tokyo. Appointed adviser to the government on film matters.

1940 Becomes president of the Japan Screen Directors' Association.

November: attends official ceremony to mark the 2,600th year of the foundation of Japan.

1941 Wife Chieko goes mad and is hospitalised.

1 December: Release of part one of *The Loyal 47 Ronin/Genroku Chushingura*, which wins the special prize from the Ministry of Education (but temporarily bankrupts Shochiku).

8 December: Japan attacks Pearl Harbor.

1942 Appointed president administrator of the Association of Cinema of Greater Japan.

1943 July: Trip to China with Yoshikata Yoda to scout locations for a national policy film that is never made.

Relocates once again to Kyoto.

Chieko's brother, cameraman Matsu Tajima, killed in an air crash.

1945 August: Hiroshima and Nagasaki bombed. War ends.

September: Occupation authorities set up film policy unit: until 1949, all Japanese films need to pass American censorship at the script stage and again prior to release.

1946 Mizoguchi elected president of the Ofuna-Shochiku branch of the newly formed Theatre and Cinema Workers' Union. Resigns almost immediately to concentrate on film-making.

1948 Industrial unrest in the Japanese film industry, especially at Toho Studio.

1949 Elected president of the (purged, reformulated and renamed) Japan Screen Directors' Association. Ends his association with Shochiku.

1951 Akira Kurosawa's *Rashomon* wins Golden Lion at the Venice Film Festival.

Marries his wife's sister-in-law, Mrs Fuji (widow of Matsuo Tajima), and adopts her two children, Takara and Mine.

1952 *The Life of Oharu/Saikaku Ichidai Onna* (Shintoho Studio) wins Silver Lion at Venice.

1953 *Ugetsu Monogatari* wins the Silver Lion at Venice (Golden Lion not awarded). Mizoguchi attends the festival.

1954 Elected to the board of Daiei Studios.

July: Visits New York and Hollywood.

September: *Sansho the Bailiff/Sansho Dayu* wins Silver Lion at Venice.

1955 Shoots *The Empress Yang Kwei Fei/ Yokihi* and *Tales of the Taira Clan/ Shinheike Monogatari*, his only two films in colour.

1956 March: *Street of Shame/Akasen Chitai* released.

May: hospitalised in Kyoto with advanced leukemia.

24 August: Dies at 1.55 pm, aged fifty eight.

Mizoguchi's Extant Films

The Song of Home/Furusato no Uta (1925)
Tokyo March/Tokyo Koshinkyoku (1929)
Home Town/Furusato (1930)
The Water Magician/Taki no Shiraito (1933)
The Downfall of Osen/Orizuru Osen (1935)
Oyuki Madonna/Maria no Oyuki (1935)
Poppy/Gubijinso (1935)
Osaka Elegy/Naniwa Erejii (1936)
Sisters of the Gion/Gion no Shimai (1936)
The Straits of Love and Hate/Aien Kyo (1937)
The Story of Late Chrysanthemums/Zangiku Monogatari (1939)
The Loyal 47 Ronin/Genroku Chushingura (Two parts: 1941–2)
Musashi Miyamoto/Miyamoto Musashi (1944)
The Famous Sword Bijomaru/Meito Bijomaru (1945)
The Victory of Women/Josei no Shori (1946)
Five Women Round Utamaro/Utamaro o Meguru Gonin no Onna (1946)
The Love of Sumako the Actress/Joyu Sumako no Koi (1947)
Women of the Night/Yoru no Onnatachi (1948)
My Love Has Been Burning/Waga Koi Wa Moenu (1949)
A Picture of Madame Yuki/Yuki Fujin Ezu (1950)
Miss Oyu/Oyusama (1950)
The Lady from Musashino/Musashino Fujin (1951)
The Life of Oharu/Saikaku Ichidai Onna (1952)
Tales of the Watery Moon/Ugetsu Monogatari (1953)
Gion Festival Music/Gion Bayashi (1953)
Sansho the Bailiff/Sansho Dayu (1954)
The Woman of Rumour/Uwasa no Onna (1954)
Crucified Lovers/Chikamatsu Monogatari (1954)
The Empress Yang Kwei Fei/Yokihi (1955)
Tales of the Taira Clan/Shinheike Monogatari (1955)
Street of Shame/Akasen Chitai (1956)

1 | Why Mizoguchi?

A true appreciation of art is always to some extent pluralistic. It would be as odd to come across a connoisseur of paintings who only and exclusively loved Picasso (for example) as it would be to come across a lover of music whose knowledge and appreciation began and ended with Wagner. It's almost a prerequisite of knowing such artists deeply for there to be other artists in the mind's eye – predecessors and contemporaries – with whom to compare them. So it is with cinema. Everyone, of course, is entitled to have their favourites, but we know from experience that such preferences shift around radically at different stages of life. The plausible contestants for the title 'greatest film director of all time' probably amount to no more than a dozen names (and maybe even this is being generous). But I think – or I hope – that it's possible to love all these great artists in different ways. So it might be that in attending a season of Bergman films at a national cinematheque, it becomes obvious, subjectively, that no one has ever grasped human psychology with such wit and penetration and intelligence as this (still living) Nordic master has; which will not stop the true film buff from changing his allegiance to the no less wonderful films of Satyajit Ray (or John Ford or Jean Renoir) when *they* in turn are showcased in well-mounted retrospectives.

It's never been contested that Kenji Mizoguchi (1898–1956) is among the greatest masters that the medium has ever known; but if this is so, he belongs nonetheless – along with directors like Bresson, Murnau, Dreyer and Ophuls – to the obscurer shadows of the inner sanctum. People know about him more than they know his actual work. Indeed, he is almost certainly less well known than his fellow countrymen Kurosawa and Ozu, about whom well-researched studies and biographies have long existed in print. By contrast, there has not been an English-language study of Mizoguchi's cinema taken as a whole since the monograph written by Keiko McDonald twenty years ago – which is as good a reason as any, I hope, for approaching him now.

Despite this relative obscurity, there is a feeling in the air that Mizoguchi is alive and relevant. The season of Mizoguchi's films curated by James Quandt of the Ontario Cinemathèque in 1996 during the run-up to his centenary had an unprecedented success in North America, touring twelve cities with sell-out screenings in each of them; while Mizoguchi's centenary itself (1998) was celebrated in England by a correspondingly record-breaking retrospective at the National Film Theatre that sold over 15,000 tickets. Nearly fifty years after his death, it appears that his cinema still has something to teach us. Partly this is a spiritual apprehension (as it also is with Ozu, surely): his films have an extraordinary force and purity. They shake and move the viewer by the power, refinement and compassion with which they confront human suffering. Thus there is a subject there – to which

Like light from a distant star: a party of travellers pick their way through the forest in *Sansho the Bailiff* (1954)

this book in different ways (and with different degrees of explicitness) will attempt to do justice. But there is also the matter of Mizoguchi's style: a specific way of setting up his scenes that speaks forcibly and directly over the gap of years to the modern viewer: the serious modern viewer, that is, who takes world cinema, and not just Hollywood, as the object of his interest and curiosity. So I think it is worth making the claim right at the beginning of this book that Mizoguchi is perhaps the greatest master ever of the method of shooting known as *extended sequence* or long-take composition – the very method, coincidentally, that is the signature of many of the most interesting contemporary film directors; in different ways of course (everyone's signature is at least slightly different), as well as for different reasons, and towards different ends: but united in opposition to that other mode of contemporary film-making which relies for *its* effects on multiple alternation of camera angles, rapid-fire editing and unremitting pace of delivery.

Is this perhaps the contrast itself between art-house cinema and commercial or entertainment-based programming? It is tempting to think so. For the time being, however, I would like simply to take note of the opposition, without drawing anything-like-polemical conclusions.[1] The comparable artists on Mizoguchi's side of the fence are directors like Chantal Akerman and Theo Angelopoulos, Peter Greenaway and Raul Ruiz, Victor Erice and Arturo Ripstein: virtuosi both of the extended 'still life' (that is, the camera held motionless on a scene for an extended timespan, without changing to different focal setups) and also of the choreographed tracking arabesque. Before *them* came Tarkovsky, and Jancsó, and Rainer Werner Fassbinder and Frederick Wiseman; and back in the 1950s and 60s there were others (Dreyer, Antonioni, Kazan, Preminger, Cassavetes). There has always been a tradition in France for this kind of patient, elaborate and concentrated 'one-scene-one-take' *mise en scène*: Jacques Rivette, Jacques Doillon, Maurice Pialat, Catherine Breillat, Raymond Depardon, Gaspar Noé and Bruno Dumont spring to mind; from Russia, there are contemporary directors such as Alexandr Sokurov (*Russian Ark* was shot entirely in a single take lasting ninety minutes); also the wonderful documentarists Victor Kossakovsky and Sergei Dvortsevoy; from Iran, Abbas Kiarostami, Mohsen Makhmalbaf, Jafar Panahi; from the Far East, Hou Hsiao-hsien, Tsai Ming-liang, Edward Yang. From Austria, Michael Haneke, Ulrich Seidl. And 'one-offs' as well: from Palestine, Elia Suleiman; from Georgia (via Paris), Otar Iosseliani; from Hungary, Bela Tarr; from England, Mike Grigsby (another documentarist). A whole raft of names in short, all of them – in one way or another – resplendent.

It goes without saying that the cinema which emerges in its different ways from this preference for the long take makes heavy demands on the viewer: minimalism, in any form, can be

---

1   In a recent letter in *Sight and Sound*, the indefatigable Barry Salt provides some interesting figures:

Your reviewer of *Requiem for a Dream* doesn't know recent American films are cut a lot faster than the 600–700 shots per minute he claims. In fact, in a sample of 512 US films from the years 1994 to 1997, the average number of shots per 100 minutes is 1,100. Darren Aronofsky [director of *Requiem for a Dream*] is boasting about getting 2,000 shots into his 100-minute movie, but even *Free Willy 2* could get across the bay faster, not to mention *The Little Rascals* (2,222 shots per 100 minutes) and dear little *Matilda* (2,400 shots per 100 minutes). And dozens of action movies in the sample go even faster, up to the equivalent of 3,000 shots in 100 minutes (for example, Serge Rodnunsky's *Diamonds in the Rough* of 1996).

Salt concludes: 'There has been a continuous movement towards faster and faster cutting in American films over the last 50 years, and most other countries have followed this trend.'

uncomfortable. There are times when such a mode of directing seems to simply slip into arid for-malism. When it does not work it can be boring and aggravating. One can feel sympathetic to the oft-voiced verdict: 'Watching *X* is like watching paint dry.' Yet, conversely, when such methods really do work, there is simply nothing to compare to them.[2]

Sometimes, it's almost as if patience with the long take – a sense of its sombre existence (even if the director isn't actually *using* it the whole time) – is the precondition for cinema saying any-thing powerful at all. I mean by this last, slightly paradoxical, parenthesis to make an important distinction: there are film-makers whose use of the long take is categorical and puristic: that is their style, that is what they always do (Angelopoulos and Jancsó are examples); and there are film-makers (Godard, Welles, Kiarostami, Wong Kar-wai perhaps) whose liking for the device goes hand in hand with a complementary skill in editing, montage, concision itself. Mizoguchi himself in dif-ferent films and at different stages of his career utilised the long take puristically (for example, in *The Story of Late Chrysanthemums/Zangiku Monogatari* [1939] and *The Loyal 47 Ronin/Genroku Chushingura*) and less puristically (throughout the post-war masterpieces – *Oharu, Ugetsu, Sansho*); and as far as I am concerned, there is no issue of quality in the preference. One way of deploying the mode is not necessarily better than the other. In short, stylistic consistency across a single movie is undoubtedly a value, but it is not the only value; as I have just said, reliance on the long take has to be balanced against the dangers of formalism. Yet whether the long take is deployed consist-ently throughout a film, or whether it is used sparingly but intelligently, it seems able to bring something to the possibility of cinema of which other forms of *mise en scène* are incapable.

So what *are* these magic properties denied to rapid-cutting MTV-style films? In brief, the long take draws us into the scene in question with a particular dramatic force and intimacy. Delivering the audience over, as it does, to real time, it delivers us over to the suspense and awkwardness that present-tense drama entails: the sense that the outcome of the scene *hasn't yet been settled*, that it is still in the air, and that we are somehow complicit in making it land rightly.

Take an example, from Jacques Becker's famous prison drama *Le Trou* (1961). The five men in the cell are making their first bid for freedom: a concrete floor has to be smashed through in order to link up with a passage leading to the underground sewers. The men have managed to fashion a crowbar of sorts from one of their bedsteads, and Becker holds the camera in close-up on the little patch of floor as the first blows of this improvised hammer rain down on the grimly resisting concrete. No editing or elision is desirable or possible here, since the point of the scene is to emphasise the brute difficulty – actually, the rank impossibility – of the task the desperate men have set themselves. We watch as the crowbar gouges the first thin chips of concrete out of the

---

2   The long take plays a special role in films that are specifically about painting. In a moment I will discuss Mizoguchi's *Five Women Round Utamaro*; here I limit myself to mentioning a few films in which the artist's patient gaze acts as a kind of 'double' or metaphorical substitute for the film-maker's own patient curiosity: *La Belle Noiseuse* (Jacques Rivette, 1991), *Van Gogh* (Maurice Pialat, 1991), *The Quince Tree Sun* (Victor Erice, 1992), *Chihwaseon/Drunk on Women and Painting* (Im Kwon-taek, 2003): long scenes in each of these movies are devoted to watching the craftsman apply paint (or charcoal) to the canvas. These sequences are all about process and therefore they belong *spiritually* to the type of cinema I am discussing here – even in those cases where the film-maker has employed some deft cheating (and 'cheating' here is only another word for editing) in order to disguise the fact that the canvas is actually being worked on by someone other than the actor who is playing the painter.

shining flat surface, gradually indenting it until it begins to form, in front of our eyes, the existential 'hole' of the film's title. I can't believe I am the only admirer of Becker to believe that the scene which emerges here is one of the most exciting and *philosophical* sequences in the whole of French cinema; indeed (it is tempting to put it extravagantly) in the whole of cinema *tout court*.

The agonising suspense that informs this scene and others in Becker's film is the same suspense, *mutatis mutandis*, that Catherine Breillat makes use of in order to underline the unbearableness of first love in such remarkable studies of adolescent sexuality as *36 Fillette* (1987) and *À nos amours* (2000). In each of these films, the central scene involves an extraordinarily powerfully imagined seduction of a teenage girl by an older man, played out in real time, with all the myriad silent changes of mood that such encounters entail in real life (on either side, but particularly on the part of the young girl of course). It is as if, in such sequences, we were watching, or being made to watch, some documentary transcript of the soul. Breillat in these scenes takes her audience to the brink of what may legitimately be imagined in cinema – *as* cinema: a freedom, it has sometimes been objected, that is perilously close to pornography. (It may be worth underlining the obvious, that pornography itself relies for *its* impact on the sustained gaze of the film-maker manipulating photographed rituals in not dissimilar slices of real time.)

Sometimes it is possible to feel that the existence of only one such sequence in a whole movie is enough to make the drama come alive. If the director can do *this*, we can usually justifiably infer that he (or she) can do all the other important things as well. Thus (to take a contemporary instance) the populist facility of a successful film like *Y tu mamá también* (Alfonso Cuarón, 2001) seems to me tamed and tempered – converted into something that really does approach art – by the film's miraculously controlled penultimate sequence, in which the three main characters, slumped round a table, at nightfall, in some godforsaken *estaminet*, drunkenly open up their hearts to each other with a candour and depth whose authenticity absolutely depends upon the fact that we are continually in their presence for seven and a half minutes without a single camera cut. Similarly, a run-of-the-mill police and legal procedural like Sidney Lumet's *Q & A* (1990) seems to me to be completely transformed – elevated into a fascinatingly complex piece of psycho-theatre – by just two or three confrontations (that is, arranged meetings, with lawyers present) where the combined acting talents of Armand Assante (playing a Latino gangster), Timothy Hutton (a straight cop, in deep water) and Nick Nolte (a 'bent' cop, and the latter's nemesis) are given full scope and measure by nothing less than the imperturbable authority of the camera's motionless, inquisitorial gravity. That particular film, I would guess, is not widely known – not even available on DVD – but the inclusion in it of these few episodes is enough by itself to 'fast-track' the movie into the top tier of the director's filmography.

Among modern movies, it is interesting to compare in this context Kubrick's *Eyes Wide Shut* (1999) with Michael Haneke's controversial study of sado-masochism, *The Piano Teacher* (2001). Both these films are 'difficult', in conventional parlance. Both have had their detractors (as well as their strong supporters): neither film was universally praised when it appeared. What is not controversial, I suppose, is that they are serious dramas (rich in cameo and in incidental detail), and that in their different ways they make a sophisticated shot at dealing with the phenomenology of a woman's inner sexual demons. Needless to say, Nicole Kidman and Isabelle Huppert are actresses of the very highest quality. Yet if Haneke's film gives the impression of going further than

Kubrick's, of mining depths which, in this instance, Kubrick does not plumb, it is at least partly because Haneke's one-scene-one-take *mise en scène* (in contrast to Kubrick's preference for edited montage) gives him the decisive edge, enabling him not just to talk about that terror which is at the basis of all drama, but to *find* it, and present it to us with unforgettable brilliance.

Bazin, Mizoguchi and Japanese Cinema

Earlier, I stated more or less openly that Mizoguchi's cinema gives us some of the most perfect instances of this method that have ever been committed to celluloid. The reader may wonder whether, or how, such a contention can ever be proven. The historical dimension of the argument has already been touched upon. Cinema itself was born with the long take, in the sense that editing wasn't developed until the late 1890s, some five years after the invention of the kinetoscope itself. The very earliest films, issued by Edison and the Lumières dating from the mid-1890s, are each less than sixty seconds long, but because they are shot and presented without cuts, they have a concentrated purity about them, a resplendence, that has survived intact to the present day. Starting from Griffith's move to Biograph in 1908, and the American public's subsequent perceived desire to 'have the story told faster', the whole history of the refinement and development of editing techniques can be seen, from one point of view, as a graduated assault on the rigidity and static-ness of the original bare, stagey, theatrical long take, in its Edisonian or Lumière-like incarnation. Yet even while these developments were taking place (it goes without saying that it's a long and complicated story, differing from nation to nation, not at all linear and straightforward), there remained among certain film-makers what one might call a *nostalgia for the long take*, an instinctive appreciation of its hidden beauties – long before those beauties (those qualities) became the subject for reflection and theory.

The greatest theorist of the long take I think was André Bazin (1918–1958): a profoundly historically minded film critic (the breed is actually quite rare) who, in his capacity as editor of *Cahiers du Cinéma* in its heyday, was at the same time a full-time reviewer of his contemporaries. Bazin outlined a teleological view of the importance of the long take in cinema's development which saw it progress from its original pristine innocence at the time of Edison and the Lumières, through a period of sublimation and repression in the 1920s and 30s (at which time, following Griffith and Eisenstein, editing and montage became the rage), to the re-discovery of its vital possibilities in the deep-focus cinema of such modern masters (I mean modern at the time Bazin was writing) as Orson Welles, William Wyler and John Ford. (He might have added – only he never cared for the director much – the Hitchcock of *Rope* [1948] and *Under Capricorn* [1949].)

Where, if anywhere, does Japan fit into this scenario? Bazin came late to the discovery of Japanese cinema, as Japanese cinema itself, you could say, came late to the consciousness of the West. 'The beauty of their film reaches us with delay, like that of light from distant stars,' he writes in a characteristically poetic essay entitled 'The Lesson of Japanese Cinema Style' that appeared in the Parisian cultural weekly *Arts* early in 1955.[3] A year away from his death, Mizoguchi isn't mentioned in the essay: it's part of the above-mentioned 'delay factor' that Bazin had only just come across him. (The main references in the essay are to Kurosawa.) Still, it is impossible not to feel that the affinity Bazin expresses for Japan could be anything other than confirmed by acquaintance with

---

3   Quoted in André Bazin, *The Cinema of Cruelty from Buñuel to Hitchcock* (1982), p. 184.

this 'master of masters' whose method of working coincides so completely with Bazin's deepest stylistic predilections. *The Loyal 47 Ronin* (1941–2), unreleased in the West at the time Bazin was writing his essay, is entirely constructed in the one-scene-one-take shooting style that Bazin describes so marvellously – far more radical, in this sense, than anything heretofore attempted by Welles or by Wyler (of course I am not saying therefore *better*). The origin of the style in Mizoguchi's cinema will be examined when we look at films like *The Water Magician/Taki no Shiraito* (1933) and the two masterpieces dating from 1936, *Osaka Elegy/Naniwa Erejii* and *Sisters of the Gion/Gion no Shimai*. Here it seems important simply to state as best I can why, in my view, the method works so beautifully in Mizoguchi's hands. And that is quite difficult of course. Significant aesthetic achievements are usually cumulative. The long take is not a formula – by which I mean that when it is *merely* a formula it is neither interesting nor worthy of study. From many possible instances in Mizoguchi's work, let us take and examine a single example, from a relatively unknown film, *Victory of Women/Josei no Shori* (1946).

Victory of Women

The setting is Tokyo in the immediate post-war era, a period of poverty and shortages and harsh struggle for existence, coinciding with an agonising spiritual reappraisal of the values (fanaticism, blind obedience, wilful worship of tradition) that had so recently tipped Japan into disaster. Kinuyo Tanaka plays a liberal female lawyer whose wartime lover was imprisoned by the regime, and who is now fighting on all fronts for a change in mentality, issuing a 'wake-up call' for the new emerging democracy – in short, for a decisive break with the past and past practices. In an important scene, a woman whom we have already briefly seen (played by Mitsuko Miura) has come to call on the lawyer, in the evening, at her private lodgings. The visitor clearly has something on her mind: as the conversation progresses, it emerges that the baby we earlier saw her nursing has suddenly died. Not so surprising perhaps in those days of want and of easy infection: there must have been many such stories. Hiroko, the lawyer, sits quietly and listens with patience and friendliness to the woman's tale as it unfolds. But there is a kind of flaw in it – somehow it is not quite as it seems on the surface. How can we be so sure, even before the dialogue teases out the real truth of what has happened, that, from the depths of her distress, the woman we have been listening to is the bearer of a terrible secret? How is it that this secret – that she has smothered her child on her breast – does not need to be *confessed* to us, the attentive viewer, in order for us to register it? There is a kind of miracle of discretion at play here, the ingredients of which may be separately identifiable, but the combination of which remains difficult to analyse.

One key element in the scene's success is that it is played out in real time, without cuts. We are present witnesses, as we would be in watching a play; and only *because* we are thus present can the epiphany strike or take fire. Acting is a second ingredient: here, as always, so subtle, restrained, completely without melodrama. Then, camera position: it is characteristic of such scenes in Mizoguchi's work that the camera at first stands back in long shot, separate from the subject, presaging, here, the documentary technique of 'fly on the wall'. It is motionless too, and therefore attentive; but the attention is delicate and reserved – the opposite of importunate. Crucially, no interposed close-up (either on the lawyer or on her visitor) 'cues' the emotion or brusquely tells the audience what to think. As Bazin remarked in analysing a similar scene from *The Magnificent*

Ambersons (1947) (the scene where Georgie Miniver scoffs the strawberry shortcake in the company of mournful Aunt Fanny), the rhetorical figure which comes closest to describing such a *mise en scène* is *litotes*, or understatement – closely linked, in its way, to ellipsis.

> The counteremphasis of the subject has rarely been pushed as far: I mean by this, the refusal to let the spectator see the climactic events of the scene . . . [In *The Magnificent Ambersons*] the entire film is partially pulled out of our reach, and all the action seems to be surrounded by an aura of inaccessibility.[4]

Inaccessible, but at the same time 'present' – as powerfully present as if we were dreaming! This sounds, of course, like a contradiction, but it is the best way I can think of to describe it.

'Hors champ'

The heightened sense of awareness that grips the viewer in the presence of such typical sequences from Mizoguchi's work is at least partially explained by the curiosity we feel concerning the off-screen space lying outside the spectator's direct line of vision. In one way, we are definitely *in* the room along with the participants of the drama. But we can only physically see so much: no matter how wide the angle of the lens, we can't see as much as if we were *really* there. This concealed

---

4   *Orson Welles: A Critical View* (1978), footnote to p. 73.

area denied to our view – what the French call the *hors champ* – expanding outwards on each side of the screen and curving backwards in an arc to take in the space behind the camera/spectator, is dramatically alive as long as the camera is running: indeed, the longer the camera is running without a cut or change of angle, the *more* charged and mysterious, the more incipiently 'active' this negative space becomes: it is almost another element of the dramaturgy.

We can relate these observations to painting. A few years ago the art historian Anne Hollander wrote a book called *Moving Pictures* which has become, in certain circles, something of a classic. In it, she re-examines the tradition of Western figurative art from the point of view of a critic who delights particularly in paintings (or drawings and illustrations) where the action is all *in potentia*: scenes where the dramatic action on display has not yet, as it were, unfolded its full course; in which, contrary to painting's usually stressed immobility, there is an element of latent movement (hence, partly, the book's punning title). It is impossible here to detail all the implications of Anne Hollander's far-reaching and influential thesis, among which the most notable is a kind of radical re-ordering of the hierarchy of painting itself, moving away from the perfection of the finished com-position towards a fuller appreciation of the merits of the sketch, the fragment, the unfinished work (because, by her definition, any action depicted, to be interesting, is *always* unfinished and partial, always encoded in time, always allegorical of movement that has not yet arrived at its zenith). Sub-versive, too – at least contrary to the old modernist pieties – is her liking for figurative art in the first place, let alone art that tells a story, art that is anecdotal and narrative; a preference that goes hand in hand with an unfashionable revaluation of 'minor' forms such as tapestry, poster art and book illustration. The woodcut too: although the book is essentially about Western art, what Hollander has to say about Japan (in the few brief paragraphs she devotes to the subject) is particularly intrigu-ing because of the way it highlights a tradition of graphic art that, more than almost any other one can think of, thrives on compositions whose main subject matter (the stern of a wooden boat, the curved expanse of a parasol, the fragment of peach blossom subtended from the branch of a tree) is at once *enlarged* and *truncated*, sliced off at the frame, leaving the viewer to imagine the much larger mass that the object is part of. It seems that before the close-up in cinema was invented, it was a defining feature of Japanese art. Size is troubling: there is often a double take in these wood-cuts – what exactly *is it* that we are looking at? And then again, in relation to the *hors champ*, since the part is substituted for the whole, the viewer is enticed into the aesthetic game by the task of reconstructing his or her own version of the missing seven-eighths of the print: the mass that extends out of sight, on either side, far beyond the limits of the picture frame.

The type of composition described here, one that Japan excelled in, must have owed something to the invention of photography (unless photography owes something to *it*!). I refer here not so much to the formal, posed studio photograph as to the casualness of the snapshot in the context, particularly, of city street scenes and of the bustle of modern life. In busy metropolitan thorough-fares, each containing a multitude of moving vehicles in the foreground and in the distance, there is no control as to what is, and is not, in the frame at any given moment. So, the rump of a horse or the rear wheel of a carriage, fleetingly and unwittingly caught by the camera, can intrude its ungainly beauty into the overall asymmetry of the frame, contributing to the general effect of ran-domness, dispersal, contingency that was so admired and emulated by (among others) the French Impressionists. Photography's underground affinity to the subject matter of Japanese prints is only one consideration, however; even more interesting is to extend that idea *forward* to the borders of cinema itself. At the risk of portentousness, one could go so far as to ask are 'Japan' and 'cinema' not *themselves* curiously congruous? I'm thinking here initially of the importance in Japanese aesthetics of the screen itself, both as an object of poetic contemplation, and as an integral part of the movable, slatted, partitioned make-up of the typical Japanese dwelling area.

The Japanese Screen

To stand in front of one of those great seventeenth-century painted screens, depicting for example a panorama of Edo or Yoshiwara street life, is to feel drawn, irresistibly, into a proto-cinematic space, the experience of which is not that different from the pleasure of reading and deciphering any cinema, but widescreen cinema in particular. Mizoguchi's career was coming to an end when, through the process of CinemaScope, commercial theatrical screens were doubling their widths; but he had seen the first of these efforts, *The Robe*, in Venice in 1953 and the signs are that, had he lived, he would certainly have wanted to experiment with the new Scope technology. His last large-scale costume movie, *Tales of the Taira Clan/Shinheike Monogatari* (1955), was photographed, in the event, in standard ratio, but – inspired by Scope's possibilities – Mizoguchi had instructed his cameraman Miyagawa to conjure up in his compositions, if he could, the atmosphere and characteristics of yet another proto-cinematic Japanese artwork, the rolling scroll or *emaki-mono*, a fantastically long hand-held cylindrical device made up of horizontally stitched silk or paper panels – sometimes up to thirty metres in length – that had been popular in the Heian (794–1185) and Kamakura (1185–1333) periods for the depiction of battles, romances, miraculous events and other miscellaneous wonders.[5]

We should return for a moment to the standing Japanese screen: no less a beautiful aesthetic object than a functional, utilitarian 'windshield', placed strategically in the public reception areas and bedroom quarters of the palaces of the nobility to keep out draughts and more generally to give shape, and privacy, to otherwise featureless apartments. Such screens either stood (supported by a wooden frame) stretched out to their full extension; or else they were self-supporting, kept upright by the individual panels zig-zagging across the floor, concertina-fashion; in which case (for the person attempting to 'read' the composition depicted on the screen) we have another rich and intriguing kind of complication. For now the composition's angles are all askew. Viewed head-on, the panorama in question now recedes, now advances towards us with dizzying effects of perspective. Once again, as in the woodcuts, the objects or people depicted on the screen tend to be broken and dissected at the seams of the panels, which slice the composition in unexpected places – giving rise to effects of magnification and distortion that would be indiscernible were the screen to be viewed standing flat. Once noticed, the viewer is struck by the way that *everywhere* in Japanese art, we are confronted by such rebuses and puzzles. Thus, while Anne Hollander in *Moving Pictures* merely hints at the fascinating complexities of space embedded inside the Japanese artistic tradition, we find another Western writer, Timon Screech, in his brilliant study of erotic

5   Mizoguchi, as I say, died before Scope came into its own in Japan. Speculations of the 'had he lived' variety are usually unprofitable, but what *is* worth saying is that Scope has probably never been handled anywhere in the world with greater beauty, inventiveness and finesse than it was in Japan in the following decade, when directors such as Kobayashi, Uchida, Ichikawa, Imamura, Masamura and Toyoda were all operating at the height of their powers.

woodcuts, *Sex and the Floating World* (1999), taking the discussion to new and even more interesting depths. For in the specialised (one can't quite say 'secret') world of the *shunga* (erotic woodcut) – a genre that in one way or another exercised the skill of practically all the great masters of
Japanese painting – the liking for experimental space and for puzzling games with perspective
stands out with a rare and beautiful particularity.

One of the interesting and playful complications of *shunga* arises from the discarded costumes
of the lovers in the print; contrary to Western art, the nude is not foregrounded in Japanese painting and woodcuts. The lovers displayed in their vigorous cavortings by Harunobe, Utamaro, Hokusai and so on are seldom completely naked. The patterns of the respective half cast-off kimonos,
crossing over each other and clashing their designs (or else rebounding in strange harmonies)
become vital elements in the visual dynamism of the picture. Which limb or limbs belong to whom?
Difficult to tell, when the torso to which the limbs are attached is partly covered by patterned
material which covers, in turn, uncovered parts of the body of the other lover. (That the lovers
resemble each other physically, and are only differentiated by their sexual organs, is another,
though perhaps adventitious, aspect of the teasing playfulness of these woodcuts that Screech
brings out.) Prior to his essay on *shunga*, the same author made a major study of the transmission
of optical science from the West to Japan in the late eighteenth and early nineteenth centuries,
and one of the most interesting fruits of this earlier endeavour is his account of a whole discourse
of looking – what Screech calls a 'scopic regime' – in eighteenth- and nineteenth-century erotic
painting, made up of covert allusions to telescopes, microscopes, mirrors, lenses and so on.

Kitagawa Utamaro, *Lovers in Summer*, from *Negai no itoguchi* (1799)

Particularly striking, in the context of our discussion of *hors champ*, is a series of late eighteenth-century woodcuts in which the inclusion of a mirror or mirrors in the *mise en scène* of the erotic tableau serves to fracture the pictorial space, 'pulling it out of reach', in Bazin's formulation, and rendering it difficult to decipher. The entire passage in which Screech analyses the phenomenon is of considerable interest to our argument, and deserves to be quoted in full:

> The eighteenth-century mirror was small and could not show both genitals and heads at the same time, so that artists had to make a choice. Either desire and the power of the organs were captured, or else the ratiocinating head. The mirror turns an actor into a voyeur of him- or herself, locked in an embrace with the partner. Users are both doers and seers. A small Edo mirror showed one's own genitals detached and exposed as well as at an angle that could not be achieved with one's naked eye. The organs were objectified, even as sensations were felt in them; it was difficult to appreciate they were one's own, even in climax. When a mirror is shown in a picture . . . inclusion allows the viewer to see the depicted sexual act from a second angle, or [else it allows] extra erogenous zones to appear, such as the back of the woman's neck where the hairline met the skin (deemed erotic in the Edo period). A notable feature of *shunga* is to show the genitals *only* in the space of the mirror, thus relegating them from the regular space of the picture. [Conversely] the organs *are* depicted, so the mirror is turned away to reveal nothing. The viewer is, then, not given double exposure of any one part of the body, but a fractured view of the body in multiple sections. Momentarily, confusion reigns over the ownership of the parts, and the capacity for 'adversarial encounter' . . . is diminished.[6]

Shunga, of course, it needs to be stressed, is only one genre among others in the total spectrum of the Japanese woodcut – though as I have said most of the major artists practised it, and a surprisingly high percentage of all the woodcuts ever made seem to get back to its protocols in one way or another. The point to be grasped, however, is the more general one, that Japanese painting and design were *always* geared, in this rather unique way, to the challenge of visual complexity; and that this tradition, naturally and harmoniously, fed into the new art form of cinema when the Japanese came to take up that art.

Mizoguchi and Utamaro

Kenji Mizoguchi was fascinated by painting throughout his life – he had trained as a painter as a young man – and one of his most intriguing films (though it is probably a minor work) takes as its subject matter the life and milieu of Kitagawa Utamaro (1756–1806), possibly the greatest of all the portraitists of the 'floating world'.[7] Among a host of outstanding contemporaries – we are talk-

---

6   Timon Screech, *Sex and the Floating World: Erotic Images in Japan 1700–1820* (1999), p. 234.

7   'Floating world' is the usual English phrase used to denote the Japanese word *ukiyo*, referring to the demi-monde society of feudal Japan. Originally, in ninth-century Heian Japan, *ukiyo* had a Buddhist connotation and meant sad or grievous. Gradually over the centuries its meaning changed to mean floating, casual or elegant rather than merely melancholy. Liza Dalby glosses the phrase thus: 'The idea behind this ukiyo . . . is that life may be disagreeable and impermanent, but as we have to live it anyway, we might as well enjoy it and indulge in what worldly pleasures there are' (*Geisha*, 1983, p. 269).

ing about the 1790s, the golden age of the *ukiyo-e* woodcut – Utamaro seems to have excelled by the sheer range and variety of his subject matter: in addition to the work for which he is best known (which might be summarised as psychological portraits of women in love), he painted idyllic outdoor scenes, Yoshiwara festivals and drinking bouts, pairs of famous lovers, beauties from history and legend, scenes of lightly veiled erotic mother-love, bathers and shell divers – along with toilet and boudoir scenes galore, and some of the greatest erotica that has ever been produced. According to Richard Lane, one of the leading current authorities on *ukiyo-e* print-making, '[Utamaro] used practically all the devices invented by Japanese artists to display female beauty – but with many embellishments distinctly his own.'[8] It is this sense of range, of openness to life's bewildering richness and variety – the idea that life must be seized vividly, on its own terms (and not, for example, in the terms prescribed by stultifying academic tradition) – that Mizoguchi wished to bring out in his post-war film *Five Women Round Utamaro/Utamaro o Meguru Gonin no Onna* (1946), adapted from the novel by Kanji Kunieda.

Five Women Round Utamaro

Thus the movie starts *in media res* with a dramatic contrast set up between the old official court-approved style of painting (called *kano*, from its Chinese origins) and the new, contemporary, dynamic, 'plebeian' form of painting known as *ukiyo-e* (literally: paintings of the floating world). Seinosuke, a samurai apprenticed to a *kano* master, is visiting an Edo print shop with his fiancée, when he comes across a painting by Utamaro that boasts, in an attached epigram, of *ukiyo-e*'s superiority to the official style of the shoguns. Enraged, Seinosuke makes his way to the brothel where the *ukiyo-e* master is supping with friends, and challenges him to a duel; but the quarrel is settled when Utamaro counterchallenges with a duel of his own invention – a contest of painting: 'Let's see who can do it best!' And naturally, it is Utamaro who emerges victor, by the deft embellishment he applies – a single stroke – to the portrait that Seinosuke (who has taken first shot) produces as his own staid contribution.

This single brush stroke is enough to make the given painting 'come alive'. That, in a way, is what cinema itself is doing – what it has always done, since the days when the Lumières first breathed life into the static snapshots of domestic bourgeois life, allowing us to see not just a 'portrait of a baby' but the actual, living, breathing toddler making his hesitant poignant first steps towards us (and toppling over when he comes to the kerbstone). So *Five Women Round Utamaro*, just because it concerns painting, turns out to be full of scenes that remind us of the pure miracle of movement; remind us, then, of the way that cinema (despite painting's undoubted survival in different vigorous manifestations) has taken over from the older art form as privileged locus of the representation of ordinary existence. In a famous episode from the film, Utamaro paints the naked back of the courtesan Takasodé. Against the law, the lady in question has expressed her wish to be tattooed, but the tattooist is so awed by the beauty of the pale expanse of skin he has to operate on that he's inhibited from initiating the enterprise. At which point Utamaro appears, and without hesitation sketches live on the woman's back the perfect design – the *only* perfect design (a depiction of the infant prodigy Kintoki with his long-haired nurse) – that 'fits' the unique curves of her body.

---

8   Richard Lane, *Images from the Floating World* (1978), p. 138.

Tattooing is only tattooing, of course: a 'minor art form'. But for the purposes of our discussion the scene is an exquisite allegory. For what Utamaro is engaged in doing, it seems, is abolishing at a stroke the traditional distinction (with all its strange longing and poignancy) between *looking* and *touching*; the 'live-action painting' he has just pulled off looks and touches, so to speak, at one and the same time; marries, in some utopian way, the respective qualities of desire and possession. And moreover the tattooist's art (metaphorically speaking) lives, breathes, moves as painting has never done in its existence So the finished design, Utamaro tells Takasodé, will 'live' on her skin, and during her lifetime (she is to be tragically short-lived) 'share the heights and lows of all your passions'.

Movement, once we come to think about it, is everywhere in *Five Women Round Utamaro*. In the procession of courtesans that forms the background to the opening credits, the elaborately coiffeured and costumed women on their high-platformed wooden clogs progress by a kind of strange and stately march that involves bending alternate knees on every second step, while bringing the opposite leg round in a wide sweep that grazes the ground in a semicircle. How can this strange gesture be painted, one might wonder, except in the cinema? Or rather, how can it be *better* painted than it is here? Here, the gestus is formal and formalised. But the sinuosity of line which the scene reveals so beautifully is in fact part of a wider 'looseness' or general elegance that the film makes it its business to capture – above all, perhaps, in those numerous scenes (including the film's bloody climax) where the courtesans, quarrelling among themselves or their lovers, flounce out of the room or otherwise cast themselves on the ground in gestures of haughty defiance. For there is a freedom of bodily movement possessed by these *filles publiques* that is not

available to better brought-up young maidens (such as Seinosuke's fiancée Yukie), and the film dwells explicitly on this piquant contrast also.

The painter, meanwhile (whether it is Mizoguchi or Utamaro), watches and observes – and burns to record it all! Following some obscure run-in with the authorities, Utamaro is briefly jailed and, returning to his home on licence, spends the last third of the movie's running time with his hands in manacles. His punishment coincides with a series of dramatic events that culminate in the double murder of Takasodé and her lover Shozaburo by Utamaro's ex-mistress Okita. The murder itself (beautifully filmed) and Okita's subsequent repentance fill Utamaro with a kind of holy rage to cast off his manacles and record these scenes while there is still breath left in his body. The fifty-day sentence finally comes to an end. His assistant brings out the saké to celebrate, but Utamaro refuses. 'Saké can wait,' he exclaims. 'Bring me my drawing materials. I must render Okita's spirit, the courtesan's tattooed body, Oran fishing – I'll draw them all!' Meanwhile, over the end credits famous prints by Utamaro rain down, one after the other.[9]

Provisional Conclusion

In this introductory chapter I have tried to look close-up at some of the formal reasons why Mizoguchi deserves study. I have emphasised his mastery of the long take, and the main aesthetic quality that goes with this: a sophisticated sense of the present-tense 'aliveness' of the medium. Perhaps also some of the strangeness (weirdness, even) of Japanese art and cinema has made itself felt: because what we are entering here *is* strange, and fascinating, and different from what Western moviegoers are used to. And I am certain that this anthropological quality in our receptiveness is not something to be ashamed of. It is there, in any case, whether we like it or not. Yet by the same token, 'exoticism' can never really be the issue. The next chapter will look at the broader context of Mizoguchi's cinema, first of all in relation to Japanese history, and then (in so far as it is illuminating) to the private history of the film-maker himself.

---

9   The film is finely anatomised by Dudley and Paul Andrew in their indispensable handbook *Kenji Mizoguchi: A Guide to References and Resources* (1981), pp. 115–18.

2 | The Japanese Context

History

The political history of Japan, viewed in its entirety and over the centuries, presents to the Westerner a series of extraordinary enigmas. First there is the whole business of the dual fount of rule. Nominally governed by the emperor and his court, based in the ancient city of Kyoto, Japan from the early Middle Ages was in fact administered 260 miles away in the eastern capital of Edo (modern Tokyo) by a series of hereditary military rulers or shoguns, in theory the vassals of the emperor but de facto the ultimate source of power and authority.

Connected to this odd system of governance is the second strange fact about Japan's history: namely, that despite cosmopolitan encounters in the fifteenth and sixteenth centuries (particularly with the Portuguese), the country, uniquely in the history of nations, chose at a certain stage of its development to isolate itself from the rest of the world. For 217 years between 1636 and 1853, the last of the hereditary families of shoguns, the Tokugawa, closed the country down to all foreign commercial contacts, with the grudging exception of the Dutch, who were allowed to maintain a small trading station at Nagasaki on the tip of Kyushu, the most westerly of Japan's four main islands. By shogunate decree, no Japanese sailors, on pain of death, were allowed to take part in ocean voyages, just as – equally on pain of death – no foreigner was permitted to set foot on Japanese soil. But it is another strange fact that, despite these draconian constrictions on intercourse with the outside world, Japan prospered in the two centuries in question – if not politically, then at least in the sense that the country lived in peace (more or less), fed its population, and continued to develop its own autonomous internal system of culture.

All this came to an end, as is well known, in July 1853, when Commodore Perry's ships steamed into Tokyo Bay. Perhaps it was the sight of those ironclad vessels, or perhaps it was merely the march of history catching up on Japan (if these two things are not in fact the same); in any case, the shogunate's confidence vis-à-vis the foreigner was thrown for the first time into disarray. Here, then, is the next 'strange fact' about Japanese history, that, in its dilemma as to what to do (a spiritual as much as a political dilemma), the shogunate found itself deferring more and more, almost against its own better counsel, to the powerless and discredited emperor's court in Kyoto. If the shogun's government itself was broadly in favour of accepting the trade treaties offered by the United States and the other great powers (probably because it felt it had no other choice), the revived court, under the Emperor Komei (1831–67), turned out to be virulently anti-treaty and anti-foreign. Yet Komei was at the same time unwilling to jeopardise, by overt opposition to the shogun, an institution that had, with or without imperial consent, governed the

Mt Fuji at dawn: from *Thirty-six Views of Mt Fuji* by Hokusai (early 1830s)

country for the best part of 700 years, and which after all paid for the court's not inconsiderable expenses.

Meanwhile, a third force in the land, represented mainly by daimyos (major military landowners) and senior samurai from the western domains of Satsuma and Choshu, rallied to the emperor's cause, but with none of the emperor's concern for the safety of the shogunate. These men were fiercely anti-government, and even more virulently anti-foreign than the Kyoto court party. Their slogan or war-cry was *Sonno Joi*, perhaps best rendered as: 'Respect the Emperor and expel the foreigners!'

Nothing is more strange in the whole of Japanese history than that the proponents of this latter view should in due course, and as the upshot of a titanic power struggle, become the enthusiastic architects of Japan's full integration into the modern world. The very forces of feudal reaction became, in a few short years (1865–73), the instruments of feudalism's destruction. Historians, with the wisdom of hindsight, can speculate as to how this came about. It is true, for example, that the nearness of the western provinces to the continental land masses of China and Russia can be seen in two opposite ways: on the one hand, living there, close to the nearby international sea-ways, made these western daimyos and samurai alert to the imminent threat of the foreigner. On the other hand, it can be argued that just this propinquity made them (more than it did other Japanese) susceptible to the possible benefits to be gained from contact with the enemy. The historian can say this quite easily: yet the breakthrough still required individual men with sufficient foresight, intelligence and courage to convert that opportunity into an advantage; and it happened (it need not have happened) that they emerged at the time.

Other vital strokes of chance contributed to the course of events, the foremost among these being the death, in 1867, of Emperor Komei (possibly by poison). The heir to the throne was a fifteen-year-old boy, Mutsuhito, known to history by his coronation name of Meiji. Meiji's upbringing until this point had followed to the letter the education deemed suitable for Japanese princes for over 1,000 years, which is to say, readings and lectures in the Confucian classics (in the original Chinese); skill in the composition of poetry (a skill kept up after he became emperor: in the course of his lifetime Meiji composed over 100,000 of the short verses known as *tanka*); finally intimate knowledge of court etiquette and religious ceremonial. Yet, despite this unpromisingly impractical background, Meiji turned out to be a natural moderniser, with none of his father's hatred of foreign ways. On the contrary, in his adoption of Western dress and etiquette and his friendliness to foreign embassies, he took the lead in aligning Japan's polity with that of the other great powers. Throughout his long reign (he lived until 1912), and in the face of numerous back-slidings on the part of his subjects towards the safety of the old feudal ways (the most famous of these probably being Saigo Takamori's Satsuma Rebellion of 1877), his commitment to modernisation never wavered.

The key question that attaches to the subsequent history of Japan from the Meiji period up until World War II is: where and why it all went wrong – when the renewal of confidence apparently augured so well. It can be argued, plausibly enough, that the flaws were there from the start, and that they showed themselves in Japan's aggressive foreign policies. Formosa (modern Taiwan) was annexed from its feudal loyalty to China in 1874, followed by Ryukyu (Okinawa) in 1879. In 1876 Japan imposed a 'friendship treaty' on Korea, the terms of which included – only in reverse – exactly the same inequities (concerning extra-territoriality and the setting of import tariffs) that Japan claimed to suffer from in its own previous treaties with the great powers. Japanese claims in Korea were in fact the pretext for two crucial wars of expansion on the continent – against China in 1894–5 and against Russia ten years later – victories which assured for Japan, by the early twentieth century, an unchallengeable military pre-eminence in Eastern Asia. All this can be interpreted (if the historian is so inclined) rather blackly. Yet at the same time, it seems unlikely that these wars were any more specious in their origin, or more violent and cruel in their conduct, than other wars and annexations that were currently being prosecuted elsewhere round the globe by American and European colonisers. No war is pleasant; but Japan's wars on the continent were relatively swift, and their settlement (certainly, that of the Russo–Japanese War) by contemporary standards equitable.

The irrevocable breakdown of liberal values, and the subsequent slide towards totalitarianism, is probably more plausibly dated from the middle of the 1920s. Up until then, parliamentary government, introduced along with a written constitution in 1889, had more or less functioned following the Western model. The qualification 'more or less' is important however: the military ministries, by tradition, had always been independent entities, headed by senior serving officers from the army and navy, rather than by civilian cabinet ministers. Such men tended not to feel themselves beholden either to the legislative chambers or even to their own cabinet colleagues. In retrospect, the collapse of world markets following the crash of 1929 was probably the crucial turning-point towards despotic military nationalism – threatening as it did to decimate Japanese exports, particularly its lucrative silk trade. Bearing in mind that Japan's population had more than doubled from the beginning of the Meiji era until 1930 (from thirty million to sixty-five million), one can see why, from a nationalist point of view, the pressures towards renewed expansion – onto the continent and southwards into the Pacific – began to seem attractive.

The coup d'état known as the Manchurian Incident which, in 1931, secured for Japan a large slice of northern China and its markets, was carried out without reference to, or permission from, the civil government back in Tokyo: it was an army initiative, and certainly contrary to democracy. In Japan itself, a series of assassinations of moderate parliamentarians and non-nationalistic military personnel in the mid-1930s served to push the country further into the hands of the nationalist cliques. For though the perpetrators of these crimes – mainly fanatical young army and navy officers – were usually caught and punished, their deeds struck a popular resonance which, disastrously, played into the hands of the expansionist military hierarchy.

Behind all these ructions and in a sense accounting for them – at the very least allowing them to happen – we must consider the extraordinary position occupied at the apex of society by the imperial institution itself. As alluded to earlier, it was the Imperial Restoration of 1868 and the unity that followed from this that was responsible for Japan's re-entry, after centuries of isolation, into the modern 'comity of nations'. And while many if not most of the features of the restored Japanese throne could scarcely be differentiated from the type of modern constitutional monarchy that had evolved in contemporary Europe, a part of its meaning and prestige harked back to a more ancient and inviolate absolutism. The emperor himself, of course, was only human (sometimes all-too-human); but in another way he functioned as a god. However this bizarre ideological construction is to be understood – part religious, part secular; part 'believed in', part manipulated by political forces – by the 1930s, it turned out to be fatal to the health of the country. For the existence of the institution, and the respect that was owed to it, meant that almost any crime could be justified if its perpetrator claimed to be acting for the honour and glory of the emperor. Meanwhile, the emperor found himself powerless, even if he had the strength and wished to use it, to descend into the arena of politics, and to act as a force for restraint.

It is not within my scope here (the reader will probably be pleased to hear) to trace the precise steps and timetable by which Japan moved into the fatal embrace of fascism. As is well known, the country entered World War II in December 1941 with the notorious raid on Pearl Harbor. Yet it is important to remember that, one way or another, Japan had been continually at war (in China) for the whole of the previous decade, ever since the Manchurian Incident, and certainly since the invasion of mainland China that took place in July 1937. What is interesting, and puzzling, to anyone who is curious about these matters, is the extraordinary cruelty and arrogance with which the nation prosecuted its doomed programme of military expansion. Reading about the treatment of allied prisoners on the death railways, or about the massacre of civilians in Nanking, or about the enforced slavery of 'comfort women' to service Japanese troops in the battlefield, the modern student of Japan is bound to ask: did the Japanese have to be so brutal? Is there something to be said here about the 'true nature' of the national character?

Undoubtedly, some things *can* be said; though whether they combine to resolve a mystery, or merely leave an enigma standing, is extraordinarily hard to make out. Looking back, for example, it is possible to argue that the outstanding openness to the world that allowed Japan to modernise itself in those few brief years during the 1870s was always a kind of aberration. The true spirit of the nation (by this argument) was constantly xenophobic: a legacy of its years of isolation. That xenophobia had 'lain low', so to speak, during the period of transformation, only to emerge (more virulently, according to laws of repression outlined by psychoanalysis) at a later stage of history.

This sounds plausible. Yet how then to explain both the earnestness and the success with which, in the sixty years since the war ended, Japan has followed the path of peace and democracy? Here, then, is another 'transformation' – another 'facet of national character' – and who is to say which is the true one?

Biography
The puzzling twists and turns of Japanese history outlined here (somewhat simplified, naturally)[1] make up, of course, the background against which Kenji Mizoguchi grew up and pursued his

---

1   The whole question of Japanese 'barbarism', in particular, has been the subject of much debate and can only be alluded to here. Not cited in my introductory outline are two incidents from the 1890s – the massacre of the Chinese troops at Port Arthur in November 1894 during the Sino–Japanese War, and the brutal murder of Queen Min of Korea the following year by Japanese fifth columnists – which throw the issue of 'civilised standards' (and their failure) right back into the heart of the Reform era. (Donald Keene subjects these episodes to a detailed and searching analysis in his brilliant historical study *Emperor of Japan: Meiji and His World 1852–1912*: see Further Reading.) The Russo–Japanese War itself was appalling in its disregard for casualties – according to Ian Buruma, a dress rehearsal for World War I (2003), p. 45. Nor, for reasons of space, does my brief account go into the rather important issue of the repression of socialism and communism. Up until the mid-1920s the injustice involved here doesn't seem to have been much worse than anywhere else. In 1925, however (the same year that universal suffrage was introduced in Japan), so-called Peace Preservation Laws introduced draconian measures against left-wing dissent that were acted on viciously. These measures were extreme by any standard: in 1928, parliamentary legislation actually made it a capital offence to agitate against private property or Japanese state policy, though, as Marius Jensen points out, no one was actually executed for this crime.

career as an artist. The novelist and scriptwriter Matsutaro Kawaguchi, a childhood friend and life-long collaborator of the director, remarked that, politically, Mizoguchi was an opportunist. 'When Marxism was prominent in intellectual circles he followed that fashion. Then, during the war, when communists were persecuted, he veered to the right. After 1945, when democracy was established, he became a democrat,' Kawaguchi told the French writer and theatre producer Ariane Mnouchkine in an interview published in 1964. 'Mizoguchi followed the currents of the epoch, like a twig on a stream.'[2] The seemingly damning nature of this statement is qualified moments later in the interview, however, by the observation that – in Kawaguchi's opinion – this is how artists *ought* to live! 'For an artist (and I include myself here) "ideas", as such, aren't important. The most important thing is to be open to life – to be open to that stream as it floats by.' Mizoguchi's great gift, according to Kawaguchi, was his peerless apprehension of beauty – wherever its traces were to be found. It was here that one could find constancy, both in his personality, and in his work as a film-maker – an ideal believed in; a cause served faithfully over a lifetime.

Many, many questions are raised by this ambiguous and (despite the qualifications Kawaguchi offers) slightly resentful judgment. So it is important to stress that it is only one colleague's point of view. Against the verdict which underlines Mizoguchi's aestheticism may be placed the testimony of another collaborator, Yoshikata Yoda, the most important of all Mizoguchi's scriptwriters, to whom it was always obvious, in interview, that Mizoguchi was 'a man of the left' whose single most defining character trait was an 'undying hatred of oppression'. It's possible of course (and even likely) that both points of view are correct in their way. Yet their surface incompatibility is maybe as good a place as any to open up the question of what is known about Mizoguchi's life and personality in the broadest sense, and also how his beliefs (if we can establish them) feed into his art.[3]

As far as the bare facts are concerned, Mizoguchi, I think, has been fairly well served by posterity. There are (as yet) no fully fledged biographies in English, but there is lively and far-ranging testimony about his life from a host of contemporary witnesses. Yoda, mentioned above, wrote an engrossing account of his twenty-six-year collaboration with the director that will be much cited in the pages that follow. On a smaller scale (but similarly intriguing and close-up) are Mnouchkine's interviews with other artistic collaborators of the director, published in *Cahiers du Cinéma* forty years ago. Here we can listen to the idiosyncratic voices of cinematographer Kazuo Miyagawa, set

---

2   These and following quotations from Mnouchkine's interviews are to be found in the *Cahiers du Cinéma* dossier on Mizoguchi published 'hors série' (special issue), September 1978: translations by the author.

3   In this connection, it is interesting to cite a genuinely committed witness of the century like Alain Resnais. In a recent interview he uses precisely the same metaphor of floating on the stream that we have found Kawaguchi quoting in Mizoguchi's case:

S'il fallait une comparaison, je choisirais plutôt l'image du bouchon de liège qui flotte au gré de la rivière quelle que soit la force des courants, les remous, les reflux. Je me sens comme ce bouchon de liège, donc je considererais que le siècle, l'histoire, est une sorte de courant, de fleuve. [*If a comparison must be made, I'd choose the image of a piece of cork floating on a river at the mercy of its currents, its surges and its whirlpools. I feel myself to be like this cork stopper - to the extent that the epoch, or history itself, is merely a sort of current or river.*]

(*Cahiers du Cinéma*: 'Le Siècle du Cinéma' (Hors série, November 2000, p. 70.) Elsewhere, Resnais calls this position an 'engaged disengagement'.

designer Hiroshi Mizutani, assistant director Eiji Takagi, Daiei production planner Hisakazu Tsuji, in addition to the comments of Matsutaro Kawaguchi that have already been quoted. Mizutani, one of the greatest of all Japanese production designers, published a beautifully detailed memoir in 1973, containing much interesting material about the director. In addition to this, there is Tadao Sato's critical study of the films published in 1982, containing, in particular, a thoughtful account of Mizoguchi's relationship with his sister. More biographical details emerge in the writings of Matsuo Kishi (1970) and Hideo Tsumura (1977), and in the memoirs of key actresses such as Kumeko Urabe (her association with Mizoguchi lasted over thirty years, from 1924 to 1956) and the legendary Isuzu Yamada. Summarising the various different strands of Mizoguchi's biography in English is an excellent short outline of his life drawn up by Dudley and Paul Andrew as an introduction to their handbook *Kenji Mizoguchi: A Guide to References and Resources* (1981), to which may be added passing references to the director's private life in the work of reputable Western experts such as Keiko McDonald, Donald Kirihara and Michel Mesnil (see Further Reading). Finally, no student of Mizoguchi can fail to be grateful for the information contained in Kaneto Shindo's prize-winning documentary about the director (1975) which brings together a huge collection of disparate witnesses, encouraging each of them to talk openly – indiscreetly, even – about their professional connection to the director.

So there is much biographical material available, none the worse for being (for the most part) anecdotal. From this testimony it is possible to make a few first shots at Mizoguchi's character and circumstances. As far as the latter are concerned, what needs to be said is that Mizoguchi emerged from a relatively humble background. His father was a carpenter by trade who went bankrupt after a misplaced entrepreneurial venture in 1905, at the end of the Russo–Japanese War, when Mizoguchi was seven years old. The failure necessitated a childhood move from the relatively middle-class Hongo area in Tokyo where he was born to the much more plebeian – if lively and even raffish – district of Asakusa, near to the theatre and brothel quarter. The move coincided with the birth of a younger brother, and the disappearance of his older sister, Susumo or Suzu, who – a drain on the family finances – was 'put up for adoption' or in other words sold into geishadom. Still, Suzu doesn't disappear from the story – quite the contrary: she continued to play an important part in Mizoguchi's adolescence, firstly round 1913, when her professional contacts found him his first job (as an apprentice kimono designer) and subsequently, in 1915, when their mother died, and Suzu brought her younger brothers into her own house and looked after them. Tadao Sato points out a parallel between the trajectory of Mizoguchi's life in his teens and the plots of numerous melodramatic *shimpa* dramas, some of which (*Nihonbashi* and *Taki no Shiraito*, for example, adapted in both cases from stories by Kyoka Izumi) Mizoguchi was himself to bring to the screen in the late 1920s and early 30s. Such novels and plays – popular at the time, but now considered dated and maudlin – characteristically recount the sacrifices made by geishas on behalf of the lonely young men they are involved with: on the one hand putting up money for their education, on the other hand making themselves scarce (indeed, doing away with themselves altogether: suicide is a constant plot element) when it becomes clear that no permanent union will be possible in the face of impassable social barriers.

In Mizoguchi's own case, there would be no such melodramatic ending: Suzu was his sister, not his lover. She eventually married her aristocratic protector, Viscount Madsudaira, and managed to make a successful life for herself. But this aspect of Mizoguchi's early life is relevant because the subject of women's suffering is fundamental in all his work; while sacrifice – in particular, the sacrifice a sister makes for a brother – makes a key showing in a number of his films, including some of the greatest ones (*Sansho the Bailiff/Sansho Dayu* [1954], for example). The support Suzu gave Mizoguchi, in the absence of a father whom he heartily disliked, continued to a relatively late date: in fact up until the time he entered the film industry in 1920, at the age of twenty-two. During the preceding years there had been a number of false starts and (as it were) enforced periods of idleness connected with his truncated formal education. Too poor, in 1911, to continue paying for their son's primary school training, the Mizoguchi parents sent him to stay with an uncle in Morioka (northern Japan) for a year – a period coinciding with the onset of the crippling rheumatoid arthritis that was to plague him during adolescence, and which was to leave its permanent mark on his body in a lop-sided walking gait that afflicted him for the rest of his life. The year 1912, aged fourteen, and back home with his parents, was spent almost entirely in bed, fighting the disease. Formal schooling in any case was over for him. 1913 brought in its wake Mizoguchi's first real contact with the world of work. Suzu, as we have seen, helped him to secure an apprenticeship designing patterns in a factory that manufactured the light cotton Japanese summer robe known as *yukata*. The 'fine arts' interest that Mizoguchi was beginning to evince (however embryonically) was kept up when he enrolled, in 1916, for a course at the Aoibashi Yoga Kenkyuko art school in Tokyo, an independent establishment that specialised in the teaching of Western painting techniques. Sato tells us that Mizoguchi's attendance here was enthusiastic if intermittent, and that during this period of his life he spent a great deal of time at the public baths (good for his rheumatism). When he was not thus employed (productively enough, one might think: baths are a good place for future storytellers – soaking up the atmosphere of the quarter can sharpen an ear for dialogue of all kinds, especially the demotic), he pursued his new craze for opera, particularly at the Royal Theatre at Akasaka, where in due course he began helping the set decorators in the design and construction of stage scenery. Then Suzu intervened in his life once again: in 1917, she was instrumental in finding him a post on the Yuishin Nippo newspaper in Kobe as a designer of advertising spreads; but though the future director apparently enjoyed the milieu and even contributed articles and some poetry to the paper's culture pages, he quit the job without warning after less than a year in order to return to the bohemian delights of Tokyo.

The initiatives involving Suzu are instructive. As women are the centre of Mizoguchi's art, so they were at the centre of his existence. The 'bare facts', or some of them, can be stated quite easily. In his twenties – as a young film-maker based in the Kansai region – he frequented the tea houses, dance halls and brothels of the great cities of Osaka and Kyoto. In a famous incident early in 1925 Mizoguchi was severely wounded in a knife attack by a jealous girlfriend. Hospitalised, and removed from work for three months, he returned to his old haunts on his recovery, and the following year married an Osakan bar hostess named Chieko Saga. There are different verdicts about the success of this marriage. Kaneto Shindo, in the documentary cited above, takes a cynical view of it. He implies that she was stingy with money and that the pair quarrelled frequently. But other acquaintances who were closer to the director than Shindo ever was testify on the contrary that the union was a happy one – at least, during the early days and during the 1930s. Tragedy struck at the outbreak of the Pacific War. In 1941, at the time of the release of the first part of *The Loyal 47 Ronin*, Chieko went mad, compelling Mizoguchi to place her in care (his great fear was that he had given her syphilis, though tests proved that neither she nor he was infected by the disease). To complete the matrimonial side of the story: a little after her death in 1951, Mizoguchi married her widowed sister, Fuji, adopting the two young girls from the latter's previous marriage, whom he brought up by all accounts with affection. (Yoda gives a somewhat darker account of family life: 'I never once saw him smile at a child'.)[4]

Kinuyo Tanaka

Whatever the truth about his marriage, it is also true that Mizoguchi loved actresses, though the meaning of love here has to be defined carefully. Two important women in his life have already been mentioned: Kumeko Urabe and Isuzu Yamada. But there is another actress who is more important than either of these. It is not overstating the case to say that the greatness of Mizoguchi's films cannot be accounted for without also taking into consideration the irradiating presence of a single star, Kinuyo Tanaka. She is not, of course, the *only* star in the Mizoguchi pantheon. Japanese cinema is full of wonderful actresses, many of whom will be discussed in this study – Machiko Kyo, Kyoko Kagawa, Takako Irie, Michiyo Kogure, Ayako Wakao. Nonetheless, Tanaka stands apart from all these in the degree to which we identify her with Mizoguchi's films: she (or rather, what she stands for) is one of the key reasons that his work is so precious to us. This kind of relationship between a particular actress and a director's work is not, of course, unique in cinema. For a period during the 1950s and 60s two major directors in Italy, Rossellini and Fellini, could be said to have expressed themselves in a similar way through the genius of their spouses (Ingrid Bergman and Giulietta Masina respectively). There is also the case of Josef von Sternberg, whose collaboration with Marlene Dietrich across six major films in the 1930s is inseparable from the flowering of that director's dark genius. Godard, too, obsessively painted his wife, Anna Karina. More recently, in China, the coherence of Zhang Yimou's oeuvre until recently owed much to the presence in nearly all of his films of the same charismatic actress, Gong Li.

We have to ask, therefore: what is it, morally speaking, that Tanaka brings to Mizoguchi's art? Stoicism and sacrifice (projected as part of a woman's 'duty') are an element of the composite image, along with dignity, integrity and a certain rather complicated submissiveness. Encasing the whole picture is a very special brand of beauty, elegance and deportment. (Tanaka's asceticism, as opposed to sensuality, separate her from the examples just given: the sultry neurotic ripeness projected by Bergman, for instance, or the sexual, satirical and even burlesque persona of Dietrich). Moreover, Tanaka's 'image' is not *just* an image: the actress is, or was, a live human being. Whatever vision of womanhood emerges from these extraordinary movies is put there by *her* as well as by the director; which means that it corresponds, in some authentic and serious way, to the truth of Tanaka's own being.[5]

---

4   I have met these children, now grown up: certainly they speak of *him* with affection.

5   Tanaka was born in 1909 in Shimonoseki (southern Japan) into a wealthy local family that removed itself to Osaka in 1919 when it fell on hard times, following a depression in rice prices. At more or less this time, she gave up school and took up study of the *biwa* (five-stringed traditional lute), soon becoming a child star at public performances, before moving over to cinema (Shochiku Studio) in 1924, at the age of fifteen. It is important to take on board that Tanaka was exceptionally well known long before her collaboration with Mizoguchi, working during the 1920s and 30s with many of

Importantly, Tanaka and Mizoguchi were never physically lovers, which didn't prevent contemporaries from gossiping and speculating. In Kaneto Shindo's documentary which came out in 1975 nearly twenty years after the director's death, the actress speaks freely and openly – and yet also with discretion – about the nature of her relationship with Mizoguchi. First, though she travelled with him frequently – accompanying him, for example, on his journey to Venice in 1953 to present *Tales of the Watery Moon/Ugetsu Monogatari* at the Biennale – she reports to Shindo that she 'knew very little about his private life'. There is a story about a reporter phoning her one day and asking her, in relation to an article he was writing, whether it was true that she and Mizoguchi were engaged? Caught unprepared by the audacity of the question, Tanaka apparently answered without thinking: 'Oh no, he's not the right husband for me!', and although this was indeed the truth, she was mortified by the blunt way she had stated it. How could she have blurted out such a thing? What would Mizoguchi think if he saw her comment in print? Shindo, the director of the documentary (who also doubles as interviewer) has his own opinion about Mizoguchi's shockability. 'You *were* the great love of his life,' he insists. Tanaka: 'Don't exaggerate.' Shindo: 'Yes, he told me [on the set of *Oharu*, when they were having dinner together] – he told me that he was in love with you.' Tanaka: 'He was drunk, no?' Shindo: 'Not at all!' After a pause, Tanaka replies with great simplicity: 'He loved, through me, the women I played.'

'He loved, through me, the women I played.' It's only a phrase, of course, and perhaps one shouldn't read into it more than a mere phrase can bear. Yet the comment is beautiful and suggestive. It speaks of a sublimation that is at the heart of Mizoguchi's art – a repression, a sense of held-back longing, an unhappiness. The partnership was of long duration and it may be worth outlining it briefly. *The Woman of Osaka/Naniwa Onna* (1940), the film on which they first worked together, is no longer extant, alas. The first surviving film in their collaboration is a *jidai-geki* (period drama) genre piece, *Musashi Miyamoto/Miyamoto Musashi* (1944), where Tanaka plays a young girl from a samurai family learning to overcome the longing for vengeance she harbours against the murderers of her parents and elder brother. Other later 'period' films with Tanaka include *The Life of Oharu/Saikaku Ichidai Onna* (1952) where she plays a seventeenth-century courtesan; and *Sansho the Bailiff*, in which she is the wife of a provincial governor of the Heian (i.e. early medieval) epoch whose uncompromising ethical ideals, directed against government corruption, cause the family and their two children to be exiled. In *Ugetsu Monogatari*, set during the mid-fifteenth-century Onin War, she plays a simple potter's wife, emblem of faithfulness. By contrast, in *Five Women Round Utamaro* she is a prostitute and murderess. The more modern roles should be briefly itemised here too: *The Love of Sumako the Actress/Joyu Sumako no Koi* (1947) dramatises the world of avant-garde theatre that became popular in the Taisho period (1912–26), and produced extraordinary stage personalities such as the eponymous heroine played by Tanaka. *My Love Has Been Burning/Waga Koi Wa Moenu* (1949) focuses on the trials and tribulations of a pioneering feminist of the 1880s. (The heroine of this movie, Eiko Hirayama, was – like Sumako – a

Japan's leading directors – Gosho, Shimazu, Ozu and above all Hiroshi Shimizu, to whom for a period she was married. While pursuing a career as an actress (the Larousse Encyclopedia says she took more than 230 roles in all, though this is hard to believe) she latterly became a film director in her own right, the first woman in Japan to do so: *Love Letter* (1953) and *The Eternal Breasts* (1955) are both remarkable. Tanaka died in 1977.

genuine historical personage.) Further into the twentieth century, *Miss Oyu/Oyu-sama* and *The Lady from Musashino/Musashino Fujin* (both released in the same year, 1951) examine the velleities of the Japanese upper classes. In *Victory of Women*, briefly commented on in the previous chapter, Tanaka plays a crusading liberal lawyer, whereas in *Women of the Night/Yoru no Onnatachi* (1948) she is someone who might, perhaps, have been one of that lawyer's clients – a refugee from the war, thrown into the world of prostitution as a mere matter of survival. Tanaka's final role for Mizoguchi, in *The Woman of Rumour/Uwasa no Onna* (1954), also has a contemporary setting; here she plays the manager of a modern, well-run geisha house, forcibly at odds with an estranged daughter who shows little enthusiasm for inheriting the business.

By my calculation, the films starring Tanaka account for over a third of Mizoguchi's surviving work, roughly twenty hours of viewing time: twelve movies altogether, if we count only the extant ones. Four have contemporary settings; three go back into the post-Meiji period during which Japan was emerging as a modern nation; while the remaining five are set in earlier feudal epochs dating from the twelfth up until the eighteenth century. It is tempting to run them together, retrospectively, to form a single, continuous 'ur-film'; and since it is the same wonderful actress who appears in major roles in all of them, the historical canvas thus outlined acquires a unity and discursive amplitude – a *completeness of vision* – for which it is difficult to find immediate comparisons. None of Mizoguchi's contemporaries – neither Ozu, nor Naruse, nor Kurosawa, nor any of the other great masters – explored so many different and contrasting aspects of Japanese culture; in none of them is the balance between past and present so finely and discriminately maintained. Such contentions I hope to demonstrate. But I can say one thing here in anticipation: the emphasis on women is crucial. By *foregrounding woman as the suffering subject of history*, Mizoguchi makes his own 'intervention' on the subject of cruelty that was discussed earlier. His films acknowledge that Japan's civilisation, for all its great beauty and antiquity, is somehow problematic 'to the core'. Somehow, there is an ineradicable buried violence in it which it will be the task of his movies to encounter, to explore – and to expiate.

The Japanese Film Industry

'The beauty [of Japanese film] has come late to us, like light from a distant star', Bazin wrote in 1955. A series of Japanese films that won top prizes at important Western film festivals in the early 1950s served to put Japanese cinema on the map; but the technical and artistic expertise they displayed did not, of course, come out of nowhere. Japan has had a long tradition of cinematic excellence: it is and always has been one of the major film-making countries of the world. The Japanese fascination with cinema goes right back to the form's invented origins. The first kinetoscopes (standing boxed peepholes) were introduced into Tokyo in 1896, followed a year later by projected screenings in front of audiences, thanks to the arrival on Japanese shores of the Lumière brothers' Cinématographe and of Edison's rival Vitascope system. The first custom-built cinema (the Denkikan, in Asakusa, Mizoguchi's childhood district) dates from 1903, and in fact the proliferation of 'picture palaces' in Japan predated their introduction into the United States by several years. (Japan had no nickelodeon era.) Independently built studios served the indigenous Japanese market: in 1909, fol-

Dignity, integrity . . . a certain complicated submissiveness: Kinuyo Tanaka in *Miss Oyu* (1951)

lowing the example of Edison's Motion Picture Patents Company, the main companies – Yoshisawa, Yokota, M. Pathé and Fukuhoda – amalgamated to found the first of Japan's 'majors', Nikkatsu, still going to this day. Other studios emerged at well-spaced intervals: Shochiku (1920), Kawai (1926), Shinko (1931), Toho (1937), Daiei (1942), Shintoho (1947) and Toei (1950).

To service the industry, artistic personnel were needed. The earliest well-known film directors are named by Anderson and Richie (in their indispensable *The Japanese Film: Art and Industry* [1959, new edition, 1982]) as Shozo Makino (born 1878, a Nikkatsu director) and Norimasu Kaeriyama (born 1893) who worked from 1914 onwards at the main rival studio of the time, Tenkatsu. Unfortunately, it is hard to say much about the quality of this early work: the great Kanto earthquake of 1923 (in the wake of which the Nikkatsu studio moved to Kyoto) destroyed all but a tiny proportion of the movies that had been made until then. But from the mid-1920s the picture is much clearer: the latter years of the silent epoch (in Japan this lasted well into the 30s) and the first years of the talkies brought onto the scene a series of directors whose work, by any criteria, is of major lasting quality. These directors, who are more or less contemporaries of Mizoguchi, include: Yutaka Abe (1895–1977), Keisuke Kinugasa (1896–1982),Yasujiro Shimazu (1897–1945), Daisuke Ito (1898–1981), Tomu Uchida (1898–1970), Mansaku Itami (1900–46), Heinosuke Gosho (1902–81), Tomotaka Tasaka (1902–74), Yasujiro Ozu (1903–63), Hiroshi Shimizu (1903–66), Mikio Naruse (1905–69), Shiro Toyoda (1906–77) and Sadao Yamanaka (1909–38). I risk making this list a long one, for it was the anonymous collective craftsmanship of these directors working together (unsung internationally at the time) that laid the artistic foundations from which Japan's post-war successes sprang, as it were, fully armed. One notes, in passing, how prolific many of these directors were: the eighty-six works that constitute Mizoguchi's filmography weren't unusual: Gosho (in a career that lasted until 1968) made around 100 films, and Ito almost as many. Notable, too, is the overall quality of the work, even among the second-tier directors, Gosho indeed being a good instance. Probably his name doesn't figure on many people's lists of the classical or top-flight directors.[6] Yet 'classical', in the literal sense, is exactly how he must be defined. Post-war movies as different as *Dispersing Clouds* (1951), *An Inn at Osaka* (1954), *Growing Up* (1955), *Fireflies* (1958) and *Rebellion in Japan* (1967) are united by wonderfully constructed scenarios and marvellous transition scenes: they are tender, touching and wise beyond ordinary standards of judgment. It seems to me, then, that what is striking about Japan, in general, is not just the output of the few major directors who existed at the top, but the extraordinary quality and evenness of its overall product. Indeed I would go further and argue that directors of the classical age such as Gosho and Ito are *technically* as fine as, if not finer than, all but a handful of the very best world directors working currently.

Demands of the Studio

The films of these directors were 'artistic': but they were not for that reason, in the modern sense 'art-house'. The distinction between commercial and experimental branches of the industry was not as marked in those days. Culture (in an almost Shakespearean way) was unified, with no

---

6   See my essay 'To Love is to Suffer: Reflections on the Later Cinema of Heinosuke Gosho', *Sight and Sound* (1986), pp. 198–202. Arthur Nolletti Jnr has recently written a full-length study of the director: *Laughter Through Tears: The Cinema of Gosho Heinosuke* (2004).

unbridgeable passage between high and low. Film was still the product of an industry, of course. Movies by the directors just cited were expected to make money, and on the whole did so. Directors may have had a high degree of independence, but they still had to find studios (and corners within studios) that suited their individual temperaments. In a career lasting the best part of thirty-five years, Mizoguchi worked in total for nine different production houses. Often (but not always) his moves from one company to another arose out of disagreements with individual producers over the direction his movies were heading in. Mizoguchi was exceptionally demanding: perhaps no Japanese director was more so. And the need he felt to protect his autonomy was a continuous obsession in his career. He quit Nikkatsu, where he had been taken on in 1920 and nurtured for eleven years, in 1932, when he went to work with Takako Irie in her independent production house that had been set up under the aegis of Shinko. Two years later, in company with producer Masaichi Nagata, he moved to a new production outfit, Daiichi Eiga (secretly funded by Nikkatsu's rival Shochiku). When that in turn went bust in 1937 (not before permitting Mizoguchi and Nagata – with Yoda's aid – to produce some of the most aesthetically radical films of the 1930s) he transferred his allegiance to Shinko, moving on to Shochiku two years later after falling out with Shinko's obtuse and nationalistically inclined then head of production.

Shochiku looked after Mizoguchi during the difficult years of the war and in its immediate aftermath. Altogether he made thirteen films there (including four that have subsequently vanished), abandoning the company only when its management failed to back an ambitious project of his to bring to the screen an adaptation of the work of the great seventeenth-century writer Saikaku. That project in turn took shape as *The Life of Oharu*, one of Mizoguchi's greatest and most austere post-war triumphs, produced in 1951 by courtesy of the Shintoho studios in Kyoto. (Even at this stage, however, there had been blips on the way, giving rise to temporary touchdowns, during 1950, at Daiei and Toho.) In 1952 Mizoguchi found himself finally settling at Daiei for what were to be the concluding eight films of his career.

Comparisons with the careers of other major directors would have to be made systematically to determine if this odyssey is typical: my feeling is that it was par for the course. At any rate, the tension it testifies to, between art and commerce, is surely one of the givens of film-making. Even at Daiei, where Mizoguchi had once again teamed up with Nagata, now one of the most powerful producers in the industry, the right to artistic autonomy could never be taken for granted. Here, for example, in 1953, the company wanted a more upbeat – a more 'marketable' – ending for *Ugetsu Monogatari* than Mizoguchi was inclined to provide; and it was the director, not the producer, who was forced in this instance to give way. Such exterior and adventitious pressures, as I say, are part of the process of film-making and it is probably not necessary to examine them here. Each studio had a culture – a body of unwritten rules – that it was impossible for the directors they employed to be impervious to.

Yet it would be wrong, in any case, to exaggerate Mizoguchi's oppositional posture, especially later on in his career when he had become widely known. His friendship with Masaichi Nagata, a major figure in the industry, has been remarked upon; he also knew and was on equal terms socially with other powerful studio bosses – Shiro Kido and Matsutaro Shirai at Shochiku, Iwao Mori at Toho (an old friend from Nikkatsu days). Mizoguchi himself at different stages of his career occupied official and honorary posts in the industry. In 1938, for example, following the release of the 'national-policy' film *Song of the Camp/Roei no Uta* (now lost), he was appointed as a national film consultant by the government, shortly afterwards in 1940 becoming president of the Association of Japanese Film Directors. We will look at Mizoguchi's attitude towards Japan's war effort later: here it is only necessary to say that, emerging at the far end of the conflict with an officially unblemished reputation (deservedly or not we will postpone discussing), he found himself for a brief period, during 1946, acting as head of the Shochiku–Ofuna branch of the All Japan Film and Theatre Employee Union – a trade union that had been set up under the aegis of the occupation in order to combat the 'feudal practices' that were felt to be rife in the entertainment industries. Mizoguchi, in one way or another, was never a very convincing or (shall we say?) democratic union chief. Kyoko Hirano, in her excellent book about the film industry during the American occupation (1992) quotes him as addressing his fellow union members in the following terms: 'I am your union chairman . . . please be prepared to follow my orders!' (orders which, it soon became clear, would never to be directed towards strike action). Left-wing he may have been by sentiment; but Mizoguchi had his fair share of 'boss mentality'. Yet all directors do, to some extent: one could say it goes with the territory.[7]

The Early Twentieth-Century Cultural Scene

Japan's modernisation during the Meiji and Taisho periods brought in its wake, as might be expected, great innovations in the world of the arts. It was altogether a vigorous and innovative epoch. By the same token, since art has always been a major element in Japanese life, the continuities too have significance. One might have imagined for example that the kabuki theatre, with its bizarre feudal plotlines and extravagant stylisations, would be a casualty of Japan's entry into the modern world. Not at all. Apart from a brief (and unsuccessful) episode in the 1890s when theatre managers experimented with bringing contemporary events such as the Sino-Japanese War into the plays they were offering the public, kabuki continued much as before: indeed, in the early years of the century, it went through what many commentators think of as a second Golden Age. The much more rarified Noh theatre, too, which, following the fall of the shogunate was for several years in danger of extinction, experienced a revival of its fortunes under imperial protection. (Emperor Meiji himself was fond of this art form, and from the mid-1870s performances of the famous plays were frequently staged in his presence in the residences of principal officers of state and members of the nobility.)

At the same time, completely new forms of theatre such as *shimpa* and *shingeki* were making their presence felt. *Shimpa* can be best translated as modern melodrama; whereas *shingeki* was the movement that brought into the Japanese repertoire the works of modern playwrights such as Ibsen, Shaw, Chekhov and Sudermann. (Mizoguchi's film *The Love of Sumako the Actress*, discussed in Chapter 7, goes into this milieu in detail.) Concurrently, European literary naturalism was being brought into Japanese consciousness through the novels and short stories of writers such as Ogai Mori (1862–1922) and Soseki Natsume (1867–1916), each of whom had made prolonged pioneer visits to the West and returned with a complicated admiration for it. Nor should the

---

7   Mizoguchi remarks blandly of this incident: 'Ofuna asked me to make *Victory of Women*, and at the same time made me president of the union. It was impossible for me to continue working in these conditions. Therefore I resigned.' ('Kenji Mizoguchi Talks about His Works', *Kinema Jumpo* no. 80, January 1954; quoted in *Cahiers du Cinéma* no. 95, May 1959, my translation.)

graphic arts be ignored: painting too was going through a revival. The traditional skills of print-making honed by the great *ukiyo-e* artists expanded to encompass cosmopolitan Western techniques, above all, in the fields of perspective and oil painting.[8]

Literature, too, is a major part of culture, and was crucial to Mizoguchi's spiritual development. Dating from the time of his adolescent illnesses, the future director was an omnivorous reader: Japanese novels and poetry as a priority, but also classics of world literature in translation (an eclectic assortment: Shakespeare, Balzac, Zola, Dostoevsky, Tolstoy, Maupassant, Sinclair Lewis). Before the war, favoured authors included contemporary stars of the 'Japanese renaissance' such as Fumio Niwa, Saisei Muro, Kafu Nagai, Naoya Shiga and Junichiro Tanizaki – discussed further later in this volume. In the post-war years Mizoguchi's interests expanded to take in a renewed study of the early modern Japanese classics: one finds him extensively immersed at this stage of his life in the writings of Iharu Saikaku (1642–93), Monzaemon Chikamatsu (1653–1724) and Akinari Ueda (1734–1809): important films, we shall see, came out of each of these enthusiasms. Other noted Japanese writers whom he acknowledged as especially his own were the Meiji master Koyo Izaki (1867–1903), along with Izaki's literary pupil Kyoka Izumi (1873–1939), whose subtly contrived *shimpa* novels Mizoguchi adapted for the screen three times in the late 1920s and early 30s. Less well known internationally, but significant to Mizoguchi because of their wit, their 'local colour' and a certain demotic realism are a trio of mid-century writers: Hakuche Mazamune, Mantaro Kuboota and Sakonusoke Oda.

Early Masters in Cinema

The directors active at Nikkatsu when Mizoguchi first arrived there in 1920 were Tadashi Oguchi ('my first real master'), Osamu Wakayama, Kensaku Suzuki and Eizo Tanaka – alas, none of their work remains. The Andrew brothers' short biographical sketch tells us that Tanaka, for whom Mizoguchi worked as assistant in 1922, taught the future director among other things how to construct authentic Tokyo sets and also how to create *Stimmung* – atmosphere. Tellingly – in view of Mizoguchi's later predilection for this method of shooting – it was an exceptionally complicated travelling shot on rails, brought off while working under Tanaka's supervision, that earned Mizoguchi promotion, at the age of twenty-four, to the director's chair, following a strike called by the studio's *onnagata* (male actors playing female roles: the practice – which had continued wholesale into cinema from Japan's theatrical tradition – ceased about this time, in part because of the failure of the strike). Mizoguchi's other main influence at Nikkatsu was the charismatic Minoru Murata (1894–1937) who, like Eizo Tanaka, had previously worked at Shochiku under the respected pioneer film teacher Kaoru Osanai. At Shochiku, in 1921, Murata was responsible for directing *Souls on the Road*, one of Japan's earliest film masterpieces, a systematically unsentimental study of contemporary poverty that apparently marked Mizoguchi profoundly. After his switch to Nikkatsu, three further masterpieces followed: *Omitsu and Seizaburo* (1923), *The Woman of Seisaka* (1924) and *Osumi and Her Mother* (1924). (Incidentally: it was as Murata's personal assistant that Yoshikata Yoda first entered the film industry, in the early 1930s.)

---

8   See Shuji Takashina, J. Thomas Rimer and Gerald D. Bolas (eds), *Paris in Japan: The Japanese Encounter with European Painting*, (1987). Excellent text and fine illustrations.

Film Influences from Abroad

Like everywhere else in the world, the Japanese industry in its infancy responded to Hollywood. To take one example among many: as David Bordwell has documented so well, it is impossible to account for Yasujiro Ozu's comedies of the 1920s without looking sideways to the comedies of the great Harold Lloyd. Similarly, Anderson and Richie have a fascinating section in their book on the legacy of the Japanese actor Sessue Hayaka, whose success in the American studios, in the 1910s, was to make him the first of Japan's international matinée idols. Influenced by his example, a number of other actors crossed the ocean to California to try their luck in the studios, and brought back with them to Japan (along with their newly anglicised names: Henry Kotani, Thomas Kurihara) a raft of new American directing methods. Some of these innovations – such as a brief vogue for actually directing films in English – proved more ephemeral than others; but there seems little question that the American emphasis on speed, stylishness and 'modernity' had an exceptional impact in these years – above all in the field of comedy. Comedy, in the end, was not to be Mizoguchi's forte, but the young director responded to this influence too, evincing, like many of his generation, a particularly deep admiration for Chaplin (*Woman of Paris*, 1923, appears to have been the key film here). Throughout the 1920s and into the difficult, xenophobic years of the 30s, Japan continued to import foreign movies on a fairly regular basis – as many as 300 titles a year. At different times during this period, Mizoguchi saw and responded to films by Ernst Lubitsch, Josef von Sternberg (whom he met in Tokyo in 1936), King Vidor, René Clair and Jacques Feyder (*Pension Mimosas*, 1935, little seen now; the Belgian-born director is among the great forgotten masters). After 1937, when Japan invaded mainland China, those foreign conduits dried up (a government decree banned their import); but in the post-war period of readjustment Mizoguchi managed to see, and to record enthusiastic verdicts on, a number of newly imported masterpieces of world cinema: *La Grande illusion* (distributed in Japan in 1949), *Bicycle Thieves* (in 1950), *Rome Open City* (the same year) and also of course the 'film of films', *Citizen Kane*.

Painting

Mizoguchi's training in watercolour and Western oil techniques at the Aoibashi Yoga Kenkyujo during World War I continued to fertilise his later thinking about film aesthetics. Thus, for example, in an interview published in *Eiga Hyoron* in 1952, we find him pondering the possibility of contemporary film capturing the 'curiously suggestive intensity' of a certain type of ink painting that flourished in the Ashikaga period (1392–1596), connecting this train of thought a moment later to the 'spare, astringent' oil paintings of Ryuzaburo Umehara (1888–1986), the so-called 'Japanese Renoir', and one of the heroes of his youth. In this connection, it is typical of Mizoguchi's long-range faithfulness to his origins that, years after attending the Tokyo art school, he should have arranged for one of his revered teachers there, Mitsuzo Wada, to be on hand to provide artistic and technical advice on the two ambitious colour films he made for Daiei at the end of his career, *The Empress Yang Kwei Fei/Yokihi* and *Tales of the Taira Clan* (both 1955). Thus, if Mizoguchi's eye for beauty was innate – it was also unusually 'literate'. The dialectical play in his films between colour and black-and-white, between line and volume, between movement and stillness, between portraiture and landscape, had received a priceless grounding in these adolescent studies.

Contemporaries

Mizoguchi was probably the most *cultivated* (in the sense of educated and knowledgeable) of all the classical Japanese film directors. An autodidact whose knowledge came equally from life as from study, his intellectual curiosity was phenomenal. Film, painting, literature and music were always, in his eyes, part of a single continuum. For all that, it is a difficult matter to follow precisely the contours of Mizoguchi's response to these exposures. By their very nature, influences (some deep and perdurable, others multiple, quicksilver, effervescent) are tricky to pin down. The artists mentioned above were all, at different stages of Mizoguchi's life, spoken of approvingly by the director; but that may be as far as it is safe to go. To take an example: in one of his always provocative essays, Robin Wood points out certain formal similarities between Mizoguchi's *Sisters of the Gion* and von Sternberg's film from two years earlier *The Devil Is a Woman*.[9] The comparison is plausible and suggestive (Wood is never less than a brilliant interpreter). Still, whether Sternberg was – overall – a *more* important influence on Mizoguchi's artistry than (say) Vidor or Feyder is, in my opinion, hard to judge definitively. What is plain is that Mizoguchi 'kept an eye on' his contemporaries in the film world – humanly as well as artistically. At different times his recorded comments on his colleagues are both waspish and affectionate. For Ozu (for example) he seems to have harboured a lifelong uncomplicated reverence. About Mikio Naruse, on the other hand (by any criterion one of the greatest of all Japanese directors), he was less than generous: according to Hideo Tsumura, Mizoguchi's verdict was that Naruse's cinema 'lacked balls'. What about Akira Kurosawa finally? Twelve years Mizoguchi's junior, and plainly the greatest of the post-war directors, the younger artist was not as much an 'influence', as a spur to emulation, and a rival to outfox.

And yet also influential in the end, why not say so? Without Kurosawa's radical re-invention of the period film in movies like *Sanshiro Sugata* (1943) and *Rashomon* (1950), Mizoguchi's great last flowering of historical drama (*Oharu, Ugetsu, Sansho, Chikamatsu, Yokihi* – the films which, for many viewers, make him 'count' today) would surely not have taken the shape that it did.

---

9 Robin Wood, 'On *Sisters of the Gion*', in J. Quandt and G. O'Grady (1996).

3 | Mizoguchi at Work

In Mizoguchi's case – more perhaps than most – the 'life' and the 'work' turn out to be peculiarly hard to disentangle. It was not that he was any more prolific than his contemporaries: as mentioned, the eighty-six films he made over the course of thirty-three years can be matched, in terms of pure volume, by the output of a surprisingly large number of Japanese directors, particularly those beginning their careers in the silent epoch when movies, anyway, tended to be shorter and more mass-produced. All movies – even the most populist and unpretentious ones – require reserves of work, concentration and single-mindedness if they are ever to get off the ground. Filmmaking is an exigent profession, requiring intricate and painstaking work as well as vision. But with Mizoguchi, this emphasis on 'preparedness', on the sacred seriousness of art, was taken to a much higher level than it was with all but the most austere of his contemporaries. He demanded complete dedication from all the people he was involved with: cinema, as an art form, deserved nothing less if it was to take its place where Mizoguchi believed it belonged, in the exalted company of music, painting and poetry. I sometimes think how easy it would have been, during the course of a career which, like everyone's, suffered ups and downs, for Mizoguchi to have relaxed a bit – to have regressed now and again into cynicism, worldliness or commercialism. Not all Mizoguchi's films are by any means pure masterpieces; but in none of them – even the minor ones – does the viewer get the feeling that anything less than the director's whole energy, taste and sincerity have been deployed in the adventure of their making.

Script

'A good screenplay', says Jean-Claude Carrière (with the air of only just avoiding stating the obvious), 'is one that gives birth to a good film.'[1] This simple view was shared by Mizoguchi. Hisakazu Tsuji, director of planning at Daiei Studios in the early 1950s, has left a very clear account of the different stages involved in the construction of one of Mizoguchi's most famous movies, *Ugetsu Monogatari*, and summarising the production calendar for this film provides useful clues to Mizoguchi's working practices.

In this case, the original idea for the film came from the director himself, inspired (as we shall see in Chapter 4) by two separate tales of the supernatural by the eighteenth-century writer Akinari Ueda, onto which Mizoguchi wished to graft another, more naturalistic fable by Guy de Maupassant. Two scriptwriters were engaged for the task in hand, both of them old and trusted

---

1   Jean-Claude Carrière, *The Secret Language of Film* (1995), p. 148.

Mizoguchi adjusting Raizo Ichikawa's costume during rehearsals for *Tales of the Taira Clan* (1955)

collaborators: the first a friend from schooldays, the novelist Matsutaro Kawaguchi (whose comments about Mizoguchi's politics have already been noted), the second, Yoshikata Yoda – after Kinuyo Tanaka, the single most important collaborator Mizoguchi ever worked with.

From the very first moment, Mizoguchi introduced an element of competition into the enterprise. Instead of asking them to pool their thoughts, he proposed that two writers create their own independent versions in whichever format they preferred. Kawaguchi's draft, presented swiftly, took the form of a short story, Yoda's a more traditional scenario. Mizoguchi read and harshly criticised both, yet apparently in rather vague terms, since his own ideas were still very much in embryo. (The painter Salvador Dali seems to have been invoked as a point of reference, yet without further enlightenment to either of the collaborators.) Mizoguchi now instructed Yoda to take Kawaguchi's text and fashion out of it a second script, in which he would be allowed to combine elements from his own adaptation. When Yoda had completed this task, Mizoguchi presented the new version to Kawaguchi, suspecting – perhaps even hoping – that the novelist would not like it much. 'He's left out all my best bits', Kawaguchi exclaimed indignantly, before knuckling down to write what would become the third version. This in turn was handed on to the film's producer, Masaichi Nagata (also, as we have seen, an old friend of the director), of whose comments and criticisms the director took note.

It was now time for a fourth version. Who would write it, Kawaguchi or Yoda? Kawaguchi, discountenanced, begged off the project at this stage, pleading deadlines in other literary work,

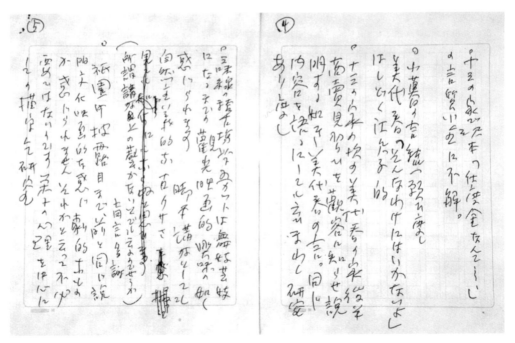

Letter from Mizoguchi to Yoda requesting changes in the script of *Gion Festival Music* (1953). Among other remarks: 'I don't understand why she says this.' 'Too Edo-style' [for a film that is set in Kyoto]. 'Too much repetition.' [À propos a scene involving a young geisha with a samisen]: 'This isn't a tourist film!'

so the script was handed back once again to Yoda. Alas, Mizoguchi's comments on this new version were as acerbic as they had been on the previous one (Tsuji tells us that phrases like 'incomprehensible!', 'cretinous!' accompanied numerous squiggles and exclamation marks in the margins). Yet despite these fierce criticisms, Tsuji says, there was a feeling now that the project was beginning to gather focus. Away from his scriptwriter, Mizoguchi was reading prodigiously and screening a lot of films, as well as going off himself on long solitary walks to meditate. Every so often he would phone Yoda (now busily employed on the fifth version) in order to recommend such and such a book or such and such a movie, to add a possible further flavour to the 'soup'. If Yoda hoped that on reading this fifth draft Mizoguchi would be any more satisfied, he was in for a disappointment. 'Is this all you're capable of?' Mizoguchi demanded in tones of refined irony, before sending the script back for yet more revisions.

Five months had now gone by. Before the next (sixth) version of the script appeared, Mizoguchi's team had begun to construct some sets. Costumes, too, were being designed and manufactured: the pre-production, in other words, was under way (we will come back to this in a moment from another angle). Yet the script itself was by no means completed: once the sets had been built, the script needed to be modified in relation to *them*, and in relation also to conversations Mizoguchi had been having in the meantime with the cameraman (Kazuo Miyagawa, perhaps the greatest of all Japanese cinematographers) and with the chief electrician on the set. Tsuji himself, now that Yoda had temporarily departed from the scene, was called in on these just-prior-to-shooting conferences, to 'tweak' aspects of the script in response to the director's suggestions. The results of this final revision were written up on a blackboard prominently displayed on the set, which came to function as the ultimate authority for the lines that were to be spoken by the actors.

That, then, was the gestation of one particular script: it has taken a long time to describe because, as we have seen, it took a long time to create.[2] Yet if a script is an important (indeed vital) ingredient in the film enterprise, it is only ever the starting-point: the chrysalis that turns into the

---

2   Information taken from the interview with Hisakazu Tsuji conducted by Ariane Mnouchkine and reprinted in the *Cahiers du Cinéma* Mizoguchi dossier (1978), pp. 17–22. It is instructive to hear of the experience in Yoda's own words, eight years after Mizoguchi's death:

> I made 20 films with him and it's only in retrospect that his instructions are comprehensible to me. He used to say: 'In your scenario, I want to have the whole human picture: what's constant in life and what is transient; the good that's in man and also the evil. On top of this, the effect on the audience has got to be one of beauty.' So I tried to make my scenario beautiful, and then he would say to me: 'It's *too* beautiful. Life isn't a bed of roses! Don't make it so diffuse. The script has got to be crystallised, concentrated. Not too beautiful, not too ugly, not too dirty, not too clean.' Such a balance was evidently hard to obtain! Even with all this explained, it's difficult to summarise what he wanted, because 'realism' itself wasn't enough, there was also a religious element, and a sort of humanism to express – above all in the later movies. It was never enough for him that the scriptwriter looked at a thing from the outside. What you looked at had to be taken into you and devoured, almost. He used to say to me: 'Wring the life out of the thing; we need to taste its blood . . . It's not enough to see man in diagram, I need to see the *inner workings of the soul*.'

(Yoshikata Yoda and Kazuo Miyagawa in conversation with Ariane Mnouchkine: *Cahiers du Cinéma* Mizoguchi dossier (1978), p. 24. [Quotations from this source shortened henceforth to '*Cahiers* Mizoguchi dossier'. Unless otherwise stated, translations are by the author.])

movie-butterfly (to borrow another concept from Jean-Claude Carrière). A film is also – perhaps pre-eminently – a work of visual symbolism. Pictorial motifs, in this sense, exist prior even to the first draft of the script, for it may have been a single image, encountered in sleep or in reverie, that set off the desire to make the movie in the first place. (Films, you could say, are always being *dreamt* into existence.) As I mentioned earlier, Mizoguchi trained as a painter when young, and right at the beginning of any new enterprise he would set down his thoughts in a multitude of sketches. In his notepads, the buildings, costumes, faces, landscapes of the film began slowly to take shape. Fantasy was important, but (film being a realistic art form) so was the rival pressure of 'truth to life' – especially for period films. On each of his projects Mizoguchi engaged the services of a picture researcher (after the war this was usually the task of a single collaborator, Hachizo Miyajima) who would be sent off to relevant libraries and museums and instructed there to copy by hand into specially prepared notebooks (of course we are in the era before Xerox machines) the entire visual sign system of the particular era in question: trades, weapons, costumes, transportation, religious ceremonies and so on. The information contained in these folders, assimilated and interiorised by Mizoguchi, formed the basis, in due course, for his all-important discussions with the art department.[3]

Art Direction

The art department got seriously into gear after the fourth or fifth version of the script had been completed – some three or four months down the line. Anyone who has had the chance to see a cross-section of Japanese films from the classic period will acknowledge that the visual splendour of these movies is one of their chief claims to glory: the taste, the restraint, the care taken over costumes and architecture are obvious even to the uninitiated eye. Mizoguchi's authority and instinct led him to collaborate with some of the finest masters in this field, including Yoshiji Oguri at Nikkatsu in the 1920s and 30s, in addition to Kisaku Ito and (above all) Hiroshi Mizutani at Shochiku and Daiei after the war. Japanese film directors, in general, had a high degree of visual education: but there was something exceptional in the level of expertise, scholarship and connoisseurship that Mizoguchi brought to the films he was involved in. Kurosawa, whose own period sets possess a remarkable plastic beauty (I am thinking of the mist-shrouded feudal castle in *Throne of Blood,* with its huge banqueting spaces and acres of polished oak floorboards – but many other examples could be given) acknowledges the paramount debt he owed to Mizoguchi, when he writes:

---

3   A word or two more should be added about Miyajima, one of the last surviving members of the Mizoguchi 'team' (still alive as I write in 2004). He joined Daiei in 1951 as a *fukozu* (specialist in the study of people's manners and customs) and worked with Mizoguchi on six films: *Miss Oyu, The Life of Oharu, Ugetsu Monogatari, Crucified Lovers, Gion Festival Music* and *Tales of the Taira Clan.* In the course of his career, Miyajima researched and compiled over ninety thick notebooks that are still in his personal possession. His testimony about Mizoguchi was published in a brief moving memoir: an antidote to the more disabused accounts of the director's intransigence which make up (justifiably, no doubt) such an inordinately large part of the legend. For Miyajima, Mizoguchi's 'strictness' was only professionalism: he stresses on the contrary his 'democratic tendencies' (the democracy of specialists: professors are specialists – but so are gardeners and cleaners), his astonishing human curiosity, and finally the kindness that Mizoguchi showed in all his dealings with Miyajima himself.

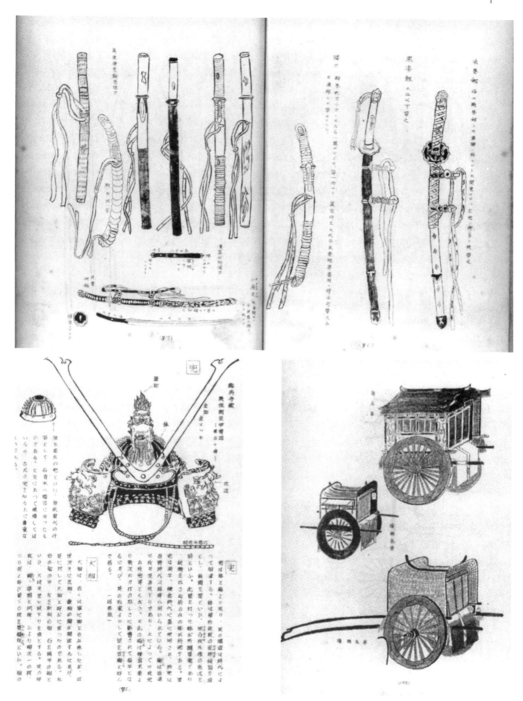

The ceaseless search for authenticity: sketches from Hachizo Miyajima's 215-page research dossier used as a basis for the production design of *Tales of the Taira Clan* (1955)

The first director to demand authentic sets and props was Kenji Mizoguchi and the sets of his films were truly superb. In my opinion, there is no question but that the quality of the decor influences the quality of the actors' performances. If the plan of a house and the design of the rooms are done properly, the actors can move about in them naturally. If on the contrary I have to tell an actor 'Don't think about where this room is in relation to the rest of the house', natural ease cannot be achieved. For this reason, I have the sets made *exactly like the real thing*: it . . . encourages the feeling of authenticity.[4]

'He was so terribly difficult to satisfy', the production designer Hiroshi Mizutani adds, 'because he knew so much! And then he used to change everything the whole time. He was like a painter who is ceaselessly correcting his canvas as he goes along' (*Cahiers* Mizoguchi dossier, p. 12). Again: 'What was inspiring about him was that he never settled for the known, the safe or the ordinary. He constantly tried to break out of his past accomplishments, striving for the new.' Mizoguchi's instruction to his visual collaborators would alternate, alarmingly, between the suggestively vague and the terrifyingly precise, but serious historical authenticity, as I have said, was always the grail that he sought. His meticulousness, in this as in everything purely professional, was legendary. On one famous occasion the art director of *Ugetsu*, Kisaku Ito, was upbraided for providing the wrong (i.e. historically incorrect) type of paving stones for a particular location. 'We haven't the money to get the right paving stones,' the art director pleaded. 'So find it!' was Mizoguchi's curt reply. Thus at enormous cost and with equally enormous labour, the stones were duly found and laid. Yet when the scene in question came to be shot, other rival artistic demands intervened, which meant that the slabs in question were covered with leaves and consequently invisible to the viewer. Ito's feelings of frustration may easily be imagined. Still, as a point of principle, Mizoguchi respected the knowledge and dedication of the technicians, craftsmen and artists whom he had chosen so carefully. He was in fact – so everyone says – an excellent listener. Installed on the set, he was preternaturally alive to the moment, assimilating at lightning speed the remarks of collaborators and diverting them towards his own artistic ends. In his dealings with actors (with some of whom, as we'll see in a moment, he had the most complicated of relationships) he was open to finding the best way of interpreting a scene.

Engagement and Training of Actors

Different countries have different traditions, yet the best work in cinema is usually designed from the beginning with particular players in mind. Unlike the theatre, where the writing needs to be rich enough to sustain multiple interpretations through the ages, a film is (generally speaking) a one-off affair in which dialogue, though still important, is subordinated to the actor's physical appearance and bearing. Getting the casting right is always important where performance is concerned, but absolutely crucial in cinema. Tanaka tells us in one of her interviews that Mizoguchi was prepared to wait five years to bring together the exact band of actors he wanted for *The Life of Oharu*. Naturally – like all directors – Mizoguchi had strong views on the *kind* of actors he wanted to work with. So what should be their provenance, by preference? Often, he preferred

---

4   Akira Kurosawa, *Something Like an Autobiography* (1982), p. 197.

actors who came from the theatrical tradition, which, as we shall see, was immensely alive for him. He loved everything to do with the milieu of the stage – the effortless sense it gave out of secrets and depths and deceptions; also, of course, the ease and elegance of the actors themselves, whose traditions and training would ensure a minimum sophistication in whichever roles they undertook.

Still, cinema, of course, is more naturalistic than theatre. In some cases, Mizoguchi evidently felt that stage actors were not the best agents to convey that crucial sense of ordinariness and restraint on which the 'truth-quotient' of cinema depends.[5] He was happy with unknowns – people who came from nowhere, so to speak, but who seemed to contain, in their eyes, in their bearing and in their gestures, some residue of lived experience which would more than compensate for a lack of formal training. In which case, the problem then was to get them to see that pure naturalism was not enough either, and that performance and fantasy are always at the bottom of art. There is no theatre – no cinema – without *playing,* Mizoguchi maintained. Isuzu Yamada's testimony, delivered at the time of the director's death, is lucid on this point:

> I remember one day, as I bent down to pick up a handkerchief, he said, 'That's Isuzu Yamada's way. Have you ever thought about the best way for the *character* to do it?' Near the end of this shoot [*Osaka Elegy* (1936)] I was supposed to enter the house and, seeing my brother and sister eating *sukiyaki,* say in a strong Osakan dialect, 'I'll have some *sukiyaki* too.' I changed the accent in dozens of ways and used every possible intonation, but Mizoguchi was never satisfied. Despite countless rehearsals, we stopped for the day without completing the scene.
>
> This was a tremendous shock for me, especially since [up till then] we had been working so smoothly. When I got home, I couldn't eat. My depression was intensified by my knowledge that the previous scenes had felt exactly like scenes from my own life. But now I no longer knew whether I was the character or the character was me, because the two had become mixed up inextricably.[6]

Disentangling this mixture (by performing, so to speak, just to the 'south' of the personality you possessed in real life) was the route to effective film-acting, but the actor was ultimately alone in finding the secret of how to do this. On set, Mizoguchi didn't give signals, for he expected his cast to have prepared themselves as thoroughly as possible before the shooting began. If it was a period film, then the actor or actress would have been instructed to study books and to have found out as much as possible about the everyday texture of the time in which the story was set. Naturally, once they were given a script the actors would have to have studied it carefully. Meanwhile, the

---

5   Hideo Tsumura recalls an episode involving Kawaguchi's wife, Aiko Mimasu, a distinguished stage actress to whom
    Mizoguchi gave a small but important part in *Street of Shame/Akasen Chitai* (1956). As Tsumura recounts it:
       Mimasu [playing a prostitute] gets out of the taxi and walks away and the camera follows her. The action
       was rehearsed again and again but Mizoguchi didn't like the way she did it. According to the actress, she
       repeated the action 80 times. Mizoguchi told her straight: 'Mimasu-kun, you are married to my friend, but
       you are a bad actress.' And he grumbled at her: 'You need to walk on the earth. Don't walk on the boards.
       You're not on the stage!'
    (Hideo Tsumura, *A Man Called Mizoguchi Kenji,* 1977 [translation kindly provided by Kimitoshi Sato].)
6   'Learning from My Mentor', in J. Quandt and G. O'Grady (1996), p. 14.

shooting schedules were arranged as far as possible to follow the story sequentially, thereby allowing the actors the opportunity to grow into their roles, and to develop with the story as *it* developed.

On the set, on the day in question, there was a feeling of excitement and engagement. As already noted, a large blackboard was prominently displayed, on which was chalked up the final version of the script to be shot that day – often, alas, considerably different in detail from the lines that the actors had memorised. The morning rehearsals were arduous, geared towards finding the most natural and fluent way to speak the lines (and changing them on the blackboard as necessary). Beyond the lines themselves what was being sought was a level of play – of relaxation almost – whereby the drama could 'take off' and the film itself come to life. Mizoguchi used to say that if *he* could respond to the emotion invoked, the audience would respond to it too. 'Be the mirror of the personage you're playing, reflect him, be natural!' That, in a way, was the most he ever asked of them.

If it was exciting for the actors it was also painful. Many examples of Mizoguchi's unbelievably demanding standards have been cited over the years. Tanaka recalls an occasion when she inadvertently (but perhaps forgivably) let her guard down. Shooting was over on *Sansho the Bailiff*. The following day she would be needed for only a few hours to record the famous song where she laments the loss of her children. Shooting had been hard over the previous months and Tanaka had been dieting in order to look haggard in the role; so on the evening in question – the evening of her 'release' – she took herself off to a restaurant, and celebrated by ordering a steak. Next day, at the recording station, Mizoguchi was sarcastic. 'What is this "happy voice" I'm hearing?', he asked, after the first shots. 'It's not the voice I need.' According to Tanaka, he had detected the clandestine steak! Five hours outside in the freezing winter weather and numerous exhausting runs with the sound crew were required before Tanaka's voice was 'tuned back' to a level of harshness that chimed with her performance in the movie . . .[7]

Sound

The correct timbre for Tanaka's voice is of course a sound issue as well as an acting issue. Far more than many of his contemporaries, Mizoguchi was aware that quality of sound is one of the most crucial elements in cinema. Seldom appreciated as such by the average filmgoer (in contrast, perhaps, to the more immediate impact of the photography), naturalism, or truth to nature, on the soundtrack is one of the key means by which concrete reality is introduced into the film's aesthetic equation, and maintained there. The example just given – the registering of Tanaka's lament – is, of course, an instance of the method of recording sound called dubbing: the additional layer of the actress's voice, registered after the scene has been shot, is being laid over an already existing soundtrack. Much cinema sound is built up like this – indeed some national cinemas (like the Italian) are entirely post-synched, from beginning to end. Mizoguchi, as we'll see in a moment, preferred where possible to use synchronous sound, but when he was forced to dub (as in the example just given), he made sure that the atmosphere of the recording matched to the smallest detail the environment of the scene that had been shot. That meant, essentially, that if it was an

---

7   *Cahiers* Mizoguchi dossier, p. 17: conversation with Kinuyo Tanaka.

outdoor scene, the dubbing must be recorded *outdoors*, no matter what technical difficulties this gave rise to, since an audience can always tell the difference, even subliminally, between sound that belongs in the open air and sound that belongs to the studio.

Why not, then, use synchronous sound always? Sometimes this is simply impossible. The location may be close to a natural sound source (highway, railway line, airfield), the noises from which intrude on the recording, or else on the set itself there may be arc lights involved in a highly lit scene which will generate an interfering hum over the dialogue. In short, there are all sorts of reasons. Before the mid-1950s, dialogues were recorded, cumbersomely, by the registration of sound waves on optical film – portable tape recorders came into service only at the very end of Mizoguchi's career – and the bulky equipment required by this technology imposed further restrictions on the possibilities of 'going synchronous'. So it required a strong nerve on Mizoguchi's part to insist on a naturalism of sound not available to his contemporaries. Even if the results that came from this method were raw and imperfect, they were justified because they amplified the truth of the performance. Iwao Ohtani, who was the recordist on a number of Mizoguchi's films dating from the late 1940s, testifies to Mizoguchi's determination in these matters:

At the time, a recording technician was called 'Mr Upstairs', for we mixed sounds inside an elevated booth cut off from the set, or sometimes out of sight completely in a separate recording bus. Mizoguchi was not satisfied with our situation because the cinematographer and the lighting man were close to the scene, and in our distant perch we were, so to speak, blindfolded. 'Gan san', he said (that was my nickname) 'I can't believe that a recording technician can record sounds without *seeing* what's happening on the spot.' Since I secretly agreed with him, I managed to talk the company and the assistants into taking the mixing machine out of the booth. Now for the first time we saw how the camera moved, the action took place, and the microphones were arranged! It caused me the most fantastic amount of trouble, but the quality of the soundtrack certainly did improve enormously.[8]

Cinematography

Far more obviously than sound, perhaps, images and iconography are identified in the audience's mind with the movie. The role of the cinematographer is always crucial, but especially so for a film-maker like Mizoguchi whose work is so clearly informed at all levels by the history and tradition of the fine arts. Over the past hundred years Japan has produced many wonderful cameramen. Mizoguchi worked with a number of the best of these: Tatsuyuki Yokota and Jinichiro Aojima in

---

8   Ohtani gives a couple of instances – one from *Miss Oyu* and the other from *Crucified Lovers* (1954) – that are interesting. In the former film, a long tracking shot following a low and intimate conversation between the two principal characters in a garden was rendered almost impossible to record by the crunching sound of their footsteps on the gravel. Instead of overdubbing later, Mizoguchi's solution here was to go for another take, meanwhile sprinkling the pathway liberally with sawdust. (Apparently this worked perfectly.) In *Crucified Lovers* (Ohtani's favourite Mizoguchi film), the scene on Lake Biwa where the lovers prepare to commit suicide was causing extraordinary difficulties to the recording team perched on a nearby raft. Though the live sound recording in the rough cut had minor technical imperfections, Mizoguchi determined to stay with it (and not re-record): the *emotion* was there, and that, he declared, was the thing that mattered. (These examples, and the quotation that precedes them, are taken from Takeshi Yamaguchi (ed.), *Kenji Mizoguchi Centennial Album* (1998), pp. 84–5 [translated at the author's request by Kimitoshi Sato].)

the 1920s, Shigeru Miki and Minoru Miki in the 30s and 40s, Kohei Sugiyama and the legendary Kazuo Miyagawa (as already mentioned) in the 40s and 50s. Miyagawa, who was linked at different times in his career to such interesting cineastes as Kurosawa (he shot *Rashomon* for him in 1950), Kinoshita, Inagaki, Ozu and Ichikawa, came into his own with Mizoguchi, for whom he lit and photographed eight out of the director's final eleven movies. His testimony, presented across several admiring and illuminating interviews, confirms in crucial ways what I have already said about the freedom Mizoguchi extended to his chief collaborators, while at the same time furnishing further evidence of the extraordinary sense of concentration – tension, *anguish* almost – that prevailed on the set, both during the rehearsals and into the actual task of filming.

Mizoguchi, as I say, gave Miyagawa great freedom: he never looked through his cameraman's viewfinder, or sought to compose the dynamics of the shot. He felt these things were the legitimate province of the men he employed; the point was to have a cinematographer whom you trusted, and who shared your basic sense of visual decorum. The meticulous preparation in all the other departments of the film's pre-production seems to have been geared towards leaving open one final pocket of creative freedom here. Mizoguchi's scripts studiously avoid giving any indication either of the movement of the camera or the distance that should be maintained from the players. The shape, movement, choreography and lighting of the film's shots were the ultimate secrets to be discovered on the day of the shoot. Their discovery, in effect, *defined* for Mizoguchi the process of live film-making.

Kenji Mizogichi directing *Street of Shame* (1956): cameraman Kazuo Miyagawa behind him

Mizoguchi a Martinet?

Within the framework of customary industry practices, the way that a film-maker works has a large degree of latitude. Different directors have different methods and idiosyncrasies. The fact that Mizoguchi prepared his films with the extraordinary devotion I have described could never by itself, of course, be a guarantee that they would turn out to be masterpieces. And it is true that his perfectionism had a heavy human cost. Shindo's documentary is full of unhappy tales – the plaintive testimony of actresses (not just the famous ones, like Tanaka and Yamada) whom he pushed to the limit of endurance, and beyond.[9] One wonders: did he have to be so ruthless, so – discourteous? His methods in these matters strike one as being the opposite of directors like the Dane, Carl Th. Dreyer, who would famously offer his actress sweets from his pocket if a particular take went well; or else, to take another example, the great Jean Renoir who (like his father, the painter) took enormous pains to contrive a sense of general euphoria in the workplace. I have no great

---

9   In the documentary, four actresses go public with negative feelings about the director. Ayako Wakao is the most bitter ('He taunted me so much, I couldn't take it any more. Even my face was wrong, apparently.'). Machiko Kyo is severe and unsentimental about her experiences on the set of *The Empress Yang Kwei Fei*. Takako Irie, who generously supported Mizoguchi in the 1930s, is forthright about the humiliation she received while working on the same film (Mizoguchi sacked her). And the reminiscences of Kyoko Kagawa (who has important roles in *Sansho the Bailiff* and *Crucified Lovers*) are not, it seems, governed by any great tenderness towards the director. Yoda's memoirs (as I have already mentioned) are a repository of anecdotes describing Mizoguchi's extraordinarily strict behaviour towards collaborators whom he fell out with. It is worth recounting one of these in detail. Yoda says:

> On the eve of the war Mizoguchi was engaged in shooting *The Story of Late Chrysanthemums*. An actress (let us call her Miss K) had been chosen by the company for the role of Otoku. She had a sweet and melancholy beauty that went well with the role, but she was too habituated to the standard way of shooting films to adapt herself to the extremely long takes that Mizoguchi was demanding at the time. And Mizoguchi himself wasn't giving her very precise indications of what he was after. They had arrived at the scene in which the heroine Otoku, having quit the hero Kikunosuke in order not to interfere with his career as an artist, by accident sees his name in a newspaper. Remembering her old lover wistfully, Otoku starts to walk sadly . . . 'All right, Otoku, you thought you had totally forgotten your lover. You had persuaded yourself that this *was* the case, do you understand? But suddenly you re-see his name, and all the old sentiments surge up again inside you. Have you got it? Over to you!', Mizoguchi explained with a certain vehemence. Upset because the sequence had already been tried ten times, he continued: 'Please analyse the psychology of the moment, and try to expound it by integrating it into the dialectical current of the scene.' The word 'dialectical' terrified Miss K as much as if she had been charged in a court of law! 'You're not worthy to be called an actress,' Mizoguchi grumbled: 'This isn't a second rate *chambara* film! You're acting with Shotaro Hanayagi, the greatest living *shimpa* actor.' 'I really am sorry; I was doing my best.' 'Well, we have got other things to do than sit around and wait for you. You're not in an acting academy – you're on a film set!' Poor Miss K tried in vain to get the scene right for the rest of the day. Alas, all her attempts failed to please the director. Remember that publicity about the film had been put out well in advance. People were talking about this actress and the fine opportunity she was lucky enough to get in playing with the great Shotaro Hanayagi. And here she was, dying of shame at the idea of having to abandon the part because of this scene she had messed up. The upshot I'm afraid is that Mizoguchi sacked her, without pity, and brought in Kakuko Mori instead, an actress who had the relevant experience to play the scene. Mori in fact rose to the challenge, and gave an admirable interpretation of the role. Yet I myself can never forget the fate of poor Miss K.

(*Souvenirs de Kenji Mizoguchi*, 1997, pp. 75–6 [author's translation].)

experience in these matters, but I have vivid memories of witnessing the Russian director Andrei Konchalovsky working on the set at Pinewood in 1986, and how pleasantly relaxed he made the whole procedure – within the context of a necessary, impressive discipline. 'If [film-making] doesn't make you happy in your heart,' he said to me at lunch one day, 'you shouldn't do it.' Did it make Mizoguchi 'happy', and did *he* make his collaborators happy? The answer is, probably not. But happiness, equally, isn't everything in art. Niceness, defined as a general diplomacy, or ability to put people at their ease, seems not to have been Mizoguchi's forte. In a fascinating passage in his memoirs, Yoda defends Mizoguchi's 'savagery' in terms of the results achieved:

> Mizoguchi detested affectation and coquetry: he admired sincerity and honesty above everything, even if those qualities were burdened with awkwardness. All that vanity and preciosity and insincerity of sentiment that one sometimes associates with the acting profession repulsed him profoundly. He pitied actresses who could only express themselves in a stereotyped way. He wanted to strip them bare and get them to expose their naked hearts without fear of whether they and their souls would be found 'ugly'. Such an attitude could easily be taken for sadism, but in truth it stemmed from something cruelly human and forthright in his make-up. Mizoguchi had an extraordinarily subtle intelligence. When he sensed that a particular actress had talent, he would endeavour without concessions of any kind to bring it up to the surface.[10]

So it would be wrong (indeed it would be grotesque) to think of the man as a monster. 'Outside his work, he was a gentle soul,' recalls Tsuji. Parallel to his extraordinary artistic curiosity ran a curious human shyness. He blushed easily and apparently found it difficult to look women in the eye. He seems to have followed rules of his own making, governed by impulses, demons and torments that are doubtless in the last resort unreachable to outsiders. In the end, of course, what matters is the art he bequeathed to us.

---

10 Yoda, *Souvenirs de Kenji Mizoguchi*, p. 57 (author's translation).

4 | The Great Triptych

If Mizoguchi's name lives on at all in the consciousness of the general filmgoing public it is probably by association with the three large-scale historical works that were produced in successive years in the early 1950s: *The Life of Oharu* (1952), *Ugetsu Monogatari* (1953) and *Sansho the Bailiff* (1954), each of which won the same major international prize, the Silver Lion, awarded at Venice for what the jury judges to be the 'next best' film of the festival. Next best, in retrospect, seems ungenerous in relation to films that have slowly imposed themselves as among the very great masterpieces of world cinema, but that is the way of festivals. One has to be grateful for the recognitions that they do confer. It was at Venice, after all, that Japanese film was first decisively put on the map of Western consciousness, through the prize awarded to Kurosawa's *Rashomon* in 1951 and the publicity that followed from this.

Rashomon, then, brought back the Golden Lion under the banner of a younger representative of post-war Japanese cinema, while these three films by Mizoguchi had to content themselves with the Silver. Pointless to complain at this distance that the slightest of the four films should have won the highest award. The rivalry between Kurosawa and Mizoguchi is one of those structuring polarities that are at the basis of any sustained reflection on Japanese film, and even those supporters of the older master who believe (as I do) that there is no dispute as to Mizoguchi's pre-eminence will have benefited from spending some time in the opposite camp. As Bazin says, anyone who wholeheartedly prefers Kurosawa must be 'blind', but he adds the caution, tenderly, 'he who loves only Mizoguchi must be one-eyed'.[1] Our allegiances are more fickle (or perhaps I mean merely more pluralist) than they were in the heyday of the *politique des auteurs*. And that is good for us, if it can enlarge our sympathy without dampening our powers of discrimination.

More immediately (and leaving aside for a moment the Kurosawa question) there is the interesting speculation as to which, among the three films, is the finest: the quintessence of Mizoguchi, so to speak. With *Oharu*, it is the performance of Tanaka that overwhelmingly compels admiration: the sense that we are watching a film in which women's destiny and women's suffering are dramatised as never before. Thus, if the word still means anything, it is a wonderful and true film of feminism. *Ugetsu Monogatari*, on the other hand, is one of the greatest films ever about the corruption and debauchery of warfare. It is interesting that this film alone among Mizoguchi's works is popularly known by its Japanese title, implying a certain familiarity and affection. (The English title, some-

---

1   Quoted by François Truffaut in the preface to André Bazin, *What Is Cinema?*, vol II (1971) p. vii. For further reflections on the Kurosawa–Mizoguchi debate, see Appendix 1: 'Mizoguchi and French Film Criticism'.

The deceptiveness of dreams: Masayuki Mori as the potter Genjuro and Machiko Kyo as Lady Wakasa in *Ugetsu Monogatari/Tales of the Watery Moon* (1953)

times used, is *Tales of the Watery Moon*.) I believe *Ugetsu* is historically the most famous of the three: its comparative brevity, the variety of its tone and subject matter (two stories, each containing two main characters, knitted together with consummate skill), its fierce realism, and finally its flavour of a sort of ghostly aestheticism, all combine to make it one of the most mysterious and suggestive films in the whole of the Japanese repertoire.

Still, despite *Ugetsu*'s genius, it is in the end probably a less organic work than *The Life of Oharu*, and also than *Sansho the Bailiff*. All such judgments are subjective, of course, but it is *Sansho the Bailiff* which increasingly seems to be seen as the deepest and finest of all Mizoguchi's works – his *King Lear*, so to speak, the summation and quintessence of his artistry. Experiencing it in the right conditions, the viewer can begin to feel that this is one of the very few works on film whose emotional range and moral splendour can truly stand comparison with Shakespeare.

Mizoguchi and Saikaku

The Life of Oharu, the first of the three films to be considered here, tells the story of the decline into prostitution of a well-born, seventeenth-century woman who loses caste through a love affair with a man who is her social inferior. According to the harsh laws of the epoch, love affairs between members of the nobility and lower-samurai families were proscribed, and the man in question (his is a small role at the beginning of the film, taken by Toshiro Mifune) is duly executed, by beheading. The scandal throws Oharu out into the streets. The rest of the film shows her adventures as, first, a courtesan, and, latterly, while she declines towards old age, a wandering common prostitute.

The film is an adaptation of the novel *The Life of an Amorous Woman/Koshoku Ichidai Onna* (1686) by the classic Japanese writer Iharu Saikaku. Saikaku was an enormously prolific novelist and poet (he was one of the most prolific poets of all time) and his work as a whole gives an unprecedentedly vivid picture of all layers of society in the latter half of seventeenth-century Japan: a society, as I have suggested, rigid on the one hand, in the grip of Tokugawa feudalism, but on the other hand (in different places) curiously free, mobile and complicated. Though in the latter years of his life he wrote about samurai, Saikaku's main subject was the erotic life of the merchant classes, focusing particularly on younger sons with too much money to spend. He paints the picaresque affairs of these youths in the licensed quarters in a direct, witty and studiously non-judgmental fashion. Occasionally, as in *The Life of an Amorous Woman*, it is women rather than men who carry the burden of the narrative; but in these cases too the writing shares the same light-hearted and non-psychologised amoralism.

This is the first and most striking thing about Mizoguchi's adaptation. In transferring the novel to the screen, the director and the scenarist Yoshikata Yoda have moved the story at one stroke into the tragic mode: they have dared to make it serious. There are aspects of Saikaku's work that, viewed under a certain light, are not altogether hostile to this transformation, but at first glance it is nothing less than astonishing. You would have to look far and wide to find another example of an original comic masterpiece undergoing, successfully, such a radical alteration of tonality while remaining faithful (as far as plot is concerned) to the original.

If we wanted to say in a word what has happened to bring about this aesthetic sea-change, it is that the character of the heroine is, in this new version, for the first time endowed with a soul.

She becomes reflective about her fate and, in the process, psychologically interesting. Numerous sequences of the film which concentrate on capturing the sublime silent gaze of Tanaka testify to the fact that this was Mizoguchi's artistic intention – to give Oharu dignity, by providing her with thoughtfulness and memory. One of the immediate key alterations Mizoguchi makes, therefore, to Saikaku's original narrative is to reconstitute the story into the form of a flashback. (The film begins with the aged Oharu wandering into a temple and recognising in a statue of a Bodhisattva the features of her executed lover.) The picaresque nature of Saikaku's original story precludes, almost structurally, any extended dwelling on the significance of its individual incidents. His 'Amorous Woman' lives in the perpetual present tense of her serial erotic encounters. Any pathos accruing to the tale comes from the outside – from the reader's own anxieties about Oharu's feck-lessness: it is not, as it were, inherent in the original. This is not Mizoguchi's way. By recasting the story in the way he does, he is able to weigh certain events against others: he is able to compare and to analyse. He *shapes* his heroine's life through the optic of her remembrance, and, in endow-ing her with reflectiveness, distills (even as the culmination of her failures) a sort of redemption.

Plainly, what we have here on Mizoguchi's part is an effort to deepen, and to humanise, Saikaku. In exchange for Saikaku's comic heartlessness, Mizoguchi proposes that the heroine's life should be experienced subjectively, in the context of pity and suffering. Certain differences follow from this that should be noted. In the original novel, Oharu's curiosity is sexual: she is in a con-ventional sense 'bad' from the start. Certainly, there are no *pudeurs* in Mizoguchi's film; he has no prejudices at all against the body. But he stresses far more than Saikaku does – and extracts from it an appropriate dramatic irony – that the root cause of the woman's downfall stems from a higher, platonic impulse of love. It was love that founded Oharu's misfortune: she remains faith-ful both to the experience and to the man. Her subsequent encounters are not so much chosen or gloried in, as endured and put up with (though there is a productive ambiguity here – she is never exactly *deprived of* desire). In contradiction to Saikaku, Mizoguchi makes the strongest of all her instincts maternal. These are the scenes – three or four passages between mother and son – in which, it seems to me, the film presses out its strongest emotional chords, and captures the sub-limity of tragedy.

To recall the plot in brief: feudal Lord Matsudaira[2] has been looking for a concubine who will possess all his favourite traits, and Oharu, living in disgrace with her parents after the love affair, turns out (after a kind of beauty contest) to fit the bill perfectly. Taken into his house, she sub-sequently becomes pregnant, eliciting the jealousy of Matsudaira's official wife, who contrives to take the infant away from her at childbirth and bring him up as her own. Years later – expelled from the household and fallen into the path of ruin – Oharu catches sight of the child being carried in a palanquin. Her obsession now is to meet him, not (we are led to believe) to 'better' herself or her fate, but simply to hold and to gaze on the child she had once clasped in her arms: an ambi-tion thwarted, in due course, by clan bodyguards when they forcibly eject her from the palace gangway across which her son is processing.

---

2   The family name is historical: one of the most distinguished in Japan. (It was also, incidentally, the surname of the nobleman whose marriage to Mizoguchi's sister rescued her from her career as a geisha.)

Scattering his coin with a
buccaneer's largesse:
seventeenth-century brothel
scene from *The Life of Oharu*
(1952)

All Mizoguchi's genius for pathos goes into this heartbreaking scene of recognition – surely one of the greatest sequences in the whole of his work. To repeat: as an interpreter of the human heart (and by extension of the human condition), Mizoguchi shows himself far superior to Saikaku. For one thing, he profoundly understands the meaning of *ascesis*. He sees that if a society is to call itself civilised not all impulses – especially, perhaps, the sexual urge – can or should be given in to. There is something higher than sex, and the name of that higher thing is love. *The Life of Oharu* is an *ascetic* rather than an erotic film; it is fundamentally different from the book, and different, too, from a movie like Oshima's *In the Realm of the Senses/Ai No Corrida* (1976) whose one and only aim, I suppose, is to celebrate bodily *jouissance*. Nonetheless, as I have said, Mizoguchi's film is not *against* sex. Like all great Japanese art, it is superbly unmoralistic. It refuses to make the body shameful. At certain moments, Kinuyo Tanaka's performance dramatises with great force and subtlety the double-edged spell of female beauty: that, in a traditional society, for a beautiful woman who has fallen from caste, there is no *escape* from the flesh.

This can be seen most clearly in the episode where, after various adventures, Oharu finds refuge and peace of sorts in a nunnery, only to discover her past catching up with her. A lovely kimono – the innocently received gift from a previous admirer – turns out to be made of stolen cloth, and the owner of the cloth (her admirer's boss) is standing at the door to requisition it. With what superb understated mockery Oharu proposes that he take the kimono off her naked back; and with what proud fatalistic resignation she accepts the truth of the situation, that the price for his silence will be to sleep with him. He is a scoundrel of course; yet in a way she still *wants* to sleep with him, even though it will mean (what inevitably happens) being expelled in disgrace from the convent. The ascetic life calls; yet the call is fated to be unheeded. Why? Because that is life, and we are human. So it is with other brilliantly imagined sequences in the film where the viewer gets a sense of the 'other side' of Oharu's goodness: her sexuality and – along with this – her penchant for satire and mischief. Satire is the essence of the scene where she sets a cat to steal the wig from the jealous wife of another employer, causing, at a key moment, the unfortunate woman's baldness to be revealed to him. More centrally, it is the lifeblood of the great scene at the brothel in Shimabura, where Oharu's patron-of-the-evening turns out to be a counterfeiter, dragged off in front of her eyes by the police.

The staging of this last scene has extraordinary panache. There is the brothel, with its scurry and bustle on different levels, beautifully incarnated (only Welles, I think, is Mizoguchi's equal in conjuring up large-scale sets and then peopling them with figures whose complex interaction belongs to their own autonomy, rather than to some pre-arranged choreography). In the midst of it all, scattering his newly minted coin with a buccaneer's largesse (while doing his best to impress Oharu): the counterfeiter. And what we feel about Oharu, who has been bored and reluctant to participate until the moment of unmasking, is a quickening, when that unmasking takes place, of *complicity*. She is at one with the outlaw, because she is an outlaw herself. So in the wake of the fiasco, the owner of the brothel is right to expel her from the premises (as the abbess was right to expel her from the nunnery). Quietly and delicately, she declines to kowtow to the system. Spiritually, if not legally, she is the owner of her body – as entitled to withhold it as to grant it.

The secondary roles in *The Life of Oharu* – the brothel owners, the jealous husbands, the fawning admirers, the miscellaneous rogues and companions our heroine meets on her journey – are all imagined, it seems to me, with a particularity and sense of comic sharpness that belong firmly to classic art, in which knowledge of human nature is inseparable from a precise knowledge of 'type'. This may be one of the ways in which the film is not, after all, so different from the original. Running through Mizoguchi's adaptation, the comic tone of Saikaku is never wholly abandoned. *Chaplin wo toritai*, he said: 'I wanted to shoot the film *à la Chaplin*.' On the other hand, comedy pure and simple does not sum up Saikaku's writing either and somewhere they meet in the middle. I say this because, while it is undoubtedly true that the attitude taken by Saikaku towards erotic encounters is a sort of uncomplicated cheerfulness (his philosophy in these matters being that an opportunity should never be wasted), still there are other places in his oeuvre where one senses a more reflective sobriety. He is, in a way, a great realist as well as a great comic painter, and this would have appealed to Mizoguchi. His work sings the joys of the body, but is not blind to the degradation and unhappiness that haunts all ruthless and energetic pursuit of sexual pleasure. Not ideologically, and not (certainly not) as a 'frontal attack', but poetically and in the interstices of his anecdotes, Saikaku shows towards the social fact of prostitution a melancholy *ambivalence*:

> Some of them [prostitutes at the bottom of the pyramid] earn their money to help out aged parents. Others, with no other means of family livelihood, are forced into the clandestine trade. Mothers leave their babies with grandmother. Older sisters sacrifice younger sisters. Uncles, aunts, nieces – all exploit one another just to keep body and soul together. They are so poor that on rainy nights they have to borrow high wooden clogs and parasols, as they cannot afford to buy any. Never staying more than one month at one back-street shelter, they move from place to place or seek new hiding-nooks. They wheedle new landlords. They insinuate themselves into the good graces of neighbours with gifts of cheap wine. They buy their firewood with what little cash they possess. Soon the smoke will vanish from their kitchen. They know nothing of the pleasures of moon-viewing, nothing of the beauty of snow, nothing of the happiness of the new year. Oh the ignominy, the misery, the pity of it all![3]

Tales of the Watery Moon

Like *The Life of Oharu*, *Ugetsu Monogatari* is a literary adaptation, taken, in this case, from several pre-existing sources. In film criticism, it seems to me that works that are wholly original have a special value. Other things being equal, we like the fact that a given classic springs, as it were, fully armed out of nowhere. There is something astonishing and grand about a film like *Citizen Kane* being, in addition to all its other attributes, completely 'invented'. But Welles's other works *were* adaptations, and, for the most part, there is no diminution of power or of genius. Likewise, most of the plots of Bergman's films come out of his own imagination but – to cite another Scandinavian master – the majority of Carl Th. Dreyer's films do not. On the contrary, *Vampyr, Ordet, Gertrud* etc. are supreme works of adaptation, finer than the originals they spring from. Bresson too, in masterpieces like *Les Dames du Bois de Boulogne* (1945) and *Le Journal d'un curé de campagne* (1951), is engaged in a similar task of refinement: that is, he extracts from the original literary artefact what is most vivid and intelligent about it, retrospectively endowing the original work – perhaps for the first time – with its real (or platonic) shape and harmony.

---

3 Iharu Saikaku, *The Life of an Amorous Man* (1684), translated by Keiji Hamada (Tokyo: Charles E. Tuttle Co., 1963), p. 87.

It doesn't of course always work like this. Cinema history is full of dull adaptations – adaptations that do no more than bring the given work to the screen respectably. I believe that *Ugetsu Monogatari* belongs to a wholly different category than this: as in *The Life of Oharu*, the adaptation shapes a radically new work out of its sources. For, though it comes from an attested literary origin, you can't really call *Ugetsu Monogatari* a formal adaptation: it is not like (say) *The Leopard* or *The Magnificent Ambersons*. Instead, ideas are taken from different stories and woven together with an extremely bold freedom into a new synthesis. The script is a triumph of bricolage: mixed, mingling, audacious. Yet the end result – miraculously – has the organic wholeness of a fairy tale.

Ugetsu Monogatari, the literary text, published in 1776, is itself a disparate collection of tales, set in largely different time periods, written by the novelist Akinari Ueda (1734–1809). Mizoguchi chooses two of them and reconstitutes them into a single narrative, binding into the mix a couple of tales from yet another source, the nineteenth-century French writer Guy de Maupassant. The two stories in question by Akinari are known in English as 'The House amid the Thickets' and 'The Lust of the White Serpent', the first set in the fifteenth century (a precise date, 1455, in the middle of the Onin War), the second far earlier, in Japan's aristocratic Heian past (tenth to twelfth centuries).

In 'The House amid the Thickets' an averagely prosperous farmer named Katsushiro travels to Kyoto to sell his silk, leaving his wife behind to look after the house. His business completed, he attempts to return home, but is waylaid by robbers and subsequently falls ill. The illness turns out to be protracted and, what with one thing and another, it is seven years before he feels able to make the journey home, spurred on by the guilty knowledge that his wife will surely be waiting for him.

On his arrival he is greeted by her in a friendly fashion and spends the evening and night in her company, but the next day when he wakes up she has vanished. Enquiries in the village elicit the fact that his beloved spouse died and was buried two years after his departure, so that the woman he met the previous night was not his wife, but her ghost. Overcome with remorse, Katsushiro visits her grave in the company of the old man who buried her, who proceeds to recount the pathetic tale of Tegona, a maiden of long ago of great beauty who, abandoned by her husband, cast herself into the waves. (The story is found in the *Man'yo-sho*, Japan's great eighth-century anthology of poetry.) Both men weep; and Katsushiro composes a thirty-one-syllable poem which takes as its refrain: 'I loved my wife every bit as much.'

That is the tale in its essence. Readers who know the film even casually will immediately recognise similarities with incidents in the movie: the story's outline in fact provides the film with one of its two main structuring polarities. Of course there are differences – for example, alterations of class and characterisation. Genjuro in the film (the part taken by Masayuki Mori: Katsushiro in the book) is a peasant not a landlord, and his wares are pottery not silk. The film is much clearer than the tale both about his furious ambition (in the book he is lazy) and also about the corresponding fact that, despite everything, he loves his wife (this is true in the tale too, but ambiguously presented there). So he stays away in the film a far shorter period: a year or two at maximum, rather than seven; and he has, in addition, a son to come back to, a little child of three. Above all, the film invents, what is missing from the tale, a *reason* for Genjuro's delay, in the form of a bewitchment, or seduction.

This additional part of the story, then, is provided by the second of the Akinari tales that Mizoguchi drew on, 'The Lust of the White Serpent', rather different in character from 'The House amid the Thickets', and, in turn, adapted by Akinari from a Chinese original. In this tale, which is set in the eleventh century, an innocent young man named Toyoo (the son of a rich fisherman) is out walking in the country when he meets a mysterious woman, to whom he offers his umbrella while they are standing together sheltering from a downpour. The following day, having dreamt about her, he goes to her mansion to retrieve his property and, hearing that she is a widow, is won over by the pathos of her loneliness. When it appears that he is ready to pledge himself to her, she gives him an ancient sword as a keepsake, which however turns out to be stolen. Questioned by the police (yes, there were police in eleventh-century Japan!), Toyoo takes his interrogators to the mansion, only to discover that it – and the lady – have vanished into thin air. Though he might have been 'spinning a yarn', the police believe him – plainly he has been the victim of witchcraft.

Two stories – two vanishing women. But this second one is not yet over. The young man fails to learn his lesson, for when by accident he meets the lady again (in the neighbourhood of Tsuba market, where he is staying with his sister) he accepts an implausible explanation for her disappearance. Soon afterwards, when they are visiting a shrine on a picnic, an old hermit recognises the woman as a wicked spirit, causing her to make a second sudden exit, this time by leaping into a ravine.

She is still however not dead or accounted for! The boy's father, impatient to get the young man settled, arranges for him to marry a suitable young lady of his acquaintance who has served at the imperial court – but guess who this young lady turns out to be? When the imposter-wife is 'rumbled' for the second (or is it the third?) time, she and her attendant turn into writhing snakes with tongues of flame who ward off all attempts to snare them. An old abbot of the nearby Dojoji Temple comes up with the answer: Toyoo's father is instructed to cover the main serpent with a monk's robe, saturated with a preparation of mustard incense. This seems to do the trick; and (it is a story with a happy ending) Toyoo is released from his haunting.

Out of this long and complicated tale (it is the single longest tale in the collection) Mizoguchi fashions the exquisite episode in the film of Genjuro's bewitchment by Lady Wakasa – perhaps one of the greatest screen enchantments ever, in its musical and dreamlike limpidity. And I think the first thing to comment on is Mizoguchi's daring in seeing that the tale could be used in this way; that, by providing a reason for the delayed return that is not really given in the earlier story, it dovetails into Katsushiro's tale with no sense of strain or incongruity. As soon as it is established that the second story deals with the tactics of an enchantress, the problem of the different epochs in which the tales are set dissolves too. Granted, then, that the lady who materialises out of nowhere, as the peasant is selling his pots in the marketplace, should dazzle him out of his wits, it is not an additional surprise (indeed it is a positive aspect of the enchantment) that she should come from literally another world and another age. Everything about the lady is old-fashioned: that is her rarified charm. Few things in the finished film are handled more suavely, I think, than the way Mizoguchi governs the transition between the real, present-tense world of war of survival and making a living, and the archaic imagined world of art and luxury and erotic reverie into which Genjuro is irresistibly drawn. The viewer does not feel (any more than Genjuro does) the sudden break or sharp contrast that might be felt to exist between the marketplace and mansion-house.

For it is part of the magic of dreaming that distinctions of time – distinctions of epoch – have no special meaning or significance.

Let us see what Mizoguchi and his scriptwriters are doing here. First and foremost, they are truncating the longer story. But as with Mizoguchi's handling of Saikaku's *The Life of an Amorous Woman* (in order to shape *The Life of Oharu*) so his choice of incident from 'The Lust of the White Serpent' – both what is chosen and what is discarded – carries in its wake certain consequences for the tone of the transmuted material. In Akinari's original, the proliferation of incident – in particular, the multiple appearances and disappearances of the phantom – imposes a sort of cumulative comic effect (the corollary of which is that we feel the young man is very ineffectual). By cutting down the meetings between Genjuro and Lady Wakasa to a mere two in the film – and in other ways being ruthless with the details of the plot – Mizoguchi permits the tone of the incidents to become graver and more poetic. The supernatural (wayward, absurd and flashy in Akinari's original) is reined in and somehow de-emphasised. There are no white-fanged serpents in the movie; nothing, in fact, but Genjuro's awakened senses to tell him, when it is all over, that he has encountered a wilful, evil demon. And in fact, the really memorable aspects of the episode – Lady Wakasa's extraordinary dance of seduction, and the bath Genjuro shares with her to seal their tryst; or later on, the Sanskrit lettering inscribed on Genjuro's back that ushers in the final terrifying showdown – are all inventions (brilliant inventions) by Mizoguchi and Yoda.

Mizoguchi in all this shows a supreme mastery of structure: the art of *Ugetsu Monogatari* is before everything else the art of the *screenplay*. The Lady Wakasa episode we have just considered is indeed just an episode (a sort of excursus, or subplot), yet its integration into the main plot is what gives the whole film its resonance and beauty. In one of the film's supreme touches, Mizoguchi juxtaposes Genjuro's life of luxury (the bath with Lady Wakasa, followed by the picnic *à deux* in an idyllic meadow) with the scene of his wife Miyagi's murder – she is speared to death miles away, on a lonely path, by drunken soldiers. This is one of the most famous scenes in all Mizoguchi's cinema, and we shall come back to it. For the moment it is necessary only to take note of the consummate *structural* irony that holds these two episodes together, with the juxtaposition itself extracting the maximum pity and pathos.

There is, as I have said, yet another plot ingredient. The destiny of Genjuro and his wife are tracked against the destiny of another couple, Tobei and Omaha; and the comparison between these two couples (more particularly, between the main male characters) is itself a constitutive part of the film's meaning and impact. If the film has a governing theme, it is that war unleashes madness. This madness affects not only those who are engaged, first-hand, in the fighting, as soldiers, but the civilian population as well. Genjuro and Tobei, civilians caught up in the anarchy of the times, make the mistake of seeing war as an opportunity. With Genjuro, this takes the form of avarice, a belief that by selling his pots he will make himself rich, whereas with Tobei, vainglorious and clownish, it manifests itself as the fantastic conceit that his destiny is to become a great warrior. Mizoguchi and Yoda took this last strand of the scenario from Maupassant's ironical short story 'Decoré' (published in the collection *Les Soeurs Rondoli* in 1884), transposing the kernel of its Second Republic intrigue back into medieval Japan, and onto *this* they have woven strands of yet another Maupassant tale, 'Bed 29' (about a husband who comes across his wife in a hospital for venereal diseases). As the sources on which the movie is based multiply and ramify, the genius involved in seeing they *could* all fit together becomes, I think, more and more compelling. The trick, in each case, is to take what you need, and discard the inessential. So the different rivulets of plot feed into an ongoing stream, and in the process become lost to their origin.[4]

Naturalism and Aestheticism: the Mizoguchian Dialectic

In *Ugetsu Monogatari* we may observe more clearly than in almost any of Mizoguchi's other films the two contrasting sides of his genius. On the one hand, he is the supreme aesthete of Japanese cinema: the Japanese artistic traditions, already refined, are expressed, in his work, with a sort of ultimate refinement and mastery. On the other hand (and, somehow, it is no contradiction), he is also the great poet of engagement. He seeks to register the suffering which he sees all around him, the pain and dislocation of warfare (experiences that he himself, and every Japanese of his generation, had lived through). Visually, *Ugetsu* shows incredible elegance. Kazuo Miyagawa's camera – in such scenes as the mist-haunted journey across the lake or the bathing scene with Genjuro and Lady Wakasa already mentioned, or in the famous 360-degree pan that greets Genjuro's return to the 'house amid the thickets' – glides across the canvas with extraordinary fluency. Mizoguchi, as I have noted, always placed the highest possible emphasis on detailed accuracy in matters of costume and set decoration. There is a famous photograph of the director on the set of *Ugetsu* discussing with his actresses the cut or design of a kimono. He kneels and touches the stuff like a master couturier; his posture denotes composure and authority. Knowledge of these things ought to be the possession of all theatre and film directors. Yet out of the thousands of beautifully costumed *jidai-geki* films that jostle together, summing up and defining the Golden Age of Japanese cinema, Mizoguchi's films remain, I think, the most visually distinctive of all. If there is

---

4   The body of any good screenplay passes through multiple drafts, so that significant transformations from the original literary material can be difficult to trace with complete accuracy. The script gestation of *Ugetsu Monogatari* was discussed in Chapter 3, using as my main source of information Hisakazu Tsuji's commentary, found in the interview with Ariane Mnouchkine published by *Cahiers* in 1964. Joanne Bernardi goes into the matter from a slightly different angle in an essay on the script in *Mizoguchi the Master* (1996), bringing in further contributions from Masaichi Nagata, Yutaka Miyada and Kisaku Ito. With all these multiple inputs two points need to be borne in mind to bring us back to the primacy of the auteur. First, no one denies that the idea and origin of the synthesis was Mizoguchi's own. It was he who brought the four main texts together (the two Akinari tales and the two short stories by Maupassant), and brought them together, what is more, under the aegis of a governing idea: that the horrors of war should, for their full effect, be filtered through an atmosphere of beauty, refinement and ghostliness. Yet, needless to say, the screenplay itself is not the film. The critic is or should be concerned primarily with the final artistic product. Screenplay, budget, choice of actors, locale – these are all interesting factors, and part of film history. But the synthesizing power lies, if at all, with the director (this of course is what auteurism means). Joanne Bernardi intelligently reminds us:

In fact, Yoda's script does not include any indication of the wandering long duration shots, the predominant crane shots, or the distance from the camera at moments of violence. Nor does it mention the frequent dissolves and fades that create delicate time lapses, or the film's prevalent grey tone, and its haunting soundtrack.

And she quotes Yoda himself from his memoirs:

He [Mizoguchi] wanted to leave everything open-ended . . . he gave life to the film shot by shot. The images that were created seem connected in a profoundly natural way. The very act of undergoing bitterness and tension in bringing the entire work together seemed to guarantee its final impeccably unified structure.

one sartorial icon to sum up the 'look' of a Mizoguchi film, it might be the veiled sedge hat with muslin side curtains worn by women of rank when they venture out unaccompanied (or accompanied by minimum retinue). This is the headdress that Lady Wakasa (Machiko Kyo) is wearing when she first accosts Genjuro in the marketplace. Equally, it is the costume that Tamaki (Kinuyo Tanaka) wears as, accompanied by her children and nurse, she treads warily through the forest in the opening scenes of *Sansho the Bailiff*. Lady Murasaki in *The Tale of Genji* reports '*tsubo shozoku* gives a dignified look, like a nun slyly averting her eyes as she goes out sight-seeing'. (The writer is being ironical.) According to Ivan Morris, 'hats like these in due course went out of fashion, and it became the custom to cover the head with a kimono when walking in the streets. Such head kimonos, called *katsugi*, soon became custom-made.'[5] *Katsugi* are also part of Mizoguchi's visual repertoire: Kinuyo Tanaka is wearing one of these lovely flowing veils in the opening scene of *The Life of Oharu*. Hard to describe the peculiar delicate modesty that is expressed in the bending pose, the gliding footwork and the averted posture that go with this way of dressing: the visual symbol of a spiritual self-possession – a feminine modesty – that is prized by Mizoguchi above everything.[6]

---

5   Ivan Morris, *The World of the Shining Prince* (1964), p. 60.

6   It may be appropriate to bring in another of Mizoguchi's collaborators at this point: Kusune Kainosho (1894–1978) was a famous 'fauve' painter in the early years of the last century, celebrated for his realistic *nihonga*-style portraits of geisha and demi-mondaines. (*Nihonga* was a style dedicated to Japanese subject matter but highly influenced by Western oil techniques.) During the 1920s, in the wake of quarrels and controversies in the art world, he moved over to cinema, becoming an associate of Mizoguchi at the time of the shooting of the now-lost film *Life of an Actor/Geido Ichidai Otoko* (1941). A cultivated and flamboyant homosexual, Kainosho soon became an intimate of the director (for a long time he

Everything related to Japan's tradition of refined aesthetic spectacle comes together in the central moment of *Ugetsu Monogatari* when Lady Wakasa dances and sings in front of Genjuro: costume (a kimono of extraordinary splendour); gesture (Machiko Kyo's sinuosity of body set off by the deft movements made by her fan); music (a *biwa* composition, played by Wakasa's elderly female attendant); finally the song itself, undercut in due course by the sinister bass chant emanating as the ghost's lament from her father's empty helmet. The staging of the scene is clearly influenced by the traditions of the Noh theatre. That, of course, is a male preserve, and Machiko Kyo, the central actor of the scene, is nothing if not a beautiful woman. So we could say that the effort on Mizoguchi's behalf is to find a *modern equivalent* of Noh – a stylisation that will fit into, and not betray, cinema's essential ground-note of naturalism.

For naturalism is the other pole the film works on. No film known to me is finer than *Ugetsu* in conjuring up the sense of panic that besets a civilian population when the source of law and order descends, itself, into banditry. Given the congruence of dates (the film came out in 1953) it is hard not to think of Mizoguchi's own experience of Japan's engagement in war eight years earlier as providing the fundamental inspiration. Here in *Ugetsu*, he excels himself in the piteous visual depiction of ruin. The roving camera catches to perfection the multiple dispersions of the villagers as they scatter in different directions in front of the military juggernaut. This film is uncanny, too, in dramatising the *lulls* in the fighting, the cautious returns when danger is over, to find food and reconnoitre damage: returns cut short by a fresh batch of marauders, and a new bout of fleeing into the hinterland. These early scenes are marked also by the masterly use of soundtrack. The cries of the soldiers precede their arrival: it is their anticipatory hallooing, rather than the actual discharge of firearms, that is the grim sound of warfare. Mixed in with the mêlée, the audience makes out the crack of bamboo, the sounds of dogs barking, and the wailing of babies.

The wailing of babies. This is the sound that lingers with us at the end of the single most famous sequence of the movie: the single-take crane shot I already mentioned in which Miyagi flees from her encounter with the soldiers. The spearing of Miyagi occurs when she has her back to us and it seems at first to be merely a blow or a jostle. (So, in real life, it sometimes only slowly dawns on us how dangerous a situation really is.) The deep-focus travelling shot which subsequently captures, in the same image, the staggering Miyagi (foreground) and in the distance, across the ricefield, her drunken assailants, jubilant in the possession of her stolen purse, must be, in its bleak absurdity, one of the most pitiful moments in all cinema – since crowning this pity (the scene has a sort of *classical* horror) is the sobbing of her child, still bound to its mother as the woman lies dying in the pathway.

The scene's impact derives from two sources: on the one hand, the absence of cutting; on the other, the fact that the camera is placed so far back from the incident as it unfolds (close enough however for its horror and meaning to be unmissable). By means of these devices (are they even 'devices'? – the word is hopelessly inadequate) the viewer is *positioned* (that is what '*mise en scène*'

---

lodged in his house). As one of the country's leading experts on the history of Japanese costume, Kainosho was extraordinarily useful to Mizoguchi both in the pre-production period and during actual shooting. His greatest skill, apparently, was to make the costume 'live' on an actress. According to the critic Doten Fukao, Machiko Kyo's 'sexual, almost godly extravagance' in the role of Lady Wakasa owes an incalculable debt to Kainosho's skill, taste and knowledge. (There is an informative chapter on Kainosho in the Japanese-language centennial volume.)

means) as a helpless bystander, cognisant of the event but powerless to do anything about it. Other scenes in the movie share this same casual, out-of-the-blue horror, and the same grim realism: such episodes, for example, as the rape of Ohama (Tobei's wife) by the group of ruffians in the precincts of the temple. Elsewhere, death has a macabre, surrealistic flavour to temper its suddenness, as when Tobei purloins the head of the defeated general by murdering the general's attendant who has just helped his master commit suicide. The grim comedy of Tobei's action doesn't, however, belie its depravity. This is the true face of war: decent men (and Tobei, at bottom, is portrayed as decent) lose their humanity and perform shameful deeds. Then they blink and wake up. Their enthusiasm was a madness; their glory an illusion. Can it even be said, about the outcome of such adventures, that, when they return to their wretched fields, the men have learnt anything about their true natures?

Sansho the Bailiff

Let us now move on to the third of the three films in our 'triptych'.[7] The story of *Sansho the Bailiff*, we are informed by a caption that immediately follows the film's opening credits, is 'one of the

---

7   A triptych is of course a religious painting in three panels, usually hung over the altar in Catholic churches. The phrase used here makes oblique reference to the French critic André Bazin's classic short book on Orson Welles (1950, revised 1958) which contains a homonymous chapter called 'The Great Diptych'. *Citizen Kane* and *The Magnificent Ambersons* are the films in question, judged by Bazin the most perfect in Welles's career. I mentioned Bazin in my introductory

oldest and most tragic in Japan's history'. It belongs in the mists of antiquity 'before mankind had yet awakened as human beings'. Mizoguchi's immediate source was a short story written in 1915 by the great scholar–novelist Ogai Mori (1862–1922). Mori was an important bourgeois public figure as well as a writer. A military doctor by training, of samurai birth, in 1902 he was appointed director of medical affairs in the war ministry, at a crucial period of Japanese expansionism. His training had been in Germany in the 1880s, and the early part of his career shows an admiration for contemporary European models. His importance in modern literary history may be gauged by the fact that his writing inspired in different ways four of Japan's most famous twentieth-century authors – Tanizaki, Akutagawa, Kafu and Mishima. The first three of these (Mishima belongs to a later generation) were all incidentally favourites of Mizoguchi, and he admired them for the same reason that he admired Mori: because they looked back at the past so tenderly and passionately.

It appears that Mori's pro-Western stance altered in 1912 with the death of the Emperor Meiji and the subsequent suicide of the emperor's high-placed aide-de-camp, General Nogi. The deed had an enormous impact on Japan and on Mori in particular, causing him to abandon his cosmo-politan preoccupations in favour of a more concentrated, serious and intensive investigation of his country's historical landscape. The stories that followed – including *Sansho* – are all very short: not novels, not even novellas, more, in a way, like court reports or fragments from the chronicles. (Robert Louis Stevenson, a near contemporary in Europe, aims for a similar laconicism in a novel like *Weir of Hermiston*. Another comparison might be with the short stories of Kleist.) The writing, henceforward, is extremely economical. Psychology and commentary are banished in favour of a pared-down forensic description. Mori's tales are 'low-key' in that they studiously avoid rhetoric and sentimentality. But they are not without poetry, and the intensity of suffering they evoke is often beautiful and moving.

Sansho, one of these tales, appeared in 1915.[8] It is set in the eleventh century ('the mists of antiquity'). The story is about thirty pages long, and Yoda's script does not veer wildly from the main outlines of Mori's plot. Naturally, there are a lot of small changes, the details of which are always interesting. One important difference between the tale and the film is that in the film ver-sion, Mizoguchi allows the hero Zushio – who has been kidnapped with his sister and transported to a sort of slave labour camp run by the eponymous Sansho – to be tempted by the morality of his oppressors. Such a temptation would run expressly against the counsel of his beloved father, whose moral precepts, delivered verbally years ago to the children before he left them for exile, have sus-tained them so far in adversity. Zushio's hardening of the soul and submission to evil (he becomes

---

chapter. For me he is a truly noble film critic – maybe the finest in the literature. In his capacity as editor of *Cahiers du Cinéma*, he was largely responsible for introducing to European audiences the great wave of Japanese film-making that took off after the war and which lasted until the national industry fell into ruin in the early 1970s. Although he never wrote at length about Mizoguchi, his passing comments were always admiring, while his general essays on Japanese cinema (collected together and translated into English in *The Cinema of Cruelty from Buñuel to Hitchcock*, 1982) are of the greatest interest and intelligence. His achievement is considered further in Appendix 1.

8   J. Thomas Rimer's translation of *Sansho* appears in T. W. Goossen (ed.), *The Oxford Book of Japanese Short Stories* (1997). A two-volume selection of Mori's tales is also available in translation – David Dilworth and J. Thomas Rimer (eds) (1977). Masahiro Shinoda's film *The Dancer* (1990) dramatises an episode from Mori's life when he was a student in Berlin.

a 'trusty' and tortures runaways by branding them) are in turn overcome at the sublime moment when he and his sister decide in the forest glade to stand up for themselves, and in doing so save the life of a dying woman whose last moments have been entrusted to their care. It is a complicated and beautiful sequence, which does not need to be analysed here (beyond clarifying the plot detail, that the sister Anju trumps his resolve, by sacrificing herself for his freedom). But this change of heart introduced by Mizoguchi and absent from the original serves to give the film a vital extra emphasis: there are now, as it were, *two* redemptions – Zushio's initial redemption from evil, *in addition to* the final redemption (the reuniting of mother and son). Of course they are in a way the same thing – they are two stages of the same trajectory – but this is only another way of stating that Mizoguchi strengthens Mori's story, by clarifying its meaning and giving it a greater intensity.

For I think it is undeniable that the ending of the Mori tale is disappointing. The writing tails off and loses momentum, whereas in Mizoguchi's version, the final third of the story is every bit as engrossing as the first part. These are the episodes following Zushio's escape which describe his accession to noble office and his return to Sansho's compound (this time as governor of the province) to free his fellow slaves. Then, in the midst of triumph, comes the great (and surprising) moment of renunciation: his ambitions achieved, Zushio renounces his titles and goes off in search of his mother. The scenes in question are all, so to speak, correctly calibrated: there is dignity and fullness in them, as well as speed and excitement. They take their place as part of a rising arc of tension which ensures that, in the film version, the climax when it comes will be momentous.

Impossible to avoid, it seems to me, the emphasis here on the climax. Of all the great endings in Mizoguchi's cinema, the ending of *Sansho the Bailiff* is surely the greatest, the most cathartic. The critic Gilbert Adair (an enthusiast after my own heart) is not being excessively hyperbolic when he writes: '*Sansho the Bailiff* is one of those films for which cinema exists – just as *it* perhaps exists for the sake of its last scene.'[9] Few things in the whole history of film match in emotional intensity these final drawn out moments in *Sansho* when it dawns on the blind decrepit woman, seated alone among the seaweed outside her beach shack, that the man who has thrown himself at her feet with such tender submissiveness is in fact her long-lost son. The dialogue in the scene is electrifying, reaching its pitch of pathos at the moment when Zushio forces himself to tell his mother that she will never see her daughter Anju in this world again. At the same time, the whole force of the recognition really comes through touch; it is physical. Zushio holds her in his arms, and the mother responds, hesitating at first, while she traces the contours of his face with her hand. As she touches the amulet (the little heirloom of the Bodhisattva Kwannon he is carrying with him) her hesitation becomes certainty, and a floodgate of emotion is undammed. Tamaki: 'Zushio . . . ? It's you, my son!' Zushio: 'You understand now. I have come to find you.' Tamaki: 'But are you alone? Anju ought to be here. [Groping round with her hands] Anju, where are you?' Zushio (turning away, overcome with grief): 'Anju has rejoined her father.' Tamaki (still not understanding): 'He's in good health, your father?' Zushio, explaining through his tears: 'Now there are only two of us – just you and me.' And he goes on, scarcely able to get the words out: 'I could have come here as a governor. But I preferred to resign my office and to follow my father's teaching. Please forgive me, mother!' Tamaki (with a final supreme effort of lucidity, as she flings herself into his arms):

---

9   Gilbert Adair, *Flickers: An Illustrated Celebration of 100 Years of Cinema* (1995), p. 121.

'There's nothing to forgive! Without knowing what you have done, I know that it's because you have listened to your father that we are finally able to be here together!'

There is no need to labour the obvious. The scene is very grand: as Adair says, 'the grandest'. A detail of its effectiveness that is seldom discussed is the importance of the musical accompaniment. The music in this scene, and above all in the rising chords of the final climax (as 'The End' is flashed up on the screen) has a power exceptional among Mizoguchi's endings. The appropriateness, or not, of music in cinema excites strong partisanship, and those ascetic minimalists (who include Mizoguchi among their number on different occasions) are surely right to complain that too *much* music can be ruinous. Yet the other side of the argument can be compelling also. Sometimes, the underlying presence of music is the single greatest factor that differentiates cinema from theatre. Many instances could be given from *Sansho*, and I limit myself only to the most notable. One of the most beautiful moments of the film is the scene in the forest glade when Anju mistakes the cooing of a turtle dove for the sound of her absent mother crying out and beckoning to her – the plangent lament 'An – ju . . . Zu – shio . . .' taught to her in the camp by a girl who had previously encountered Tamaki in captivity. Both the sounds – the birdsong and Tamaki's voice – are present on the soundtrack simultaneously, overlying each other, so that Anju's confusion is in a way our confusion too. The birdsong *is* the mother's voice, or else they are interchangeable. On stage, this would be at once too literal and too symbolic; but the context here is filmic realism, and the miracle of hearing the mother's voice (if we call it a miracle) breaks no rules of naturalistic psychology.

It is impossible to think of *Sansho* without remembering this song: it's at the centre of the movie. As in so many of the great films of history (*L'Atalante*, *Jules et Jim* and so on) the song is above all what the audience takes away with it. The beautiful words are given in the Mori original as a lament sung to ward off sparrows from a patch of seaweed Tamaki is guarding:

> How much I yearn to see Anju – be gone!
> How much I yearn to see Zushio – be gone!
> Little birds, if you are alive and can move
> Fly away before you are driven away.

In the tale, as I say, we hear the song only at the climax ('hear' it, of course, is a manner of speaking in the case of a written text). In the adaptation, however, it becomes the keystone of the tale's moral architecture. For in the first place, as I have said, it is the *discovery* of the song, carried to the camp by a stranger as an accompaniment to her weaving, which awakens in the children the possibility that their mother is still alive. And after this, at key moments of their plight, it is the song which gives them heart – mystically transported to them across the water from the island where their mother, sold into the stews, has never ceased hoping that they are alive.

This idea of the voice carried (impossibly) across the water is one of the most exquisite things in the movie. Formally speaking, it connects the film to the classic genre of melodrama, understood in its literal sense: that is to say, drama sustained by 'melos', or melody. Classically, such musical accompaniment is the thread used to unite lovers 'telepathically' when they have been physically separated from each other. It is a key feature of the great tradition of silent cinema (which by that token was not really silent at all: everywhere, film in that epoch was sustained by music). Here, the music says in fact what cannot be said in the dialogues – it broaches the 'ineffable', for, once heard and lodged in the children's hearts, it operates for them as sustenance in adversity. And the succour it gives surely has elements of religion in it. Truly religious works of art of course are rare: especially in the twentieth century, and especially in the cinema. Even those that claim to be such (one thinks of certain films by Dreyer and Tarkovsky) reveal themselves to be, on examination, not without their complicated ambiguity. So to call *Sansho* 'religious' is to take a gamble. And yet if the word means anything at all, *some* of the aura of religion at least, I think, attaches itself to this masterpiece. It is a film about mercy and forgiveness, raised to the level of grand cosmic principle. 'Mercy' and 'forgiveness' are universal categories; and while the ethical flavour of the film derives from the tenets of Buddhism, one reason why the Western viewer responds to it so directly is surely because these themes belong in the Christian tradition also. If the ethical heart of both faiths is compassion, Christianity, somehow, is also here in the details: in the pietà-like monumentality of the final tragic tableau; and in the similarity of the goddess Kwannon's qualities as an intercessor to the mercy and grace bestowed (according to Catholic believers) by the Virgin Mary.

Religious or non-religious, then? And does it matter? The dominant political passion that *Sansho* breathes is a hatred of oppression and injustice. In this sense (and it is of course a strong sense) 'redemption' is as much secular as religious. The story takes place, as the opening title informs us, at a period of history 'before mankind had yet awakened as human beings'. It charts, imaginatively (and perhaps even anachronistically) the beginning of one such episode of awakening. In one way, the message conveyed is the purest liberalism – for the story concerns the freeing of slaves from captivity. This liberal message is kept serious by its continuing contemporary relevance. For who can say, as we survey the record of the past century, that it has been *less* notable for oppression than the eleventh century was? I myself have no doubt that this was Mizoguchi's intention. The scenes of 'camp life' in *Sansho* (realised with extraordinary conviction) can only be understood in relation to the whole dismal contemporary history of the concentration camps that blighted the middle years of the twentieth century with their catalogue of oppression and torture. The film is militant in its hatred of such oppression (and in its conviction that this oppression must be combated). But in the end perhaps it goes *beyond* militancy - by its disdain for power and power's trappings.

These reflections may have taken us an unwarranted distance from the real 'text' of the film. I hope they are not too abstract or speculative. If criticism has a duty (the word is pompous) it is to find some kind of formal equivalent in words to the object being scrutinised. A film as famous as *Sansho* has been written about many times, and a critic who comes late in the day must be content to place his contribution within a play of commentary that is already wide and multifarious. What is the central thing to say about this film? I am sympathetic to commentaries that succeed in laying out, modestly, the successive triumphs of the film's *mise en scène*: classic essays, such as Robin Wood's, which recreate in masterly detail (with fine attention to their spiritual content) scenes that I have not touched on here, such as the suicide by drowning of Zushio's sister Anju (indubitably one of the film's highlights).[10] Then again, is any account of the film complete that does not itemise the virtuosity of the opening sequence, with its superlative succession of lap dissolves: surely, in total, one of the greatest single examples of the art of flashback in cinema history? The list could go on and on, and perhaps the best a modern critic can hope for is that, by adumbrating a few of the work's finest scenes, he may inspire the reader to go to see the film again.

Yet if I ask myself how this great film stamps itself on my own mind, I would have to alight on something I have not yet mentioned: I mean the power of the film's *faces*. More almost than in any other Mizoguchi film, the faces of the actors are compelling and unforgettable. First of all Sansho himself, played by Eitaro Shindo, with his bulging eyes and wispy beard, a man obsequious to superiors (for he is only a steward, or bailiff), while implacable to those under his rule. Shindo appeared in other Mizoguchi films about the same time as this, most notably *Chikamatsu Monogatari* (1954). Still, Sansho is the role he was destined for. The actor makes him come to life; he imbues him with fullness and complexity. Similar reflections apply to the stocky, short-legged actor Yoshiaki Hanayaki who plays Zushio. I love the scenes where we see him wielding a hammer, and those other episodes where he uses a knife to cut the reeds that will furnish (for his family and for the dying woman) their simple overnight resting place. His plebeian vehemence contrasts with the lofty aristocratic idealism that can be seen on the features of his noble father Masauiji Taira (Masao Shimizu). The calm authority of the latter, as he sets off, mounted, and surrounded by weeping retainers, into exile, irradiates the film's opening sequences. Nobility in fact informs the whole majestic film, from first to last. It is the unavoidable word to describe the beauty of Kinuyo Tanaka, playing Tamaki, the mother; and also the word which best summarises Kyoko Kagawa, whose Anju is surely one of the most touching heroines in cinema.

---

10 Robin Wood, 'The Ghost Princess and the Seaweed Gatherer', in *Personal Views: Explorations in Film* (1976), pp. 227 *et seq.*

5 | Geisha, Prostitution and the Street

The films discussed so far have been set in the past, although, as I have tried to show, their interest has not been merely archeological. Just as in Shakespeare, the recourse to an historical or a mytho-logical setting allows the film-maker access to universal themes which possess, by definition, a cor-respondingly contemporary relevance. Right from the beginning of his career, Mizoguchi liked to look backwards. There was an antiquarian and scholarly element to his character that shows up, for example, in his connoisseurship of the Meiji (= late Victorian) period about which he made many films in the 1920s and early 30s. We will look at these later as well as some other films which, like the triptych, are set in the remote medieval past. Here however, I want to look at a side of the director that is more straightforwardly contemporary. In several films made between the mid-1930s and his death in 1956, Mizoguchi turned his gaze relentlessly, and with the power of a great social critic, onto the society he saw around him in Japan. These seven films (which include some of his most admired works) are set for the most part in the contiguous milieus of prostitution and geishadom.

The Tradition – and Its Representation

No doubt prostitution existed, and continues to exist, in most societies, if not all. In Japan, how-ever, it has had an especially complicated history dating back a thousand years to Heian times and beyond. Into that history is woven (paradoxically) some of the greatest achievements in Japanese culture. The various strands of this story, though fascinating in themselves, are not my concern here. One strand, however, that is worth highlighting – because it is central to Mizoguchi's nuanced relationship with the whole phenomenon – is the way that the original culture of courtesanship and high-class prostitution was superseded, during the course of the eighteenth and nineteenth centuries, by the subtly different culture of geishadom. Courtesanship, as an institution whose pri-mary purpose (beyond all the frills) was the regulated exchange of sexual favours for money, con-tinued alongside this new culture. Yet, at a certain moment during this period, the licensed quarters lost their hegemony to a newer and freer institution that was based – theoretically at least – not as much on sex as on entertainment.

Now it is true that sex, bought and sold, is part of the geisha's world too, hypocritically con-cealed in some places, in other places more or less acknowledged. Nonetheless, whether sexually inflected or not, the fact remains that the geisha's main social function was an artistic one: it was to sing and dance and play samisen at the banquets thrown by wealthy clients at tea houses. Acquiring these skills meant a long and arduous learning process, comparable in many ways,

Ambivalent by definition: the geisha's welcome in *Gion Festival Music* (1953)

strange though this may sound, to the education of a modern ballet dancer. So it is not entirely misleading to talk about a geisha's life in terms of a 'vocation'. The critic may rightly ask whether that vocation was freely chosen. Maybe not in many or even most cases: children were frequently sold into the profession by their parents. Moreover, the terms of indenture whereby the geisha was expected to pay back to the geisha house, out of her earnings, the large sums of money spent on her artistic education and on her wardrobe, were often harsh, especially if (as was often the case) the mistress of the house was cruel or rapacious. Still, as Lesley Downer and Liza Dalby among others have argued, the institution was not wholly negative – even for the women involved. In a society such as Japan's where, until recently, women were otherwise kept in the background, the geisha house – peopled and managed exclusively by women (often strong, intelligent, sophisti- cated women) – paradoxically offered a kind of utopian space, a segregated atmosphere of calm and of busyness, where the feminine world could blossom on its own terms.

That is certainly the feeling elicited by a number of films which explore this phenomenon, link- ing it (where it needs to be linked) with more traditional forms of prostitution. While geishadom was the 'subject of subjects' for Mizoguchi, it was also (and is) no less compelling a topic for his contemporaries, and continues to haunt modern directors: films on the topic form a significant por- tion of the classic corpus of Japanese movies over the last sixty years. A season of such films just from the post-war period would necessarily include some of the following: *Clothes of Deception* (Kimisaburo Yoshimura, 1951), *Epitome* (Kaneto Shindo, 1953), *Growing Up* (Heinosuke Gosho, 1955), *Flowing* (Mikio Naruse, 1956), *Geisha in the Old City* (Hiroshi Inagaki, 1957), *Not Long after Leaving Shinagawa* (Yuzo Kawashima, 1957), *The Story of a Love at Naniwa* (Tomu Uchida, 1959), *A Strange Story of East of the River Sumida* (Shiro Toyoda, 1960), *A House in the Quarter* (Tomo- taka Tasaka, 1963), *A Scent of Incense* (Keisuke Kinoshita, 1964), *Empire of the Senses* (Nagisa Oshima, 1976) and finally – a late and brilliant example – *The Strange Story of Oyuki* (Kaneto Shindo, 1992). Although these films share a common theme, it is important to stress that they vary significantly in tone and content. Kawashima's film, for example, is set in a late Edo-period brothel (definitely no frills here), while Hiroshi Inagaki's movie, as its title implies, belongs to the much more decorous world of classical geisha. And as they differ in their milieu, they differ also in their point of view – Kawashima's film being ribald, insouciant and unjudgmental; Inagaki's (despite its extra- ordinarily rich colour photography) sombre, thoughtful and elegiac. (The ostensible subject of *Geisha in the Old City* is the revival of the Dou-chu procession of courtesans in Shimabara after World War II for business and tourist purposes; its real subject is the deceptions and lies that shel- ter behind this 'jolly' initiative.)

Do such films romanticise the milieus they evoke? Art, by definition, aestheticises, subjecting even the grimmest subject matter to the transforming rigour of shape and colour and line. Films and paintings (and books too for that matter) answer to their own truth before they answer to his- torical or sociological fact. Yet of course the work of art is a representation of *something*: there is always a human and psychological subject matter which can either be handled with depth and deli- cacy, or else carelessly, dishonestly, sentimentally. In this particular subject matter the cliché that looms is a romanticised version of 'the whore with the heart of gold', a complaisant way of look- ing at a given milieu that – we may feel – should have required from the artist a harsher and more honest moral judgment. This criticism has been levelled, for example, at one of the most famous explorers of the Japanese lower depths, the writer Kafu Nagai (1879–1959), on whose stories two of the films I have cited (Toyoda's *A Strange Story of East of the River Sumida* and Shindo's *The Strange Story of Oyuki*) are based. It is easy to read into Kafu's tender and nostalgic evocations of the past, and in his avowed friendship with prostitutes, merely the contours of a cold and arid masculine connoisseurship.[1] The view which used to be held, that the role of 'appreciative' observer belongs exclusively to man, while woman must content herself with being the tractable, docile, and available object of his interest, has long since been abandoned, I think, in civilised discourse. Yet the converse danger in these matters is a sort of sanctimonious political correctness which stridently demands, in front of a work of art, that it *must* nail its ideological colours to the mast. Can the painter Toulouse-Lautrec or the New Orleans photographer Bellocq be asked to 'come out' with a judgment (one way or the other) concerning the whorehouses they haunted and chronicled? Their art would be a lesser thing if they did so.

Even so, there is no getting away from the fact that fierce moral indignation was part – perhaps even the defining part – of Mizoguchi's attitude towards this fascinating, complex and deeply embedded element of Japanese culture. The director broached the topic in seven surviving films, three of which date from before the war. The pre-war films are *Osaka Elegy* and *Sisters of the Gion* (both released in 1936) along with *The Straits of Love and Hate* (1937). (This last film is very rarely screened but copies of it exist, and who knows, one day it may become more widely known.) From the post-war period are *Women of the Night* (1948), *Gion Festival Music* (1953), *The Woman of Rumour* (1954) and finally Mizoguchi's swan song, *Street of Shame* (1956). For the sake of convenience I have chosen here, broadly speaking, to consider these films chronologically.

The 1930s

Osaka Elegy and *Sisters of the Gion* are usually thought of as a pair: not only did they come out in the same year (produced by the same short-lived production company, Daiichi Eiga) but they share the same fiery actress in the leading role, Isuzu Yamada. And although the milieus depicted in the two films differ (only *Sisters of the Gion* is specifically set in the world of geisha) their structural and spiritual affinity becomes obvious when we look at them closely. So, for example, both films, in their different ways, are centrally concerned with what it means to have to scrabble for patronage. In the pre-war Kyoto geisha world depicted in *Sisters of the Gion*, the search for an elderly rich client who can support Omocha (Isuzu Yamada) and her sister and allow them to practise their trade is shown to be a time-honoured and quasi-formal part of the business (indeed without such economic backing, the whole structure of geishadom would collapse). This search for patronage is not quite as formalised in *Osaka Elegy*. Ayako, the heroine, is a lowly company employee (a telephone operator), rather than a bird in a gilded cage. But, in a way, she *is* a bird in a cage too; in any event, the quest is the same, and Mizoguchi is exploring the same phenomenon in both films:

---

1   Edward Seidensticker, in his classic study of the author, *Kafu the Scribbler: The Life and Writings of Nagai Kafu 1879–1959* (1965), remarks pointedly about *Rivalry* (1917), one of Kafu's most famous stories: 'Nowhere in the book is there the suggestion that venereal disease might be one of the hazards of Komoyu's [the heroine's] profession.' Nostalgia is part and parcel of the flavour of Kafu's writing. 'In the old days,' he remarks somewhere, 'the keepers of doubtful houses kept morning glories and . . . lit festival fires.'

the circumstances which permit – or else force (the ambiguity is crucial in both cases) – beautiful yet hard-up young women to exchange their freedom for money.

A further structural affinity between the two films lies in the suggestion in both cases that the motive for the Faustian bargain is partly, at least, altruistic: Ayako, in *Osaka Elegy*, wants to rescue her father from debt (and later on, pay for her brother's university fees); Omocha, in *Sisters of the Gion*, gets trapped in a situation she can't get out of when she takes steps to acquire a kimono for her elder sister that will allow the latter to take part in the spring dances. The relative degree of 'niceness', or sympathy, differs considerably between the two heroines: Ayako is a softer and more immediately sympathetic character than Omocha; but what unites them more – and in doing so, unites the two movies, lending them their astounding modernity – is the fact that both women, in their different ways, are furiously rebelling against their lot.

Why should this be worthy of comment? I do not wish to exaggerate the audacity involved here. Still, in the context of 1930s' Japan, when women were expected meekly to put up with the status quo, the quality of truculent defiance communicated by Yamada (even across the gap of almost seventy years) strikes a daring and original note. The actress was only nineteen when she took on these roles. Active in minor parts at Nikkatsu since 1931, she had already appeared in three of Mizoguchi's previous movies: *The Mountain Pass of Love and Hate* (1934), *The Downfall of Osen* and *Oyuki Madonna* (both 1935). The first of these films no longer exists; while the surviving pair are fairly conventional *shimpa* dramas. Between mid-1935, when these two latter films were released, and the following year, when Yamada renewed her acquaintance with Mizoguchi, there had been a turbulent storm in her private life: entering into a liaison with an actor by whom she bore a child out of wedlock, she had been forced to face and weather out her father's very public disapproval. (He was a *shimpa* actor by profession, separated from his daughter when she was still young.) In the publicity about *Osaka Elegy* and *Sisters of the Gion* which Mizoguchi participated in at the time of their release, it's this controversial and unconventional aspect of Yamada's character that he comes back to in order to explain why she was so fitted for these roles. Of course, there was no automatic guarantee – as Mizoguchi knew very well – that, having been through rebellion in her private life (still very much ongoing at the time we are talking about), the experience could be transformed wholesale into the deep dark underbelly of her performance: the relation between art and lived experience – in either direction – is subtle. Yet sometimes the connection *is* evident; and out of the confusion and vehemence of her private rebellion, Yamada succeeded in bringing something new and dynamic to the development of Japanese cinema.

The great quality of her acting is its frank naturalism. The very first time we see her in *Sisters of the Gion* (her entrance in the theatrical sense) she is yawning and stretching as she moves forward to greet her sister's visitor. Dressed in a negligee and still, as it were, smelling of the bedroom, she casually walks over to the sink and starts brushing her teeth. The lazy and animal insolence displayed here, as in all her gestures in the movie, is not in the slightest bit studied; there is no hint of falseness here, no recourse to theatricality or melodrama. Yoda reminds us that *Osaka Elegy* was shot in the authentic Kansai dialect,

A lazy and animal insolence: Isuzu Yamada as the geisha Omocha in *Sisters of the Gion* (1936)

a language which serves to emphasise, in its particular intonation, the mean and obstinate side of human nature. 'You have to bring out this trait in the characters of our film', Mizoguchi said to me: 'Find the right imagery to describe the stink of the human body. Paint me human beings who are implacable, selfish, stingy, sensual, cruel!' For the first time in Japanese cinema the Kansai accent, which up till then had only been used in comedy, became an authentic dramatic language.[2]

Both the films are extremely compact (each of them under seventy minutes long) and elicit the feeling that the director decided he had no time at all to waste on pathos. The actions unfold simply and remorselessly. The tone is sober and prosaic, heightened or reinforced by the absence of music on the soundtrack. So, with no artificial cues for emotion, the audience is left to face a 'documentary' bareness.

Are these wonderful, strange films perhaps *too* bare? The dissatisfaction of contemporaries focused on a perceived inadequacy in the endings, as if the coolness of the films' leave-taking gestures contrived to leave their audiences stranded. A panel of film experts debated this very issue (among other topics) in the editorial offices of the leading film magazine *Kinema Jumpo*, with Mizoguchi himself present as an observer. Here is a sample of their verdicts. Kotaro Yamamoto: 'The public is shocked to be so brutally expelled from these stories.' Fuyuhiko Kitagawa: '*Osaka Elegy* ends with a scene in which people are simply walking out of the frame, and I think the public can't be satisfied with something so unusual!' Tatsihiko Shigeno: 'We ought surely to be left with a more composed tableau at the end – something more distanced.' And so on. Mizoguchi, participating in the discussion, himself had his doubts about his handling of the endings – doubts which he chose to put down to his 'immaturity' (in fact he was thirty-eight at the time, while these were, respectively, the fifty-sixth and fifty-seventh movies he had directed). He wondered whether he should have taken Yoda's advice over *Sisters of the Gion* and left out the cry of despair from Omocha's hospital bed that ends the film. Still: he stands by his artistic decision: 'The responsibility [for the endings] is mine alone,' he says finally.[3]

Are the endings actually as brutal as these critics claim? In *Osaka Elegy*, Ayako, driven out of her home by the hostility of her family (who object to the fact that she has become the mistress successively of her boss and her boss's best friend) goes down to the river. It is night time. The viewer might think (if this were a certain type of melodrama) that suicide was on her mind; and of course – melodrama or not – such an upshot is not absolutely out of the question. Before any decisions can be made, Ayako is accosted by a stranger. He turns out to be a character we have met before: a fat doctor in the pay of Ayako's former employer whose social clumsiness was responsible for her 'cover' being blown. A brief exchange takes place in which he asks her (not unkindly) whether she is ill. Her reply is brave and sardonic: 'A sort of illness – called delinquency! Can such a condition be cured?', to which the doctor responds (they are the last words of spoken dialogue in the movie) 'That's something even I don't know', before moving off into the darkness.

A brief lateral travelling shot follows Ayako as she tucks her bag under her arm and makes her way along the riverbank. In the very last shot of the film, she is walking towards the camera, her grave blank face moving slowly into close-up.

---

2   Yoshikata Yoda, *Souvenirs de Kenji Mizoguchi* (1997), p. 43 [Author's translation].

3   See 'Table Ronde avec Kenji Mizoguchi' (II), *Positif* no. 238, January 1981, pp. 26–7.

The ending of *Sisters of the Gion* is in certain respects much more rhetorical. Omocha's jealous young admirer has thrown her out of a speeding taxi, and she is lying injured in a hospital bed attended by her more conventional sister Umekichi (Yoko Umemura). Both of them in different ways are in pain (Umekichi has just learnt that she herself has been dropped by her long-term patron Furusawa). Yet while Umekichi is content to suffer in silence, Omocha gives vent, in the closing moments of the movie, to a soliloquy of profound bitterness and despair. The tirade is worth quoting verbatim, because it might be taken as Mizoguchi's own verdict on the geisha phenomenon. 'Has it [i.e. being brave, holding your head high] helped in any practical way?', Omocha demands of her sister.

Facing the world proudly: what has it done for us? Furusawa may be happy. But what about you? You meekly did as you were told. What did you gain by it? Nothing! If we're sharp in our business, we're criticised. What do they want us to do? Why must we suffer so? Why are there such things as geisha in this world? It's wrong, it's entirely wrong! I wish they had never existed!

While she has been speaking, the camera has been moving in on her face. Two brief sobs follow her outburst. Then the screen very briefly moves to darkness before the end credits appear over music.

At a time in my life when I objected more strongly than I do now to the presence of 'statement' in art, I used to think that this latter conclusion to *Sisters of the Gion* was too explicit. I no longer think this, however. The sequence seems to me on the contrary profoundly eloquent. To appreciate it properly it has to be seen in the context of the scenes that have led up to it: first, the episode in the taxi, and the shocking revelation that Omocha's erstwhile admirer, the drapery clerk Kimura, should have planned such a ruthless revenge. (We are not, in fact, shown the actual moment of violence – in a daring ellipsis, it's only reported, second-hand, to the sister.) In the hospital where Omocha is carried out of the operating theatre on the back of a nurse, an extended lateral camera movement in extreme long shot unites the two sisters as they make their way to the ward where Omocha will be cared for. The soundtrack here fuses their voices into a single lament. 'I told you so,' says one of them (which one?) 'I'll never accept that!' replies the other. Presently Umekichi reappears from behind the screen that has been masking the sisters, and tells the nurse that she is going home to collect her nightclothes. In a brief scene back in her apartment, a messenger comes to tell her that Furusawa has been offered a post as a factory manager in another city, and intends to leave her.

With no transition at all we are back in the hospital, Umekichi seated at her sister's bedside, listening to the movie's closing words, quoted a moment ago. The whole affair is tied up, it seems to me, with masterly economy – even (despite the tirade) with understatement. Endings are important because they stamp on the audience's mind a story's final irony and significance. Contemporary critics of *Osaka Elegy* and *Sisters of the Gion*, whom we have quoted, complained of being left in the lurch, yet, for a later generation, it seems to me, it is exactly this suddenness (this swiftness, this concision) that gives these endings their strange exaltation.

Of the two films, *Osaka Elegy* is perhaps the more immediately beguiling, if only because the character played by Yamada in this movie is sweeter and more vulnerable than the character she portrays in *Sisters of the Gion*. On the other hand, the interest in *Sisters of the Gion* resides in the fact that Omocha's soul is so riven. She is a more complicated figure than Ayako: bitter, resentful, duplicitous – all of these things; but she is also a free and brave spirit. While her sister Umekichi in the film belongs to the *tribe* of geishas (and might, under certain circumstances, have been content with her destiny), Omocha pays the penalty for her independence. For the career of a geisha, alas, is never simply a career like any other.[4]

Aien Kyo

Early in the following year Mizoguchi made another film whose atmosphere, character and general critique provide links with the two films we have been considering. The name of the film is *Aien Kyo* (usually translated as *The Straits of Love and Hate*). A rare copy of this movie exists in Japan where it can be seen by film researchers, although for private contractual reasons it is not currently (2004) being shown to a broader public. Some scholars and critics who have seen it, such as the British specialist Tony Rayns, rate it very highly. (In a *Sight and Sound* poll in September 2002 Rayns included it – as the only Mizoguchi – in his personal list of the ten best films of all time.) Since a number of movies from this period (*Song of the Camp* and *Ah, My Home Town* from 1938, *The Woman of Osaka* from 1940) have vanished altogether, the fact that *Aien Kyo* even exists – actually, in quite a decent print – is reason enough to look at it briefly.

Ofumi (Fumiko Yamaji), a servant at an inn in the province of Shinsu (northern Japan), is made pregnant by the inn-keeper's son Kenkichi (Masao Shimizu), with whom she is temporarily infatuated. Fleeing the wrath of the family, the lovers elope to Tokyo; but Kenkichi, spoiled from birth, proves to be a hopeless provider, and Ofumi drifts into prostitution in order to provide for their baby. A new lover, Yoshitaru (Seizaburo Kawazu), persuades her to join him in a group of travelling players (the group is in fact run by Ofumi's feckless, drunken uncle) which in due course passes through Ofumi's home province, where it is booked to perform near the inn. (Kenkichi is currently in residence, having long ago returned to his parents.) Perversely, from the point of view of his own interests, the new lover Yoshitaru sees this as an opportunity for Ofumi to take up with Kenkichi again: at least there will be security, and a home for the child. Kenkichi, for his part, though he claims still to love Ofumi, hasn't the will or the courage to force himself back on her. Meanwhile Ofumi, momentarily tempted by the possibility of marriage to Kenkichi for the child's sake, breaks off at the last moment; she won't live with a coward and deserter.

So it is back to the road for Ofumi, along with the child, and with Yoshitaru, whom she may or may not love any longer: in any case, an equivocal victory of principle over interest since, whatever happens, the future is going to be bleak for the trio.

This short summary[5] will have done its essential work if it suggests the film's melancholy and pessimism – traits that it shares, of course, with *Osaka Elegy* and with *Sisters of the Gion*. The three films, if not quite a trilogy, belong recognisably to the same family: designed by the same

---

4   For further consideration of the director's thinking on these films, see Appendix 2: 'Mizoguchi's Attitude towards Geisha'.

5   There are minor differences of emphasis from the plot summary given in the Andrews's *Kenji Mizoguchi: A Guide to References and Resources* (1981). Incidentally, the credits say the story is adapted from Tolstoy's *Resurrection*, but it seems to me that the film as it stands is so far away from the inner essence of the Russian classic as to make the citation misleading. On the other hand, *Aien Kyo*'s storyline seems to have strong similarities with that of a key Mizoguchi film from the early 1930s, *Shikamo Karera Wa Yuku/And Yet They Go*. Much admired by Yoda (who cites it frequently in his

scenographer (Mizutani), photographed by the same cameraman (Minoru Miki), scripted by the same writer (Yoda) and put together by the same producer (Nagata). As with the two earlier films there is an immediate and compelling documentary interest that asserts itself concerning the different sides of modern Japanese life. The sociology that forms the background to the events is the perennial drift to the city. We are shown what it is really like to live in the metropolis at zero level, with next to no money. Ofumi is forced to farm out her child to a wet-nurse in order to take on wretched, underpaid work in cafés ('waitressing' in these establishments is a thin euphemism for something darker). There are marvellous scenes, too, on the road with the sad little theatre troupe heading from town to town in the provinces, late for their appointments because of lack of money to take the right trains: sometimes so poor indeed that they cannot afford overnight accommodation and have to hunker down among the scenery in the pitiably furnished village halls in which they have been engaged to perform. How difficult to produce comedy (and comedy is what their provincial audiences are asking for) when there is no food in the stomach, and the baby's wail can be heard from the back of the auditorium! All this is observed at first hand, and without flinching. As austerely as in *Osaka Elegy* and *Sisters of the Gion*, *Aien Kyo* eschews the pull of 'melodrama'. In one of the movie's rare bouts of physical action, Yoshitaru pulls a knife on his rival Kenkichi, but his motive for doing so is not anything as vulgar as jealousy. In fact, the true reasons for his action (he wants to put himself in a bad light so that Ofumi will return to Kenkichi) are, like everything else in this film, held back from the audience, pulled out of alignment, de-dramatised, so that the viewer could miss the point unless he or she was supernaturally alert. That Mizoguchi doesn't help you at all – and indeed in certain ways seems to go out of his way *not* to help you – is an intriguing aspect of this movie. It defines too its single most striking feature, as a sort of puzzling perversity: the fact that it is not until half an hour into the running time that the audience is granted as much as a glimpse of the heroine's features in close-up.

Why *should* she be hidden like this? Mizoguchi's distrust of the close-up will be discussed again in these pages (notably when we come to *The Loyal 47 Ronin*). The preference seems to have formulated itself in the early years of the 1930s in reaction to the excessively rhetorical symbolism which he believed to be the mark of classic silent cinema. As Yoda tells us in his memoirs:

> The realism that [Mizoguchi] sought essentially depended on a sense of continuity in the actions and gestures of the players. He categorically rejected any artificial transition between one shot and another: he rejected, in short, the recourse to 'inserts' that are a feature of the silents. Movies only really came into their own, for him, with the advent of sound – with the talkies. 'Have you ever noticed', he once said to me 'that in the movies you always seem to have a bell-flower blown by the wind *in close-up*. For me, it's an artistic sin to attempt to insert a lyrical or a poetic atmosphere by these kinds of means. Except in cases where one absolutely wouldn't be able to understand the meaning of the scene without such a close-up, they're to be avoided! The "lyric sense" is either there – or it isn't!'[6]

---

memoirs), this now lost film (dating from 1931) is reputedly the place in which Mizoguchi first systematically tried out his one-scene-one-take camera style. The director's brutally frank naturalism (neo-realist *avant la lettre*) that culminates in *Women of the Night* (1948) found its tentative beginnings, according to Yoda, in this movie.

6 Yoda, *Souvenirs de Kenji Mizoguchi*, p. 40 [Author's translation].

During the 1930s Mizoguchi's *mise en scène* utilised close-ups rather rarely in comparison with his contemporaries; but this gave them great force when they *were* used. Here, a pensive Isuzu Yamada contemplates the hardships of a geisha's life in *Sisters of the Gion* (1936)

After the war, it appears that Mizoguchi gradually softened his line on this. In *Oharu* and *Sansho* and several of the other post-war masterpieces, close-ups are a significant part of his filmic grammar. An exchange in a 1952 interview is revealing in this context. Interviewer [Hajime Takizawa]: 'While using a long-shot, you continue shooting for an extremely long time, which is like filling a canvas with many colours, painting one layer over another.' Mizoguchi: 'But close-ups can't be avoided. Though long-takes can convey psychological conflict, close-ups are indispensable for more complicated nuances.'[7] *Indispensable for more complicated nuances.* That is quite a concession for Mizoguchi, quite a departure from his usual recourse to the Brechtian *Verfremdungseffekt*. And then I find myself linking this thought to a thought about *Osaka Elegy*: two of the greatest moments in that film (the moments, perhaps, where this film precisely *becomes* great) are close-ups of the human face: the final shot of Ayako advancing towards the camera that I have already discussed, and the beautiful close-up in the prison cell that shows Ayako mutely overhearing her lover in the process of denouncing her to the police. It is not in the spirit of denying Tony Rayns, and critics like him, their right to admire *Aien Kyo* as much as they claim they do, that I personally find myself regretting the lack of at least *one* close-up in this film which could take you into Ofumi's soul with the economy and elegance of the two earlier movies.

Contemporary Comparisons

These three films seem to me to be, whatever distinctions are made between them, distinguished works of art. Yet it would be interesting to know how typical they are, both in terms of artistry and of subject matter, of the films being made at the time. A director to whom Mizoguchi is sometimes compared is Sadao Yamanaka (1909–38) whose late-Edo costume drama *Humanity and Paper Balloons* (1936) is often taken to be a watershed movie of the epoch. Yamanaka, like Mizoguchi (whom he knew well), was the master of a terse and unfussy realism which in his case seems to have emerged out of social beliefs that were exceptionally bold and anti-authoritarian. *Humanity and Paper Balloons* is one of those gay and melancholy masterpieces of film history, like *L'Atalante*, whose tender, witty stylishness makes the viewer wish that he or she could have met its director. Yoda too – it is worth adding – adored this director, and took much from him. In 1935, at the lowest ebb of his fortunes and smitten with illness, he tells us that he found the confidence to live and fight on through a viewing (in the company of his mother) of one of Yamanaka's films, *The Village Tattooed Man*. Yamanaka, alas, died young, a victim of the war in China. His complex, lucid pessimism is summarised by Anderson and Richie in the following way:

> [Yamanaka's] objectives went far beyond mere historical reconstruction, since his interest in historical material was governed by a desire to show the emotions of which it was made, not merely its physical shape. His dialogue, far removed from the clichés of the conventional period drama and yet not too close to actual speech, aimed for the poetic: he was one of the few directors who could focus on the verbal without sacrificing the visual. He was also one of the few to treat period stories in a consistently adult manner.[8]

---

7   See J. Quandt and G. O'Grady (1996), p. 12.

8   J. Anderson and D. Richie (1959), p. 93.

The connections with Mizoguchi's spiritual seriousness don't need underlining.

Another contemporary of Mizoguchi in the 1930s was Mikio Naruse, arguably the fourth great Japanese film director in the canon (along with Mizoguchi, Ozu and Kurosawa). I have not by any means seen all of his films from this period (in any case, he is probably better known for his post-war works); but two that I have seen offer rich opportunities for comparison with Mizoguchi's work of the period. The films in question, *The Girl on Everyone's Lips* (1935) and *Feminine Melancholy* (1937), are both, in different ways, about the pressure of modernity on young women – pressures inherent in society, but also emanating from their own will and their latent sexual longings. In contrast to the heroines of *Osaka Elegy* and *Sisters of the Gion*, the principal characters are traditional marriageable 'nice girls', but in their protest against the safe, suitable alliances that are being arranged for them they show an independence of spirit (an intelligence, an integrity) comparable to that of Mizoguchi's feisty rebels. Naruse is no more reliant than Mizoguchi on the safety of a convenient happy ending. Destiny, in the films of both directors, is treated in a serious, dark and admirably unsentimental fashion.

So the films have similarities in atmosphere and in philosophy; but they also have interesting differences. One immediate and marked difference is stylistic: Naruse *does* use editing and close-up, so the films in question are immediately more 'legible'. The serious and examinable faces of the actresses in repose (Sachiko Chiba in *The Girl on Everyone's Lips*, Takako Irie in *Feminine Melancholy*, both magnificent) take us directly into their feelings. There is none of the darkness and distance – the sense of the 'non-said' and 'can't be said' – that makes Mizoguchi's films from this period both so intriguing and so oblique. Akira Kurosawa worked as an assistant director for Naruse in the late 1930s and has this to say about the shooting methods of Mizoguchi's younger contemporary:

> Naruse's [skill] consists of building one very brief shot on top of another, but when you look at them all spliced together in the final film, they give the impression of a single long take. The flow is so magnificent that the splices are invisible! This succession of short shots that looks calm and ordinary at first glance then reveals itself to be like a deep river with a quiet surface disguising a fast-raging current underneath. [For me] Naruse's sureness of hand was without comparison.[9]

Mizoguchi's method is less solicitous – less artful, less *captivating* – than Naruse's as described here; yet on the other hand, this doesn't mean that his movies aren't, in their own way, lucid – and were felt to be such by contemporaries who *did* appreciate them, even if there were certain things about them (as we have seen) that puzzled them. *Osaka Elegy* and *Aien Kyo* both came third in *Kinema Jumpo*'s list of annual ten best films, while *Sisters of the Gion* actually came first. Of course these fine movies by Mizoguchi are far from being the *only* masterpieces of the 1930s (an extremely rich decade in Japanese cinema); but they are, all three in my opinion, exceptionally living works, and a significant part of the Mizoguchian canon.

---

9   Akira Kurosawa, *Something Like an Autobiography* (1982), p. 113.

Post-war

The war came and went, with its attendant horrors. Out of its ruin came despair but also a new humanism. Early in 1948, in the company of Yoda, Mizoguchi visited the prostitutes' ward of the Osaka Municipal Hospital as research for a film he was planning about street conditions in the wake of the collapse. Two versions exist of this very famous visit. In Yoda's memoirs, the teasing voices of the prostitutes are foregrounded.

> When we entered the sick-room (according to Yoda) the girls clustered round and started shouting 'Hey, look at this little fellow – they say he's a film director! D'you think it's possible?' 'He's blushing, what a timid guy!' 'Come over here, sweetie! What brings you here? You want to sleep with us?'[10]

'We were all highly embarrassed,' Yoda concludes primly. Kaneto Shindo's documentary about Mizoguchi – already much cited – came out ten years after Yoda's memoirs, and Shindo, unlike Yoda, focuses on Mizoguchi's response. According to the Shochiku producer, Hisao Itoya, who was present that fateful day, Mizoguchi was overcome with emotion and could scarcely bring his words out. 'If you are here', he told the assembled prostitutes, 'it's the fault of men.' Then, lowering his eyes, and close to tears: 'It is *my* fault too!'

It is certainly an extraordinary incident. The passionate, discomfiting sincerity of Mizoguchi's words puts one in mind of certain Tarkovskian heroes: characters like Domenico in *Nostalghia* or Alexander in *The Sacrifice*, who feel constrained in some mystical way to take on their own backs the sins of the world. In return, the world judges them mad for their pains, and perhaps they really are mad. The scene could be understood in some ways as a public nervous breakdown. Yet the emotional logic in retrospect is easy enough to grasp, and the whole cameo, I think, is profoundly touching.

Women of the Night, the film that came out of this experience, is one of Mizoguchi's fiercest and swiftest. In stylistic terms, it is very close to neo-realism. The movie's opening credits – against a panoramic travelling shot taken at roof level in the city of Osaka (specifically, the black-market districts of Tennoji and Kamagasaki) – tell us that the story we are about to see is based on a novel called *The Feast of Women* by Eijiro Hisaito. As the film unfolds, the events depicted seem to have emerged, unmediated, out of the rawness of life itself – as if they had written themselves, or merely been 'recorded', in the manner of an on-the-spot documentary. Perhaps there is no need to *invent* anything, when the pressures and sufferings of the war turn everyone's life, so to speak, into a story. We are at the end of the war, and Fusako (Kinuyo Tanaka) is living in poverty with her brother-in-law and his mother while caring for her tubercular child. She has been separated from her husband, as well as from her sister and her parents, last heard of in Korea. How many other families suffered in such ways? In rapid succession within the first ten minutes of the movie the following catastrophes occur to our heroine: (1) The joyful news that her husband has been found turns to ashes when she arrives at the hospital to find that he has died. (2) Her son too is carried off (one of the briefest and least sentimental child deaths in the whole of cinema). (3) Her sister turns up from Korea – this is the good news but the bad news she brings with her is that their parents have died. Four deaths in a row: yet the viewer does not feel they are excessive or untypical, given the strictures and privations of the time. Fusako's subsequent descent into prostitution has the same terse and authoritative ring of truth to it. The possibility of 'going on the street' has been dangled in front of her during the film's opening sequence when the black-market stallholder shocks her by telling her that there are means at her disposal by which she can afford to buy those 'extra eggs' that she and her child need.

The child dies shortly afterwards, and the various catastrophes outlined take their toll. A turning-point of sorts comes when her sister steals from under her nose the one man whose support she has been relying on (that the man in question – her boss – turns out to be a worthless scoundrel is irrelevant to the injustice she feels she's been subjected to). Fusako toys with killing herself (a beautiful elliptical scene on a railway bridge which dispenses with the need for dialogue) but, changing her mind (or else: missing her opportunity), she throws herself onto the game with a kind of talented and passionate nihilism born out of despair.

On one level, then, we have a pure naturalistic drama: a typical 'slice of life', vivid and informative (as in the best documentary reportage). At another level, however, the shaping hand of the artist, manipulating events so that they fit in with *his* vision of the world, is also in evidence just as it is in contemporary European dramas such as Rossellini's *Rome Open City* (1946). For Fusako, it turns out, is not to be among the damned – or not permanently. There is redemption and hope at the end of this tale. In a scene of extraordinary violence, Fusako battles to save her young sister-in-law Kumiko (really only a teenager, and – in one sense – her own younger self) from joining her sisters on the game. Yoda, who helped craft the two sides of the scenario (naturalistic on the one hand; religio-humanistic on the other), didn't in the end think they really 'meshed' but I think I disagree with this verdict, and indeed to my mind, Fusako's psychological and moral redemption is both subtle and plausible.

It is important to see – and Tanaka's acting makes it wonderfully clear from the outset – that Fusako's fall from respectability was initially immense, and goes against her deepest inner nature. The steps towards her recovery of soul (one can't really use any other phrase here) are all profoundly connected with her feelings about the future generation. She has lost her own child – this was the starting-point for her despair. The beginning of her ascent out of hell, on the other hand, comes when she finds that her sister Natsuko (who has betrayed her) has become pregnant, albeit by the same wretched man who was once her own lover. She busies herself with trying to find a hospital in which Natsuko may rest and bring her pregnancy successfully to term, but despite her best efforts, the child is still-born – which throws Fusako back into even greater despair. Then comes the discovery, mentioned above, that her young sister-in-law is intent on following the same road to ruin that she herself has pursued, and in the fury of her appeal not to go down that path (we will come back in a moment to this episode's specific violence) we see operating a profound instinct of sisterly protectiveness. The girl, we are led to feel, not only represents her younger self, but also the future of Japan. Presiding over the hope she holds out, I should not omit to say, is a specifically Christian iconography: the great battle for Kumiko's soul takes place at twilight in the courtyard of a bombed-out church whose one surviving stained-glass window depicts an icon of the Virgin and Child – a last image of hope on which the film takes leave of its audience.

This Christian imagery may come as a surprise. Yet it is not so strange, after all, in the context of Japan's tradition of tolerant religious syncretism. Buddhism, Shintoism and Catholicism have always co-existed in Japan, though subjected at different times, in different centuries, to regular bouts of official persecution. The issue is not, I think, whether Mizoguchi was a Christian in his personal beliefs: I see no reason to think that he was. But I am sure he was *interested in* Christianity, in the wake of Japan's terrible defeat and devastation. His motives can only be guessed at: of all the great world religions, Christianity is certainly the most 'iconographic'. Far more specifically than in Buddhism and Shintoism (both of them discredited by Japan's defeat), Christianity in this film seems to provide in obscure ways solace and inspiration to the hearts of women, through its deep and perennial meditation on the theme of mother and child.

Perhaps more important, however, than deciding on the film's philosophy, is to register its extraordinary physical impact. As a cry of pain from beginning to finish, there are few films in the world to compare with *Women of the Night*. 'Defeat had given birth to savage customs,' says Yoda. 'It stripped both body and soul naked – it brought an evil sensuality into everyday living.'[11] The anguish Mizoguchi feels is communicated, as always in his films, through the metonymy of physical touch: specifically, two devastating rape scenes both of which involve the young sister-in-law Kumiko. What must have been shocking to contemporary audiences (it is hard to understand how they passed the censorship board) is the extended and 'two-part' nature of the violation. So, in the first of these episodes, Kumiko's rape by the young student in the upstairs room of a café is followed moments later, outside, by a sort of female collective 'gang bang', in which the café girls who are the student's nefarious associates beat her up in the street and humiliatingly strip her to her underwear.

Violent as this scene is, it pales in comparison with the movie's final showdown in the abandoned churchyard. Surrounded by a hostile gang of prostitutes, Fusako endeavours to persuade the girl of the senselessness of the path she is following – at which point the prostitutes turn on Fusako (now seen as a turncoat to the tribe) and beat her up in a savage orgy of retribution.

These scenes are uncomfortable to look at – in fact, they are almost unendurable. Yet they seem to me to be powered by a kind of holy fury – an idealism, even. *Women of the Night* in one way is a minor film in the Mizoguchi canon: its rapid, sketchlike progress seems to preclude, almost by definition, that mastery of form which is one of the preconditions for a masterpiece. On the other hand, form (in the sense of polish) isn't everything, and the film achieves that essential resolution which Aristotle calls *catharsis*. Experienced in the right conditions, the emotion that is communicated is the unmistakable one of pity and awe.[12]

---

11 Yoda, *Souvenirs de Kenji Mizoguchi*, p. 92.

12 According to Kyoko Hirano in *Mr Smith Goes to Tokyo* (1992, p. 164) *Women of the Night* 'got by' because of the approval its script secured from the occupation censor Harry Slott. Such films evidently walked a fine line. A year later, another script by Mizoguchi and Yoda, *Beauty and the Idiot* (*Bibo to Hakuchi*) fell at the last hurdle because of its 'anti-social' portrayal of drug-trafficking.

> Although at the end of the story the drug users are sent to prison, the censor judged that any reference at all to narcotics and stimulants was too dangerous, and that the film's principal theme of women seduced and turned into prostitutes . . . did not help to redeem it (p. 77).

(This is odd, because *Women of the Night* also has a sub-theme of drug-trafficking: yet in matters of censorship, consistency is never a prominent characteristic.) It is important to note that when *Women of the Night* was made the

The Brothel or 'Maison Close' – in Life and in Art

Fusako and Kumiko and the other women portrayed in *Women of the Night* engage in prostitution in the most primitive conditions possible. To say that they ply their trade 'on the street' is almost a euphemism: in post-war Osaka, a major industrial city, the very streets have been blown away, and the women congregate in open lots and bombed-out ruins close to the main roads leading to the city's slowly re-opening factories. It's from the industrial proletariat servicing these factories that they draw the bulk of their clientele, accosting them on their way to and from work. Charges, perforce, are minimal, given what the factory hands themselves are earning; and thus for the women to earn a living at all, large numbers of clients must be serviced on each working day.

The 'house' or bordello, operating in some long-established licensed quarter, must by contrast have seemed to Fusako and women like her a haven of civilisation. There, at least, one has a roof over one's head and guaranteed rice in the bowl. The dangers of a freelance existence on the street (including unprovoked attacks by strangers) are avoided or at least minimalised. In addition, there is free health inspection and medical care. Nonetheless, in the immediate post-war era, it was exactly this domiciled, quasi-official, protected status of the licensed quarter that constituted prostitution's affront to society. The brothel, it was thought, could perhaps, as a known quantity, be tackled and eradicated. Legislation began to be introduced in European countries – France, most famously – to outlaw the *maison close* and the red-light district. Japan, where the institution was as deeply engrained as anywhere in the world, in due course followed suit.

This is the social context surrounding the events portrayed in the last film Mizoguchi ever made, *Street of Shame*, released in 1956, the year in which he succumbed to leukemia at the age of fifty-eight. At the end of the movie, the brothel owner Taya congratulates himself that the threatened legislation to close the house in the Yoshiwara (Tokyo's red-light district) seems to have been defeated; but in fact, it was in that very year, 1956, that the measures in question were finally passed.[13] The *succès d'estime* that surrounded Mizoguchi's film following its release in early summer had a sociological byproduct: the movie was at least partially instrumental, so it is said, in pushing these anti-brothel measures through parliament. Whether, and to what extent, this makes the film a mere 'propaganda movie' will be discussed later. First, though, and for the sake of clarity, it is interesting to lay out the lines of the critique Mizoguchi is offering.

'Dreamland', the invented locale of the action, is an average modern brothel in the Yoshiwara. Times are hard (perhaps they are always hard?). 'Courtesans used to be rich', opines one of the girls, but – whether she is right or not – that is very far from the case now. All the girls are in debt to the brothel's shrewd, business-minded madam, Mrs Taya (the excellent Sadaki Sawamura), and

---

subject of prostitution and streetwalking was very much in the air. Hirano cites six different scripts on the topic that came before the censorship board in 1948. (It isn't clear how many of these were actually made, but at least one of them – Masahiro Makino's *The Gate of Flesh/Nikutai no Mon* – was, and became a great box-office success.)

13 The Anti-Prostitution Law, outlawing public solicitation and management of prostitutes, although passed in 1956, didn't come into force for a year, and it was another year before prostitution became a punishable offence. 'Respectable, controllable, government-sanctioned prostitution came to an end as the clocks struck midnight on 31 March 1958', says Lesley Downer in *Women of the Pleasure Quarters* (2001, p. 211). Downer goes on: 'The licensed quarters had, for all their faults, been clean, well organised and safe for both the women and their customers. Hereafter there would only be unlicensed prostitution which rapidly became the domain of the yakuza.'

one sees immediately that it's in the madam's interest (and of all madams like her) that they *should* be in debt. It gives her a hold over her employees that is, in essence, identical to the slave owner's hold over his or her chattels. As long as the girls are in debt they must work for her; and in all cases save one, the debt is so deep, and so well devised, that there is little chance of them buying their freedom. Yasumi (Ayako Wakao), the single employee to escape this regime, does so by engaging in methods that are essentially similar to the madam's – i.e. by loaning out her savings to her colleagues, while charging them extortionate interest rates (rates she is ruthless in enforcing). She 'collects', too, on an even grander scale, from her male clients (one in particular, who is eager to marry her), by promising favours she has no intention of granting.

In a sense, Yasumi is the only 'professional' among the employees. For this is the second most striking thing about Dreamland and places like it: any residual glamour that once attached to the profession of courtesanship (if only the glamour of a set-apart caste) has long since vanished or been amortised. The place and the inhabitants are dingy. The girls are not so much professionals as amateurs, involved in the game because there is no other way to keep body and soul together. Homely looking Yumeko (Aiko Mimasu), from the depths of the country, has an adult factory worker son who is desperately ashamed of her. Frumpish, bespectacled Hanae (Michiyo Kogure), cursed with a permanent cold, has an invalid husband and a child to support: prostitution, for her, was the last resort after she and her man balked at a planned double suicide. Only the reckless, insolent and forcibly sexy ex-teenager Mickey (Machiko Kyo) shows any aptitude for the game, and she, in a way, is the most amateur of all: a middle-class girl on the run from her authoritarian father, choosing a way of life which can be certain of mocking his values and exposing his paternalist hypocrisy.

As a realistic or semi-realistic critique of the sadness and tawdriness of brothels, the film has few equals and is among the most famous of Mizoguchi's works. Donald Richie calls it 'the best of all films examining the problems of women in post-war Japan'. Jean Douchet (French Mizoguchi expert, onetime contributor to *Cahiers du Cinéma*) goes much further: 'For me, along with Chaplin's *M. Verdoux* and Renoir's *Rules of the Game*, [it is] the greatest film in the history of cinema.' Verdicts like these – delivered with sincerity, by critics who know what they're talking about – naturally command respect.[14] But, much as I respond to the film's power and relentlessness, I do not myself share this conclusion. True, individual sequences are as memorable as anything in the Mizoguchi canon: for instance, the extraordinary final scene, in which the little girl from Kyushu who has belatedly joined the stable of prostitutes is 'powdered up' for work by the brothel's madam, before being sent out onto the street to solicit custom (a close-up of her timid features peeping from behind a wall as she essays her first gesture of beckoning is the grimly wordless image on which the film closes). Remarkable too, and authentically shocking in its directness, is the sequence in which Mickey taunts her father who has come to take her away from the brothel. Her previous insouciance is revealed, in this scene, as a mask to disguise deep feelings of anger and betrayal. Affecting to believe that he is simply another customer, she demands to know, with savage indifference, how much he will pay her to sleep with her. Here, as elsewhere, there is genuine psychological intensity. The remorseless gaze of the camera nudges out many unspoken things from behind the brittleness of the dialogue.

---

14 These, along with other encomia, are cited by James Quandt in the Fall 1996 Film Programme guide on Mizoguchi issued by the Ontario Cinemathèque. Truffaut was also an admirer of this film: his review of it is reprinted in *Les Films de ma vie* [1975] (*The Films of My Life*, 1980).

Nonetheless, the film to me suffers from being over-schematic. While the characters of Mickey and Yasumi (the 'miser') come over as interestingly conceived and well written, other participants in the drama (the prostitutes Hanae, Otane, Shizuko for example) remain obstinately one-dimensional. Crammed into the confines of an ugly set that seems to be excessively artificial and studio-bound, *Street of Shame* appears, at times, wooden and arthritic as a film. In defence of this style, one could point by way of comparison to the spareness of certain late works by other great cineastes which delicately walk the line between theatre and cinema: Ford's *Seven Women* (1966), Renoir's *Le Petit théâtre de Jean Renoir* (1967), or maybe Dreyer's *Gertrud* (1964). The idea here is that the staged and artificial qualities of these films' *mise en scène* represent a kind of paring back to the bone of the available dramatic grammar: paradoxically then, it is their very 'staginess' that makes them 'pure cinema'. (Perhaps something of this is what Douchet is driving at in his comparison with *M. Verdoux*.) Try as I might, however, I am unable to think of the scene (for example) in which Yumeko goes mad – in response to her son's rejection of her – as anything other than 'theatre', in the bad sense.

Mizoguchi was old and ill when he made the film, and maybe one can't help feeling that it shows. Moreover, for the first time since the war, Yoda had nothing to do with the script, and it may be that the multipart, 'choral' nature of the scenario that Mizoguchi arrived at in collaboration with his new scriptwriter Masashige Narusawa was somehow inimical to the kind of flowing, seamless, plastically rich cinema in which he usually excelled. *Street of Shame* is fuelled by a fierce and pitiless indignation, and, like all Mizoguchi's films, is impressive for its dedicated moral seriousness. But it lacks the redemptive tenderness of Mizoguchi's finest work, and strikes me as being uncharacteristically cold.

The Moral Economy of Brothels

Let us recapitulate for a moment: for the customer, as for the 'service-provider', the brothel is a house of illusions. The institution, it goes without saying, is rooted in profound ambiguity. Sometimes, as in *Street of Shame*'s Dreamland, the illusions are palpably kitsch. The large plastic scallop in the hallway on which Mickey, on her arrival, strikes up a pose as the Venus de Milo, gestures towards a world of beauty, art and refinement that can only be mocked by the establishment's prosaic reality. The gap between aspiration and gross actuality is poignant as well as obvious, and it is tempting to conclude that this is the moral economy of all brothels. So it is, in a way, and yet one can still be tender towards illusions: they are part of human life and human need. Speaking about the establishment depicted in his movie *Flowers of Shanghai* (1998), the Taiwanese director Hou Hsiao-hsien explains:

> In our patriarchal Chinese society, men visited those *maisons des fleurs* because it was the only place where love could find expression. [Arranged] marriages being the norm in this society, courtesans existed less as a sexual outlet than to respond to the human need for romance. To seduce a courtesan required money of course, but above all it required time, attention, assiduity. There was a delicacy involved: it was a 'flower' that you were paying court to. We must remember above all that in the *maison des fleurs* men were obeying rules that were set down and administered by women.[15]

15 Quoted in *Positif* no. 453, November 1998, p. 6 [Author's translation].

The brothel in *Flowers of Shanghai* is what might, euphemistically, be called a 'high-class estab-lishment', but a similar air of freedom, and one might almost say of happiness, sometimes reigned (if we are to believe witnesses) in more down-to-earth environments. The English writer Peter Quennell, visiting Shanghai in 1931, describes one such house in terms of liveliness and innocence:

[There was] a large room, looking out onto a busy street, full of women sitting round tables: to every three or four girls an ancient governess, like a peasant woman who has brought pigeons to sell at a fair. What charming and refreshing informality! The young women, girls of 15 or 16, wore trousers and short pyjama coats, dull blue over white socks and little satin slippers. None was attractive, but the indistinguishable mass chattered as glib and bold as a crowd of schoolchildren. They pulled and stroked our clothes as we went by, unafraid and unabashed, almost indifferent to our presence.

It is interesting that Quennell's appreciation of the charm of the scene should go hand in hand with an equally marked aversion to the 'glumness' and 'cyonising propriety' of its Japanese counter-parts, which he also visited. ('Cyonising' refers to lead-based make-up: Quennell disliked the way that Japanese whores coated their faces with white paint.)[16] Any serious discussion of brothels needs to take into account the obvious fact that different regimes operate in different environ-ments. Here is Nagisa Oshima attempting to formulate some distinctions in relation to his film *Empire of the Senses* (1976). (The movie, based on a notorious true-life incident in which a woman murdered her lover at the height of their combined sexual ecstasy, came out in 1976, and is set in the mid-1930s.)

Question: To avoid misunderstanding, could you define for us what is meant by the terms geisha and prostitute in the Japan of 1936 and the Japan of today?

Answer: The term geisha comprises very different professional categories. It means 'to sell one's art', but on the bottom rungs of the social ladder it means 'to sell one's body'. In that context, let me add that according to notions specific to our country, the world of sensuality doesn't in the least detract from a person's value as a human being. The notion of *koshoku*, implying both 'capacity to appreci-ate' and 'knowing how to love', has never been neglected. In another era it even used to be a condition for being a gentleman. In the tenth century, *The Tale of Genji* founded aristocratic society in Japan, and for the first time in that society a sexual culture aspired towards 'knowing how to love'. Polygamy [multiple wives] and polyandry [multiple husbands] dominated in that aristocratic class. The refinement came to an end with the brutal era of the samurai [thirteenth to seventeenth centuries], but re-emerged in the Edo period from the seventeenth to the nineteenth century. Of course, that culture was the priv-ilege of the dominant classes who practised it in houses of pleasure. No shame attached to those houses, absolutely not! . . . The beautiful tradition of 'knowing how to love' faded and died on the eve of the Second World War. Sada and Kichi, my characters in *Empire of the Senses*, are the survivors of a sexual tradition that used to exist, and which to me is admirably Japanese.

There seems to be an element of provocation here. *Empire of the Senses* is a deliberately shocking work of art. The *amour fou* portrayed in it goes far beyond any normal understanding of *koshoku*

16 Citations from Peter Quennell, *A Superficial Journey through Tokyo and Peking* (1932; reprinted 1986), p. 78.

– beyond bounds, I suppose, that most people would find defensible.[17] The main point stands, however: that, in its historical incarnation, the brothel offered to men – and in certain ways also to women – utopian respite from the boredom, solitude and utilitarianism of everyday humdrum existence. The question: 'Does the moral economy of the pleasure house issue in rich human relations or, on the contrary, in a *void* of human relations?' cannot be answered simplistically. It depends both on the place and the time. The film director Yuzo Kawashima was a prolific contemporary of Mizoguchi's, to whom it was obvious that brothels were places of high popular entertainment – or else they were nothing at all. Kawashima's response to the threat of the anti-prostitution law was to come up with a film set in the late Edo period in which the institution of the brothel was simply and lyrically celebrated. *Bakumatsu Taiyo-den/Not Long after Leaving Shinagawa* (1957, co-written by Shohei Imamura) is probably one of the most joyous films in the Japanese canon, though its joy co-exists with a distinct sense of *lacrimae rerum*. I think it is perhaps worth a short excursus.

'Contra' Mizoguchi: Kawashima's *Not Long after Leaving Shinagawa*

After a brief prelude, the credits sequence unfolds over shots of a corner of modern-day Tokyo: a bridge near a railway viaduct, to the left of which (so a voice-over informs us) lies the district of Shinagawa, the first of the fifty-four traditional 'stops' on the way to Kyoto. Though currently in decline (as we can see), the quarter still houses thirty-three brothels and several hundred prostitutes – all shortly to be cashiered following the introduction of the anti-prostitution bill. By way of a flashback, the film now introduces us to events taking place in one of these establishments 100 years previously, on the eve of the Imperial Restoration. We immediately see how busy the place is, how prosperous-looking and 'well-kept' – in all respects (save one) like a large, friendly, modern hotel.

Accompanied by a retinue of cronies, Soheiji, a humorous-looking man of the people (soon to emerge as the hero of our tale), appears in the main reception area, demanding to be served with wine ('The best! We don't want hangovers!') and be introduced to the women. Soon this fellow – a townsman (possibly a merchant) – establishes himself in charge of the party, dispensing good cheer to all newcomers, scarcely fazed when three or four angry-looking samurai (his social superiors) appear, complaining they have been insulted by the English. (We are at a time when the first foreigners were setting foot in Japan.) No deference to class superiority here! In the brothel, everyone is equal. Quick-wittedness – a certain style and easy insolence – is the currency that counts. Soon we discover that our hero has no money to pay his bill, at which point he proposes that he himself join the staff of the hostelry. No sooner installed as a waiter, he turns out to be incredibly good at it, garnering the tips of the real waiters from under their noses, to their evident jealousy and discomfiture.

Meanwhile, the real business of the house goes on, of course. We are introduced to the prostitutes, two in particular, one of whom seems inclined – out of laziness, or else out of some crazy

---

17 Which doesn't prevent Oshima, in the next breath, from making such a defence: 'Sada's name is so popular in Japan that it suffices to pronounce it to touch on the most serious sexual taboos. It is quite natural that a Japanese artist would want to dedicate his work to that marvellous woman!' The whole dialogue is quoted in Jacques Gerber, *Anatole Dauman: Pictures of a Producer* (London: BFI, 1992) pp. 143–4.

hauteur – not to take part in the bidding for clients, and sinks into debt as a consequence. The other, on the contrary – the heroine of the film, Osone – is talented, resourceful, duplicitous, and in all respects made for the game. The various ins and outs of the plot – the adventures, misadventures, various comic and bittersweet rivalries of these women – need not be itemised here. It is enough to take in that the brothel, a world in miniature, is presented as containing within its confines all the drama, playfulness and variety that anyone could possibly desire. The seasons come and go. A visit from a peddler with a fresh supply of reading material (tragedies, double suicides, romances) makes a welcome break from the inmates' routine. One snowy day, a pretty maidservant, stepping outside the building to empty a pail of slops, sees a prisoner being led off on horseback to the gallows. And there are other, more colourful incursions too, issuing from the drama of the times, as when everyone hurries out of doors to catch a glimpse of a band of Scottish Highlanders marching through town on the way to the British Legation.

In the midst of all this activity and torpor, it is possible to believe that the brothel's business does not *only* concern the commerce of sex; and that, even though sex *is* the main business it need not necessarily be described in terms of exploitation. One returns, after seeing this beautifully composed film, to the extraordinary lack of *pudeur* in relation to sexual matters which has been the historical norm in Japan and which persists to this day (as a strange mingling of 'business' and 'generosity') at every corner and cranny of the contemporary sex market. Thus, for example, in certain low-life bars in downtown Tokyo (so John David Morley tells us, in his beautifully written memoir *Pictures from the Water Trade*) it is permissible and even proper for drinkers to nuzzle up to the *mama-san*, and to fondle her breasts – and this fondling will be charged on the bill! Morley writes (with a mixture of awe and admiration):

> Magical slips of paper, little anatomies of the state of the nation and masterpieces of character analysis, are handed out [at the end of the evening] with the same authority as a verdict passed by a court of law. Few customers appeal. None, ever, fail to pay up.[18]

Other Films from the 1950s

These observations may serve as an approach to two final films by Mizoguchi on this topic, both dating from the early 1950s. The movies in question are *Gion Festival Music* (distributed in America under the title *A Geisha*) and *The Woman of Rumour*. Tucked in between such period masterpieces as *Ugetsu Monogatari* and *Sansho the Bailiff* (in the case of *Gion Festival Music*) and between *Sansho* and *Chikamatsu Monogatari* (in the case of *The Woman of Rumour*), the pair may easily be overlooked, but they are not negligible works. (In passing, it is interesting to note in this context the extraordinary productivity of the classical masters in the heyday of the Japanese studio system. 1954 – at Daiei, under the auspices of Masaichi Nagata – was in some way an *annus mirabilis* for Mizoguchi: three separate films were released (*Sansho*, *The Woman of Rumour*, *Chikamatsu*), in addition to extensive working journeys to America, Europe and Hong Kong.)

Gion Festival Music is sometimes spoken of as a remake of the pre-war *Sisters of the Gion*, but this is not quite accurate. There are indeed a number of similarities: in both cases, we have a tale

---

18 John David Morley, *Pictures from the Water Trade: An Englishman in Japan* (1985), pp. 194–5.

which contrasts two different types of geisha living under the same roof in difficult personal circumstances. In both cases, the pair have a sister relationship (but they are 'blood sisters' only in
the earlier movie); in both cases, finally, the younger of the pair questions and rebels against the
system. Yet in other respects the stories go their own ways. The characters in the two films differ,
and so too do the tales' respective conclusions.

Eiko (Ayako Wakao) is a sixteen-year-old orphan who turns up in Kyoto on the doorstep of her
mother's best friend Miyoharu (Michiyo Kogure), asking to be taken in and trained as a geisha.
(Her mother, like Miyoharu, followed the profession.) Miyoharu is reluctant: for one thing, the life
of a geisha requires a very special discipline; besides which, the cost of the training is exorbitant,
and Miyoharu, who lives on her earnings, without the support of a patron or *danna*, doesn't
believe she has the money to back such a wish. But Eiko is adamant, and in the face of her determination, the older woman accedes. She will find the money from somewhere, borrowing it, in
the event, from the powerful female restaurant manager and figure-of-the-district Okimi (Chieko
Naniwa), who in turn has borrowed it from one of her own rich male clients – alas (as we shall see)
with certain strings attached.

Miyoharu's hunch about Eiko's suitability for the profession seems at first glance to be justified
The girl is assiduous as well as beautiful, and soon shows signs that she might become one of the
most striking *maiko* of her generation. But here is the catch – and it comes, you could say, before
she has even had the chance to get started. The money put forward by the wealthy boss Kusuda

(Seizaburo Kawazu) to fund her training has this price tag attached to it: that as soon as she graduates (i.e. when she turns seventeen), Eiko shall become his mistress. Eiko, of course, does not know about the deal, and neither apparently does Miyoharu – although the worldly Okimi insists she ought to have been aware of the implicit bargain involved (for nothing in the geisha world exists without a tariff).[19]

Will Eiko go along with the plan? Not at all! As soon as it becomes apparent – on an arranged trip to Tokyo – that this is the payback, she digs her heels in. Resisting Kusuda's lecherous advances, she bites the fellow on the lips so viciously that he lands up in hospital.

Scandal – disaster – opprobrium. Eiko's wounding of Kusuda, taken in conjunction with the wrath that falls on the head of her 'elder sister' and mentor Miyoharu, puts paid to the possibility of gainful employment for the pair. Invitations to the local tea houses dry up, through the fiat of the vengeful Okimi. Miyoharu, who has been moved and shaken by the forthrightness of her young ward, comes to believe that there is only one way out of the impasse. Since they will need protection if they are to survive economically, she reluctantly takes up the offer that has been held out to her by another key player in the drama, Kusuda's business acquaintance, a cold and treacherous bachelor named Kanzaki (Kanji Koshiba) – who at least possesses the merit of admiring her.

The film ends with a tentative restoration of the status quo. Life slowly goes back to normal. Miyoharu becomes Kanzaki's mistress. Okimi calls off her embargo. The phones start ringing again. It is twilight in the Gion. As we take leave of the two women, they are glimpsed, immaculately dressed and coiffeured, setting out together down the alley for the first of the parties they will be attending that evening.

If we are to go only by its ending, *Gion Festival Music* must be judged less 'radical' than its celebrated pre-war counterpart: resignation not defiance is its keynote. Less radical perhaps, but not necessarily less truthful, or less moving. In its own way, the film is a jewel. Both actresses possess a wonderfully beguiling screen presence. Michiyo Kogure, who plays Miyoharu, is outstandingly gentle. Her softness and pliancy (her 'femininity') had already been noticed by Mizoguchi when he cast her, three years earlier, in the leading role in *A Picture of Madame Yuki/Yuki Fujin Ezu* (1950). (The kindness she brings to this part reminds me of another wonderful Japanese actress, Setsuko Hara, her exact contemporary, whose luminous performance as the caring daughter-in-law of an old provincial couple irradiates another classic film that came out in the same year – *Tokyo Story* by Ozu. What magnificent actresses Japan possessed at that time!) Ayako Wakao, twenty in 1953 (playing a sixteen-year-old), was soon to become one of the most famous faces in Japanese cinema. Her role in *Gion Festival Music* requires her to provide a kind of hardness, or dryness, that counterpoints Miyoharu's delicate pliancy. Yet Eiko's disciplined approach to her profession turns

---

19 The deal here needs to be distinguished (though perhaps there is a deliberate ambiguity on the film-maker's part) from the traditional de-flowering ceremony of the *maiko* called *mizu-age*. This usually took place when the girl was around fourteen. The lofty sums paid for it by patrons formed an extremely important part of the economy of the geisha house. In contrast to the deal proposed here, it was usually a one-off arrangement. Liza Dalby tells us in *Geisha*: 'The *mizu-age* patron was something like a male honeybee . . . After his initial function was served, he had no further relation with the lady.' (1983, p. 109). For further discussion of the phenomenon, see Downer *passim*, and Arthur Golden's novel *Memoirs of a Geisha* (1997), especially pp. 232–3.

out to be free from the snares of greed and graspingness. In Wakao's performance, the young geisha comes across as essentially innocent.

As for the world that is portrayed here: there is no let-up in Mizoguchi's critique. The power structure of geishadom is laid bare in the extraordinary scenes following Eiko's attack on Kusuda, which show the girl's fate being decided. Various interests and vanities are at stake. Kusuda (a clownish figure) has been humiliated but, lying in his hospital bed, his humiliation appears not to be his key preoccupation. More important than the insult he personally received is his anxiety about how Miyoharu treated his colleague Kanzaki that same evening in Tokyo; for on his success, or not, in fixing up the pair hung an important industrial contract. (Miyoharu's refusal to sleep with Kanzaki, on the same evening that Eiko refused to sleep with Kusuda, means that this contract is in jeopardy.)

And then Okimi, too, the district 'fixer', has also been insulted. Was it for this that she went out of her way to help an old friend with Eiko's training? The venomous contempt that she unleashes on Miyoharu in the wake of the outrage is only the counterpart of the contempt that has just been unleashed on *her* for her failure to deliver her side of the bargain. As Kusuda's bow-tied lieutenant vents his fury on her in the hospital, it is possible to glimpse momentarily (but with an extreme clarity) the grim economic reality behind the whole facade of geishadom. Step out of line and you are dead. Once, perhaps, the institution had a form of glory. But this 'spiritual' content seems to have all but vanished. Was it ever really there in the first place? Liza Dalby in her indispensable *Geisha* (1983) is astonishingly upbeat about the phenomenon:

> Today one might look back at the elaborately stylised world of the Japanese licensed quarters of the nineteenth century and see a form of cultural sophistication and civility rarely matched in the history of the world.

Balzac, too, in his great European novel on the subject, emphasised the splendours as well as the miseries of the trade. Dalby's enthusiasm for her subject is not self-evidently absurd: the customs and practices of the geisha world represent, in their way, an astonishing anthropological *fact*. But the cost it entailed in human freedom is also surely inescapable. In the nineteenth century, courtesans and geisha were probably the most cultivated women in the country. The *only* entertaining conversation between the sexes took place in this milieu. *Gion Festival Music* shows how the women who offer the service, and the men who receive it, have become, over the years, misaligned. Once upon a time (it is possible to believe) the latter lived up to their 'privileges' – but now they have sunk into boorishness.

Refinement and Licence in the Geisha Districts

A figure we haven't mentioned in *Gion Festival Music*, Eiko's crippled and feckless father Sawamoto, is played by a member of Mizoguchi's regular repertoire, Eitaro Shindo. (The following year he was the eponymous steward and slave-holder in *Sansho the Bailiff*.) The actor's authoritative and imposing personality makes itself felt in a small but decisive part in the last of the films to be considered in this chapter, *The Woman of Rumour*, in which he plays Harada, the boss of the local association of tea-house owners in Shimabara and long-time admirer of Mrs Mabuchi (Kinuyo

Tanaka), who is the proprietor of the Izutsuya, one of the oldest and most prominent of these establishments.[20]

Mrs Mabuchi is in difficulty: she is a million yen short of the sum she is looking for in order to purchase a clinic on behalf of a young doctor (Tomoemon Otani) with whom she has become infatuated; and although Harada knows that this is the reason she is seeking the loan (and that if the purchase goes through it will be directly against his interests), he nonetheless forwards her the money with a disinterested generosity – one might even call it a stylishness – that stands in stark contrast to the leeching, calculating brutality of the male protagonists in *Gion Festival Music*.

Harada's masculine authority protects Mrs Mabuchi from other dangers too – the kind of physical dangers that beset women of her ilk in this kind of milieu. Thus, when the hoodlum boyfriend of one of the geisha barges into the Izutsuya demanding that she pay back the money he claims she has stolen from him, Harada steps forward and without further ado fells the young intruder with a coolly directed blow to the shins. Plainly, this is a man who has experience in dealing with ruffians. The interest of the incident, however, for the audience, lies not so much in the proof it affords that gallantry and male courage can exist in unexpected places (we don't really see enough of Harada to judge this properly) as in the physical specificity – the sharpness, the neatness, the authority – of the man's actions. *The Woman of Rumour* is, among other things, a marvellous documentary portrait of Japanese *gesture*. For these houses of pleasure have their own laws of movement – their own 'physics', you could say – uniting the geisha to their customers. Alcohol fuels everyone's deportment. Intoxicated when they arrive, the guests become even looser (if this is possible) as the evening progresses. Geisha, too, who pour the saké, also partake of it, and are soon nudging their guests and slapping them on the wrists, or tapping them with their fans, in a vocabulary of stylised playfulness. Licence (a kind of stylised licence) prevails, as one would expect in such an environment; but in the midst of it, a strange contrasting decorum. While the house party makes merry, other geisha – in full regalia, this time, and attended by their twelve-year-old maids – make their way, in stately procession, round the outskirts of the orgy, heading for the doors and other appointments in the district. To the unacclimatised eye, the simplest Japanese action (whether of speaking or walking or sitting or bowing) has something overdetermined and mysterious about it. In *The Woman of Rumour* especially

---

20 Viewers often find themselves asking: What kind of establishment is the Izutsuya, exactly? The classic geisha house (*okiya*) was off-bounds to customers: professional entertaining was done in the tea houses (*ochaya*) nearby in the district, to which the geisha were summoned by telephone. The Izutsuya seems to be unusual in being both the domicile and the workplace of its inhabitants, and in this respect is closer to the template of a traditional brothel. John Gillett, in a National Film Theatre leaflet dated 1989, seems to be under the impression that this is in fact what it is (he uses the word throughout in his programme note). Dudley and Paul Andrew, in *Kenji Mizoguchi: A Guide to References and Resources*, characterise it as 'a tea house that fronts for a geisha house', but this is to make the establishment more clandestine than it is actually portrayed. Yoda (who, having written the script, ought perhaps to have the last word) comes up with the intriguing suggestion that what we have in this film is an *updating*: the traditional life of the *shimabara* courtesans 'transposed into the modern epoch' (see *Souvenirs di Kenji Mizoguchi*, p. 119). So it's partly geisha and partly courtesan/prostitute behaviour that is being looked at: the distinction is deliberately blurred. (It is perhaps relevant to the intrinsic ambiguity of the phenomenon that Yoda himself, in his commentary, makes little distinction between geisha and prostitutes, using either word interchangeably.)

(although it can be seen in the other movies too), the various gestures can be excavated and itemised, without our feeling that they really give up their deepest secrets. At least three main 'levels' are discernible, it seems to me. At the highest and most formal level, there is the movement of the mimes in the Noh drama that Mrs Mabuchi visits in the company of the doctor and her daughter Yukiko. (Almost impenetrable to outsiders, the stylisation of this form of drama does make sense to contemporary Japanese audiences, for the daughter and the doctor are clearly shown enjoying the play.) Connected to this, but at a slightly lower level of refinement, there are the traditional summer dances attended by Mrs Mabuchi and the doctor (not entirely cultural, this occasion: the doctor disgraces himself in Mrs Mabuchi's eyes by ogling the dancers' photographs in the programme booklet). And finally there is the deportment of the geisha in their formal regalia, commented on a moment ago, as they decorously trip around the tea-house district.

The final sequence of *The Woman of Rumour* seems to comment on these levels of gesture and at the same time to suggest how they are disfigured in the modern world. A exterior crane shot peers down on the street from an angle of forty-five degrees and takes in, first, the procession of geisha leaving the Izutsuya; next, a woman worker of the district dressed in modern Western clothing, hurrying past them on some errand; finally, coming down the street towards the procession, a party of staggering drunken revellers. Three different modes of locomotion (in shorthand: 'natural', 'inebriated' and 'stylised') make up, between them, the 'eternal' picture of Japan. At the most basic level of meaning, the image cannot but be a desolate one. We do not need a caption to read the director's intention: 'This is how it has always been, and always *will* be – until the end of time!' Yet the very fact that the scene is wordless throws it back, at a deeper level, into enigma. Here it is above all the haunting changelessness of the scene – not the judgment of its morality – that leaves the strongest impression on the viewer.

The Role of the Daughter

When all is said and done, *The Woman of Rumour* is minor Mizoguchi, and I do not want to draw inflated or metaphysical conclusions from it. It has its faults, rather noticeable. In particular, the role of the doctor is badly underwritten. If he is not to be cast as a villain (certain of his actions would seem to point in this direction), he needs to be made more lively, complex and intriguing than the film succeeds in painting him. As things stand, the scenes expounding the three-way pull of jealousy between the mother, the daughter and the doctor – scenes which should be the film's dramatic centre – lack the essential energy and inventiveness that is needed to make them convincing.

On the other hand, the relationship between the mother and the daughter (once the doctor is out of the picture) *is* presented with subtle tenderness. Yukiko (the girl in question, played by Yoshiko Kuga) has come back to Kyoto from Tokyo in order to recuperate from a failed love affair and resulting suicide attempt. Everything about her (her dress, her manner, her way of relating to the geisha) bespeaks a spiritual distance from the world she has found herself recalled to. It is only too clear that she is ashamed of her mother's profession, and – as far as her inheritance is concerned – wants nothing further to do with it.

But Mrs Mabuchi falls sick, and Yukiko finds herself, perforce, gradually taking over the duties involved in running the establishment. Whereas this upshot might have been presented darkly, and deterministically, as her inescapable destiny, the film seems to regard it, on the contrary, in a calm and natural way, as some sort of homecoming: the right choice (at least, not, egregiously, the *wrong* choice). Nursing her mother, looking after the geisha, attending to the needs of the customers and to the finances of the household, the girl at last (without the help of the doctor – he has vanished into the dark) arrives at a kind of contentment.

6 | Visions of History

Japan's love affair with history is one of the most striking aspects of the national culture. Right from the beginning of its cinema, *jidai-geki*, or historical costume drama, played a major part in the industry's output, making up, in any given year, fully half of the films produced. All studios made them. (Generally speaking, with important exceptions, the historical films were made in a company's Kyoto studios; those set in the present, in Tokyo.) Usually these films had no great historical depth to them: the vast majority were *chambara* (sword epics) – which didn't mean however that they weren't backed up by genuine knowledge of the customs of the times, coupled with scholarly accuracy in such areas as costume design, architecture and weaponry. Yet some films went even further than this: from the 1930s we find in the work of directors such as Tomu Uchida, Hiroshi Inagaki, Mansuku Itami, Sadao Yamanaka and Daisuke Ito, a deeper and more discreet level of realism, refinement and seriousness. In the best of the works of these directors, genre, as such, disappears, and the violence of subject matter that underlies *chambara* becomes infused, gradually, with tragedy and reflectiveness. After the war (and a six-year hiatus caused by the occupation's ban on 'feudal' subjects) this path is taken up again, with further refinements, by Akira Kurosawa. Mizoguchi – self-taught historian, connoisseur and scholar – had always been attached to this movement: in certain ways he is plainly the 'leader' of it. We have already looked at a trilogy of films in which these historical preoccupations were very much to the fore: *Oharu, Ugetsu* and *Sansho* are clearly his best-known films in the West: the films on which his reputation is ultimately based. However, 1954, the year which saw the release of *Sansho the Bailiff*, was also the year that produced *Chikamatsu Monogatari/Crucified Lovers* whose reputation in Japan is at least as high as the films just mentioned; while the following year – the last full working year in Mizoguchi's life – saw the release of two more majestic period films, the only two he ever made in colour: *The Empress Yang Kwei Fei/Yokihi* and *Tales of the Taira Clan/Shinheiki Monogatari*.

These three films are my main focus here; but before going into them it is worthwhile considering another 'costume' film by Mizoguchi – an absolutely key work of his career, made during World War II, and in some ways (above all in the passionate meticulousness of its period recreation) the foundation stone on which his subsequent historical movies could be said to rest.

Mistress and servant: Kyoko Kagawa and Kasuo Hasegawa as the doomed couple in *Chikamatsu Monogatari/Crucified Lovers* (1954)

The Loyal 47 Ronin/Genroku Chushingura (1941–2)

There is no point in denying that *The Loyal 47 Ronin* is a difficult work, posing challenges of a different order of complexity than those so far considered. Prints of the film, for a start, are exceptionally difficult to find, and, though Image has put it out on DVD, the film has never been properly distributed in the West. As I write, the subtitled 35mm version that is on offer for current Mizoguchi retrospectives is, in places, excessively underlit: a grave handicap in a film whose masterly visual compositions are nearly all presented, in the first instance, in long shot. Physical legibility therefore – the ability at the most basic level to identify characters – is an issue. (An audience's appreciation might be altered and enhanced were the film to be projected on a beautiful mint copy.) Another difficulty is the length of the movie: it is Mizoguchi's longest, a two-part epic, 222 minutes in all, and the action progresses very, very slowly. In a way, 'action' is misleading: the film is really about *in*action. It is about waiting for the right moment to strike, and the audience, at times, is made to experience the length of the wait as an almost physical sense of oppression. Finally, there is the whole business about *seppuku* (or decreed collective suicide) on which the film hinges. If the action is not repugnant to morality, it is still, to most Westerners, odd at least. Naturally, I do not want to exaggerate. It is my belief that the film is, in fact, extraordinarily powerful and dramatic; but the obstacles put in the way of the modern viewer can seem all but insuperable.

Let us start by going into these in a little more detail. Over and above the difficulties just mentioned, there is the obscurity of the original incident itself: the plot *donné*. Japanese audiences are well acquainted with the events of Mizoguchi's story: it is in fact one of the most famous tales in Japanese history. But Western audiences who come to the movie without specialised knowledge are initially liable to be bewildered. The events portrayed are based on a true historical incident that took place in the year 1701. As the film opens, envoys from the imperial court in Kyoto are expected on their annual visit to the shogun's castle in Edo (modern Tokyo). The ceremonial procedure was the responsibility of resident senior *daimyos*, assumed yearly on a turn-by-turn basis. On this particular occasion, it has fallen on the shoulders of a certain Lord Asano, chief of the fiefdom of Ako. Lacking expert knowledge in the niceties of imperial protocol, he has approached a court official, Lord Kira, for advice, but his queries have been answered with insolence. (The problem appears to have arisen because Asano failed to offer Kira the bribe that was customarily expected.) Goaded by Kira's taunts and obstructiveness, Asano loses his temper: he makes the fatal mistake of drawing his sword and attacking the supercilious official within the shogunal compound.

This, then, is the dramatic incident on which the film opens – with a flurry of action and violence. But my summary has made explicit background events that are only hinted at in the dialogue, and which, in the absence of prior knowledge, have to be pieced together retrospectively. So it is with subsequent scenes in both parts of this very long film. There is an additional complicating factor though. For it soon emerges that the behaviour of the film's main character, Lord Asano's chief retainer Oishi (Chojuro Kawarazaki), is governed by a need for concealment and dissemblance so great as to be almost pathological. Enigma is built into the film before it has started, so to speak. Each of the main scenes or confrontations has a subtext, or hidden meaning, which – unless one is previously acquainted with the story – can only seem to add to the general air of opacity.

But let me turn back to the problem of Oishi: Why is he a dissembler, and what is he dissembling *about*? To answer this question we need to return to the consequences of Lord Asano's impetuousness. Lord Kira has not been killed in the affray, indeed he has not even been very seriously injured. But the rules of the *bakufu* (the name given to the shogun's government) were exceptionally strict on matters of protocol and discipline. Any noble drawing his sword within the walls of the shogun's castle had to expect the severest consequences. Asano is arrested and in due course ordered to commit suicide. His retainers, of whom Oishi is the chief, become masterless samurai, or *ronin*. According to the custom of the time (whose rule of *bushido* stressed loyalty to one's feudal lord above everything) the first duty of the dispossessed retainers must be to seek vengeance – vengeance against Lord Kira and his household. But the swift execution of such a vendetta is forestalled, in Oishi's case, by a number of factors, of which the first is that the incident took place, as has been said, on the shogun's home ground, right in the middle of Edo. It's therefore impossible for the matter to be looked at as a mere private quarrel between nobles. There is a public or policy issue involved: a different, conflicting set of values to agonise over.

Second, as a matter of course, immediately after his lord's ritual suicide, Oishi has petitioned for the house of Ako to be restored under the leadership of Asano's younger brother, and this petition will take time to work its way through the system. (It would be wrong and immoral to strike before the petition was definitively answered.) Then there is a final complication: Asano's fiefdom at Ako is only the domain of the cadet branch of the family. The main clan is based in Hiroshima, and its elders have their own agenda, not necessarily the same as that of chamberlain Oishi and his supporters.

These surrounding but at the same time integral factors account for the fact that waiting ('suspense' in the strict sense of the word) is the main dramatic element in the film. Oishi (who is absolutely determined he *will* strike) must hide his motives not only from his enemies, but also, more importantly, from his followers, a number of whom are pressing for immediate action. The key issue is whether the shogun will accede to the formal request for the restoration of Ako domains; and it is the idea that Oishi does not really *want* this – indeed, it would ruin his plans – that provides the tale with its sombre, tragic irony.

This obliqueness or indirection in the film's content is matched (one might think appropriately) by a striking indirectness in Mizoguchi's camera style. It is as if the caution on the part of the main character finds its correlative, on the camera's part, in a corresponding *holding off* from the features – and particularly the eyes – of the protagonist. Seldom can there have been a film of such length in which there are so few establishing close-ups – so few opportunities of looking into the 'soul' of the main character to discern either motives or psychology. At first (and maybe, for some viewers, always), this absence is sensed, acutely, as frustrating – just as it was for us in the earlier, 1937 film, *Aien Kyo/The Straits of Love and Hate*. (Here perhaps we should revert for a moment to the contingent and accidental darkness of the only print currently available. Yet I have the feeling that even if one *could* see the film in mint condition, and properly lit as it was meant to be, those clues that we are searching for might still be mysteriously unavailable.)

Such opacity in a film could be seen as an artistic failure. Yet, once one has overcome the initial hurdles of understanding, this is not the case with *The Loyal 47 Ronin*. On the contrary, with or without inserted close-ups, the rigour and sweep of the film's *mise en scène* becomes exactly what is notable and wonderful about it, the reason I go back to *The Loyal 47 Ronin*, on the rare occasions it is shown publicly, as to a precious and compelling masterpiece. Mizoguchi's penchant for what the French call *plan séquence* (scenes which derive their shape through the seamless movement of the camera, rather than through a separately edited series of shots) finds its most pure and extreme incarnation in this work of wartime 'propaganda' commanded (perhaps against his will) by the national authorities. Many such sequences stand out, but four or five stick in the memory. From among my own favourite instances let me cite, therefore, without, at this stage, analysing them further, the wonderful ceremonial scene in Part 1 where the soon-to-be-widowed Yosenin (wife of Lord Asano) cuts off her hair prior to retiring from the world. Or there is the equally remarkably staged scene in which Oishi visits this lady's apartments and tries to tell her, without confiding it explicitly, that he is still 'on' for the execution of the vengeance (Sugiyama's camera choreography here is simply breathtaking). Then there is the exceptionally elaborate scene in which the young samurai Sukeemon attempts to persuade the shogun's nephew Tsunatoyo (betrothed to his sister Okiyo) of the justice of Asano's action (a scene that ends in one of the film's rare, explosive bouts of action when Sukeemon, catching sight of Lord Kira at the end of a corridor, leaps to his feet to despatch the peccant courtier there and then, only to be dragged back by his supporters, propelled on his knees along the slippery wooden floorboards).

Other, contrasting scenes demonstrate a majestic calmness. One such is the episode near the end of Part 1 that shows Oishi's wife closing up the conjugal mansion before returning discreetly to her family (birdsong, stillness, sweeping exterior camerawork). And then there is the climax of the whole movie, an astonishingly controlled crane shot in which we see, their deed accomplished, the vindicated *ronin* progress calmly to the tents in which each of them will ritually disembowel himself.

What is so special about a *plan séquence*? Touched upon in Chapter 1, the subject was approached again in the discussion of *Ugetsu Monogatari*. For some people, the device is simply a formal virtuosity. Other critics, as we know (André Bazin chief among them), have claimed to find in its fluid metaphysics the very essence of cinema itself. Certainly, at the very highest level, the 'extended take' is a glorious part of the repertoire of such masters as Murnau, Ophuls, Welles, Dreyer, Sternberg and Rossellini. In *The Loyal 47 Ronin* the method is practised not merely as one technique among many (or else one that can be alternated, as it is in Welles's *mise en scène*, with similarly virtuoso bouts of editing) but as the sole guiding aesthetic principle of the movie. This gives the film, at times, an exceptionally experimental feeling, as if it were a work of the purest avant-garde and not a huge, popular, historical pageant. Two things stand out about the practice. The first is that it gives the scenes in which it is utilised an exceptional sense of unity and concentration. There are no cuts within the scene; you are watching the action unfold in real time. The upshot has not yet (as it were) been decided. Anything at all could happen (anything could go wrong and move into dangerous and dramatic configurations). Yet on the other hand, it is all choreographed and artistically predetermined. There is thus a vivid tension between the poles of openness and closure; and it is *in* this tension (this 'field-force') that this particular kind of cinema comes alive.

The other main 'Bazinian' attribute of the *plan séquence* concerns respect for a scene's geographical integrity. Since the shape of the film is predicated on the total mobility of the camera, sets have to be constructed on the assumption that any part of them will be visible in any direction in which the camera happens to be facing. This gives the *mise en scène* a degree of spaciousness, reality and solidity that is not available (or not available in the same way) in films that are conventionally edited. The sets reveal themselves not as artfully built backdrops, but as real houses, constructed in 360-degree space (an effect reinforced, in *The Loyal 47 Ronin*, by the care and authenticity of the research work, and the financial means put at Mizoguchi's disposal). That vital extra degree of reality, so precious to Bazin, resides in the feeling that life and continuity exist beyond the frame – in the space that is *not* filmed as well as in the space we see. Time and again in the visual composition of the *The Loyal 47 Ronin* there is an intimation of this off-space, the area just out of view, the area not covered by the camera, in which, unseen to us, actions related to the story are quietly unfolding at their own pace. It is nothing but a bonus, then, when these hidden things *do* come into view. Every so often the camera slides round to disclose a new depth of field, a special scale and magnitude in the surroundings, a vista that we had not previously suspected – as when, for example, in the scene of Lady Yosenin's hair-cutting, the slow arc of the camera comes, finally, to rest on an enormous chamber full to its farthest dimensions of kneeling, weeping courtiers.

Mizoguchi and Mayama

Mizoguchi's version of *The Loyal 47 Ronin* (one of scores that have been filmed since the beginning of movies in Japan) was based on a cycle of plays by the renowned kabuki playwright Seika Mayama (1878–1948). The last of these was written as late as 1940: that is to say, only a year before Mizoguchi put *his* film into production. The plays in question, ten altogether, are, for the kabuki stage, exceptionally wordy and issue-oriented, their comparative sobriety and realism being, in fact, one of the chief reasons Mizoguchi chose them. We learn from Yoda's memoirs that adapting the cycle for filmic purposes involved much compression and rewriting, concentrating on the choice of episodes and the paring down of dialogue. In particular, sequences in the plays needed to be cut and repositioned so that, in a two-part movie version, each of the parts leads up to a natural climax. There was no problem about the end of Part 2 – the climax of the film (the warriors' *seppuku*) naturally coinciding with the climax of the play. But Part 1 of the movie also finishes strongly: it is the moment at which Oishi, after almost unbearable prevarications, first explicitly swears vengeance. (This avowal is delivered, sotto voce, over the dead bodies of two of his supporters, and is no less dramatic for its quietness.)

It is worth pausing on this question of strong dramatic punctuation, if only because the film is so often spoken about as though 'drama' is not among its qualities. As I have said, I believe this charge to be unwarranted, though it's not difficult (for all the reasons we have looked at) to see why and how it arises. The focus of such accusations, in Part 2, revolves round the seemingly perverse decision by Mizoguchi (although he is merely faithfully following the Mayama text) *not to show the strike of revenge when it happens*. Thus the physical release from anticipation guaranteed by a short, cathartic bout of action is denied; instead the audience has to content itself with an oral account of the deed read out to Asano's widow in a letter.

The reason usually given for this ellipsis is Mizoguchi's self-confessed lack of confidence in staging *chambara* scenes; but perhaps this puts the matter too negatively. The letter-reading scene is by any criterion extraordinarily successful and beautiful: one of the finest-staged scenes in the whole of the movie, and magnificently powerful in its emotional resonance. If there *is* a complaint about the dramatic shape of Part 2 (Part 1 is compellingly exciting) it possibly lies in the over-extended passage which follows, delineating the consequences of a love affair between the

young *ronin*, Jurozaemon, and his faithful though sorely tested paramour, Omino. Here, so near the end of the film, there *are longueurs*. Yet this minor flaw (if it is a flaw) is subsequently redeemed by the extraordinary power and gravity of the collective *seppuku* scene which brings the work to its sober, dark conclusion.

An Allegory of World War II?

Darkness and sobriety. Because the movie was being shot (from July 1941 to February 1942) at the time that Japan entered World War II on the side of the Axis Powers, it is difficult not to ask what attitude the film has towards militarism. First and foremost: *The Loyal 47 Ronin* is not self-evidently *anti*-militaristic. The film was a prestige production of the Shochiku Studios, planned around an exceptionally high budget. Plainly, in the backers' minds was the notion that a film based on one of the best-known tales in Japan, recounting as it does the determination of a group of warriors to seek vengeance on behalf of their slighted lord, was timely: if not a call to arms then, at least, a reminder of duty. The original incident, back in 1701, had occurred at a juncture of Japan's history when it looked as if there was a danger of the old samurai spirit disappearing after decades of comparative luxury. What was exemplary about the original story was exactly the stoicism and steadfastness of its heroes: the forthright way the tale reminded audiences that a samurai carried a sword, and on occasions was expected to use it.

Yet against this militarist interpretation lies the awkward fact that the film is all about *deferral*. It is as if, in the very scrupulousness with which Mizoguchi was adapting Mayama's play cycle, there lay some unresolved ambiguity about the message he wanted to convey. In Mizoguchi's version, the endlessness of the warriors' waiting takes over, so to speak, from the swiftness of the final *coup de grâce*. I can only speculate about the reason for this. We know for a fact that the film was made during one of the most painful periods of Mizoguchi's personal life when his wife, Chieko, went mad and had to be institutionalised; and it is plausible that something of this personal agony communicates itself to the film, imbuing it with its strange air of lassitude and melancholy. Ideologically, it would seem incontrovertible that the message is conservative and nationalist. The key issue – whether Oishi is, or is not, justified in taking his revenge – is the subject of an explicit argument in a scene that occurs about halfway through the movie. The shogun's nephew Tsunayoto Tokugawa is discussing the Asano case with his revered tutor Arai Hakusaki (an historical figure – one of the then shogunate's most important intellectuals). Arai champions the official neo-Confucian view based on Chinese sources, which emphasises the overriding importance of obedience to central authority. Under this ruling, vengeance would be wrong and illegal. But the shogun's nephew (who is secretly sympathetic to Asano's action and to the subsequent plight of Oishi and the *ronin*) argues the opposite point of view: that the code of honour known as *bushido* must take priority over everything, even over the rules of the shogunate.

Plainly, our own sympathies are meant to lie with the arguments of the shogun's rebellious nephew. It would be blindness in other words not to recognise that the film in the end offers a profoundly traditionalist endorsement of the wisdom of native Japanese (i.e. *non*-Confucian) sentiments, and of the correctness of Japanese samurai ethics. In this sense, the film is indeed 'nationalist': this much must be granted. Yet there are balancing considerations. First, the film is all about *arrogance* and the misery that follows from pride. It was Kira's high-handedness that set the crisis off initially; so that, while audiences would be made to think of the high-handedness of the Allied powers facing down (and, as the Japanese would see it, provoking) Japan, the film might equally be seen as a warning – and in a way *is* a warning – against *any* form of arrogance and aggression, including Japan's own.

In this context we ought to note what Mizoguchi does *not* do with the story: he does not reinterpret it in terms of vulgar propagandist bravura. He sticks to what is there – academically, even pedantically. Mayama, the author of the original theatrical text, was a keen supporter of the emperor. (There is one short and possibly anachronistic scene from the original play cycle which Mizoguchi keeps, showing the Asano clan's profound gratitude when it hears from reliable sources that the emperor in Kyoto is, like the shogun's nephew, secretly sympathetic to their cause.) But neither play nor film is a crude piece of jingoism. Part 1 was released in the very week before Pearl Harbor (thus, at the height of Japan's bellicosity), and Part 2 three months later, as the Pacific conflict moved into gear. To be sensitive to the spiritual flavour of the movie is to respond to its darkness, doubt and seriousness: to take on board the way that it meditates not so much on victory and vengeance, as on death, sacrifice, duty, and transience.[1]

Crucified Lovers/Chikamatsu Monogatari (1954)

The Loyal 47 Ronin is one of a handful of grand historical films in world cinema whose authority seems to emerge out of a unique personal style in the telling. Other examples one might point to include *Andrei Rublev* by Tarkovsky, Eisenstein's *Ivan the Terrible*, Bresson's *Lancelot du Lac*, or finally, to take another instance from Japan, the beautiful *Throne of Blood* by Kurosawa (his black-and-white version of *Macbeth*). In each of these films, it is as if the originality of the vision is only allowed to emerge by their directors' finding some skewed, intransigent and personal cinematic language uniquely honed to the story they are telling – a language for that very reason unrepeatable. So *The Loyal 47 Ronin*, exquisite and monumental, is also, like Eisenstein's masterpiece, a kind of dead-end. The director, as it were, can only go so far down that particular path. All these films seem to contain a residue of strangeness above and beyond any elucidation that a sympathetic commentary can give them. Certainly this is true of *The Loyal 47 Ronin*, and not only because of the challenging formal language in which the film is cast. The whole business of individual and collective suicide which Mizoguchi's film hinges on is itself somewhat impenetrable to the Western viewer. Lord Asano is ordered to take his own life. It is the *bakufu*'s preferred method of execution for nobles. Even if this is seen as more 'civilised' than some versions of the death penalty, there is still the problem of the triviality of the offence (on the grand scale of things) for which Asano has been indicted in the first place. He drew his sword in a prohibited environment. He struck someone (who was not injured). He dies for a brief, rash error of judgment. Many societies have had in their pasts penalties for malefactors which to modern eyes seem fierce or barbaric. It remains true that, for the Western onlooker, the institution of *seppuku* has an especially impassable weirdness. (It is, of course, exactly this 'refined barbarity' of oriental custom that Sir W. S. Gilbert, in the nineteenth century's first flush of contact with Japan, burlesques so brilliantly in *The Mikado*.)

---

1 For further reflections on this film, see Appendix 3: 'Mizoguchi, *The Loyal 47 Ronin* and the War Years'.

Chikamatsu Monzaemon, the *genroku* dramatist whose puppet play, *The Almanac of Love* (1715), forms one of the two main sources for *Chikamatsu Monogatari*, was also fascinated by suicide, this time in its specifically romantic incarnation: in this tale a pair of star-crossed lovers, in flight from the world, decide to put a joint end to their suffering. Such 'double suicides' (based in the main on real-life incidents) form the subject matter of no fewer that twenty of Chikamatsu's puppet plays (out of a total of nearly a hundred), plays whose popularity had the effect, rather in the manner of Goethe's *Sufferings of Young Werther* a generation or two later in the West, of encouraging among susceptible members of the audience the very act that was depicted. Indeed, the government was eventually forced to bring in a ban against plays that bore the word *shinju* (double suicide) in their titles.

In Mizoguchi's beautiful and classically crafted movie (released in the same year as *Sansho the Bailiff* and some twelve years after *The Loyal 47 Ronin*) we see such a pair of lovers prepare to put an end to themselves. They have fled Kyoto to Lake Biwa, a traditional scene for such deeds. Mohei (Kazuo Hasegawa), until a short time ago the trusted head clerk of an important stationery works which, among other duties or privileges, publishes the imperial almanac, has run off with Osan (Kyoko Kagawa) wife of the head of the enterprise. They are not really lovers: at least, not in the technical sense of the word, even though the world thinks they are. Mohei himself has no inkling of what Osan feels for him. Their escape takes place at dawn. Mohei guides their boat silently through the misty reeds, heading for the open lake where he brings it to a halt and approaches the woman with reverence. 'Are you ready?' he asks her, producing a girdle to bind her at the knees (it will make the drowning quicker and gentler). Osan, for her part, is overcome with remorse: it was, after all, her rashness (to be explained in a moment) that had got the pair into this royal mess in the first place. 'Because of me, you will die,' she breathes wistfully. 'Can you forgive me?' Mohei's reply is that Heaven will forgive them because (and here for the first time he tells her what he has never dared to up till now) he has always worshipped and adored her. This confession to Osan changes everything; for secretly, and without telling him, throughout all the time of their misfortunes, Osan has been in love with *him*. (So actually they have been 'lovers' without knowing it.) Flinging herself into his arms, she begs Mohei not to go through with the deed. The bringing-into-the-open of their mutual infatuation means that, from now on, they must – will – seek to live.

This then is a 'love suicide play' with a difference: a tragedy with elements of comedy – the comedy that often hovers over sexual and amatory misunderstandings. Mizoguchi and his long-standing scriptwriter Yoda seem to have first come across the story not in Chikamatsu's puppet play, but through reading Iharu Saikaku's *Five Women Who Loved Love* (1686), a novel – or more accurately a collection of tales – they had already made use of in their adaptation of *The Life of Oharu*. Saikaku's version of this story – a prose narrative, naturally, rather than a play – has, as one might perhaps expect from this writer, a cynical, satirical cruelty of tone to it: he is interested above all in illustrating his theory that women are concupiscent creatures, and that men are blind dupes to their wiles. So it is a comic tale of lust, in Saikaku's hands, rather than a tale of true love. Contrasting in moral vision to Chikamatsu's more frankly 'sentimental' puppet play, Saikaku's tale contains details and descriptions (for example, accounts of the lovers' cross-country flight and of their final execution) which are absent from Chikamatsu's scenario. And indeed Yoda in his memoirs plays down the elements from the eighteenth-century dramatist in favour of stressing Saikaku's contribution. Still, Chikamatsu's play is undoubtedly 'there' in the finished film, and not only in the title. The playwright, it should be said, has the reputation for being one of Japan's very greatest literary artists (he is sometimes called 'the Japanese Shakespeare'). According to his translator Asataro Miyamori, *The Almanac of Love* is one of his finest works. Yet to a modern reader there is something psychologically and even morally unresolved in the drama that has come down to us: something opaque and artistically unsatisfactory in its attitude towards the events it depicts. For, strangely enough, in Chikamatsu's hands the story (which was based on a real-life incident from 1676) is not tragic either. On the contrary, according to Chikamatsu, we are dealing with a 'joyous tale'. The lovers, captured and delivered up for execution, have their lives saved through the perfunctory intercession of a priest named Togan; while the tale's one possibly tragic element, the fate of Otama, Osan's maid, who has been beheaded by her samurai uncle to prevent her from prattling about the pair (actually, she had no intention of doing so) is registered with a sort of comic 'Tough luck!'.

In the Chikamatsu play, comedy intrudes further in the handling of Mohei and Osan's sexual relations. For, whereas Mizoguchi emphasises the initially platonic nature of his two 'lovers', Chikamatsu makes it as plain as Saikaku that the pair become physical lovers *before* their decision to flee together, and that they do this in circumstances close to farce. What happens, very briefly, is this. (I give the names of the characters as they appear in the film: there are minor variations from the sources.) Osan, the wife of the printing-house director, has run into financial difficulties in the course of attempts to help her feckless family. Mohei, the chief clerk, who (though himself engaged to be married) admires her from afar, offers to help her by a temporary loan 'lifted' by the use of an authorised seal from the company coffers (of course it is illegal of him to do this). Reported to the boss by a jealous colleague, Mohei refuses, through fear of implicating Osan, to explain himself, and is only saved at the last moment by the intervention of his fiancée – the maid Otama, mentioned above, who nobly claims the action was done for her benefit, and at her instigation (and, as we saw, is later executed for her pains). Despite this plea on his behalf, Mohei is marched off in manacles and imprisoned, leaving the field clear for Ishun (the printing-house director) to make a play for Mohei's fiancée, whom he has always more or less openly lusted after.

To foil this development, Osan and Otama concoct a plan together, which, if it comes off, will benefit each. Mistress and maid will swap bedrooms for a few nights. Ishun, it is assumed, will sooner or later head for Otama's quarters and in the darkness find his wife there, who (in Saikaku's version) will berate him for his infidelity and hypocrisy, or (in Chikamatsu's version) do her best, by matrimonial wiles, to win back his long-dormant love for her. An important byproduct of the stratagem is that Ishun will be shamed into freeing and pardoning Mohei.

Naturally the plan goes awry. On the very night of his imprisonment Mohei escapes from his lock-up and makes his way to his fiancée's room to hide there. Who should he find but Osan? (Only in the darkness he thinks, of course, that she is Otama.) In Saikaku's version, the elegant lady is asleep, which doesn't prevent the clerk from making vigorous love to her through the night. In Chikamatsu's story she is awake and willing (only she thinks, with the darkness serving to mask both their identities, that her companion is actually her husband). In short: however it comes about, in both play and tale, the pair become lovers by accident.

Confusions of identity like this, in what might euphemistically be called 'delicate situations', are in many ways the stuff of traditional drama: Shakespeare and Mozart are full of comparable instances, usually under the emblem of comedy, though sometimes (as in *Measure for Measure*) in the service of more tragically inflected ends. Yet cinema is above all a realistic medium, and even if verisimilitude were the only factor at issue (which I think it is not) one can see artistic reasons why Mizoguchi and Yoda felt it necessary, at this crucial point, to depart from the original sources. In the film version, then, the confusion is constructed to be far less 'theatrical' and bawdy: the events are looked at seriously, and played out in real time. So the fugitive Mohei turns up in Otama's room and finds his beloved Osan there: the room is lit, and he can see her. But before anything can 'develop' out of their initial mutual amazement, except for a few wonderful exchanges, the alarm is given and Mohei is forced to resume his flight. What follows has something of the compelling contingency that belongs not so much to drama or melodrama as to life itself. Searching the house for Mohei, a servant finds Osan in Otama's room and summons his master to investigate. Ishun swiftly enough puts two and two together; yet his jealous questioning is unable to elicit any admission on Osan's part of guilt or of wrong-doing (on the contrary: she is quietly defiant). At a certain moment of the interview she excuses herself and leaves, and in the neighbouring corridor literally bumps into Mohei, who (having managed to elude capture) is making his exit. The decision to become fugitives together is taken in an instant: they will head for freedom and Osaka. Though the world will construe their flight in only one way, the world will be mistaken. At this stage, each of them, according to their own lights, is in flight from separate acts of injustice.

The film is a fascinating and rarified study of a situation which could not, probably, any longer happen in the modern world (at least not in the West): a situation in which the notion of *personal service* or *personal allegiance* is only the sublimation of a profound romantic longing. Crucial to the psychological interest – and to the nobility – of Mizoguchi's film is that Mohei should not 'know' that he is in love with Osan, nor she with him – exactly because, across the rigid class barriers of the time, such love would be literally unthinkable. And – here the film, in artistry and psychological power, is simply leagues ahead of either of its two sources – such love continues to be unthinkable even *after* it has been declared, declared in the most pressing circumstances imaginable. Thus as Osan, in the boat, flings herself into Mohei's arms, Mohei retreats from the embrace with a sort of shocked and protesting delicacy: it cannot happen, he seems to think, even though (as he realises) it *is* happening. *Chikamatsu Monogatari* comes alive here through its beautiful sense of *pudeur*, of holding off, of not going through with the enterprise: grasped dialectically, of course, in the context of a situation whereby the lovers must, and eventually do, acknowledge the implacable force of their desire for each other.

Thus in the immediate aftermath of the aborted suicide pact, Mohei's whole effort is to separate himself from Osan, arguing that if they are caught together (and if they remain together, they *will* be caught) his beloved mistress faces certain execution. Since she has 'chosen life', *her* life at least (he reasons) must be saved – his own life doesn't matter. She on the other hand is franker about her longings: they have chosen not to die: therefore their future course of life can only be *together*. The playing out of this tension governs the last quarter of the film and forges some of its most brilliant and memorable sequences. It is on the foothill of Mount Atago that Mohei's delicate evasions are finally shattered by his physical need to touch, to grasp and to hold onto the object of his longing. What happens is this: Osan's foot has been injured, forcing the pair to take shelter in a simple peasant's hut. While the peasant is tending to her needs, Mohei, scrupulous in following his self-imposed vow of 'going it alone', slips off down the mountain path, abandoning her. Osan senses his departure and follows him with piteous pleading. (A wonderful crane shot picks out her frantic pursuit.) At the foot of the hill Mohei crouches in the undergrowth, hiding from her. As Osan passes, she stumbles and falls to the ground, and Mohei can bear it no longer. Darting out from his hiding place he takes her leg in his hand and starts kissing it, before moving to a more general and unrestrained embrace. 'I'll never abandon you', he cries, 'as long as I live!'

It is difficult to exaggerate the sheer physical charge of this beautiful and profound embrace, all the more powerful in that it has been postponed for so long. The lovers, in typical Mizoguchian fashion, cast themselves on the ground in utter abandon. Mizoguchi, we learn from Yoda, had actively studied *shunga* prints (albums of erotic drawings) in preparation for the 'look' and atmosphere of the filming. But for all that, the primary flavour of the love that is being examined here is not as much erotic as (in the deepest sense) romantic. Everything – custom, morality, and even self-interest – conspires to prohibit their union; yet nothing in the end can keep the lovers apart. This is the film's simple moral economy. So Chikamatsu, after all, had a point, perhaps, in calling it a 'joyous tale'; though what he means by joy seems to be not at all what Mizoguchi means. For Mizoguchi, a 'happy ending' is irrelevant. Better the scaffold than pardon! As the captured lovers

are conducted to their execution, bound together back-to-back on horseback, a woman in the crowd (she used to work at Ishun's now confiscated stationery factory) gives voice to the general consensus: 'Madame has never looked happier, nor Mohei more calm and serene!'

Romanticism in Japan: Mizoguchi and Tanizaki

I have used the word 'romantic' to describe the feelings that inform and give value to *Chikamatsu Monogatari* and which, in my opinion, serve to differentiate the movie (at least for a Western viewer) from an earlier and more aesthetically stringent work such as *The Loyal 47 Ronin*. The adjective, it must be admitted, is difficult to define in this context. Japan had no equivalent to the literary and artistic movement of Romanticism that swept Europe from the end of the eighteenth century onwards and to which we in the West owe so many of our habitual assumptions both about life itself, and about how life may be depicted in art. In using the term here, it might be argued, I am applying a concept that has little or nothing to do with Japanese culture. Or is it that Mizoguchi himself, in adapting his sources, has conferred on the tale a 'romantic' and anachronistic meaning or value that is incongruent with the events being depicted?

I do not wish to invent complications. To my mind, there is nothing in itself objectionable about a modern film director mining the past to make stories that belong, in their psychological ramification, to the present: indeed this modernising tendency is to a certain extent inevitable in any adaptation. Conversely I do not think that the genuinely universal quality of certain basic human predicaments should be underestimated, such as the exigence of desire. The passion to which I attach the word 'romantic' is anyway there, if only latently, in the original tale. Saikaku was schematically cynical and disillusioned about such things; but surely we can believe that Chikamatsu knew what it meant to portray his two characters as being 'in love', even if he did not actually use the term.

Nevertheless, there is something difficult, excessive, hysterical even, attaching to the corners of this film (the centre of which, I repeat, seems to me extraordinarily simple and noble): something at any event that is worth pausing over and trying to draw out a little more explicitly.

Let us return, then, to the premise given in all three versions of the story: that the passion we see depicted arises from, and is a variation of, a servant's devotion to his mistress. This is a classic premise in Japanese fiction and movies. A film that came out around the same time, *Shunkin Monogatari* (1954), Daisuke Ito's adaptation of Junichiro Tanizaki's tale of the same name, embarks from a similar starting-point. Only here, the proof of devotion is taken to limits that would seem to most people, Japanese included, hyperbolic. Thus, following an attack on his mistress by a jealous lover that has left her permanantly scarred, the hero of the tale, a household servant like Mohei, blinds himself with needles in order to avert his importunate and unworthy gaze from his mistress's now-blemished beauty. It is plain from the way the story is told, both in the original and in the film, that this gesture is supposed to demonstrate *the utmost sublimity of passion*; but for an ordinary viewer the impact of the deed surely belongs more to the realm of the grotesque.

As a matter of fact, Tanizaki was one of Mizoguchi's favourite authors. With *Miss Oyu*, one of a trilogy of 'bourgeois dramas' made between 1949 and 1951, Mizoguchi had already adapted one of his tales for the big screen (not wholly successfully as I shall argue in the following chapter): it too deals with a strange love affair that is 'also' a relationship between mistress and servant. The relationship is too odd (too sophisticated, too 'decadent') to come under any such general heading as romanticism. What is interesting about Tanizaki's writing is its evolution away from an earlier Western influence (in the Taisho period) towards a clear espousal of fascination with Japanese cultural values in the 1920s, the period in which *Shunkin Monogatari* was written. The exquisite meditation on Japanese music that forms an important subplot of *Shunkin Monogatari* acquires an ironical shade in the light of Tanizaki's previous pro-Western cultural line:

> I could hear Western music on the rare occasions (*the author wrote in 1915*) when it was performed by Japanese, or in excerpts on phonograph records; but how directly and how grandly it sang of the sorrows and joys of human life as compared to the etiolated, somnolescent sounds of the *samisen*, or the curiously perverse, retrogressive, superficial *joruri*. Japanese vocalists sing in voices trained to produce unnatural falsetto tones, but Western singers sing boldly and impetuously, like birds or wild beasts, sending forth their natural voices so ardently they risk as it were burning their throats. Japanese instrumental music produces a delicate sound like the murmur of little streams, but Western music is filled with the sound of surging waves . . .[2]

The Wagnerian fullness that Tanizaki describes so ecstatically has never been part of Japanese art. The original puppet plays that Chikamatsu composed so prolifically at the beginning of the eighteenth century were small-scale affairs, definitely not 'surging' oceans. The puppets were manipulated from below by a single puppet master, while the words of the plays were chanted by a nearby singer, accompanied on stage by a lone samisen player. Mizoguchi, in his adaptation, gets rid of the chanted element (transforming the traditional *joruri* into spoken monologue); but in contrast to, say, *Sansho the Bailiff* or *The Empress Yang Kwei Fei*, the score of *Chikamatsu Monogatari* sticks strictly to Japanese rhythm and instrumentation. Indeed, this has always seemed to me a great part of the film's beauty and authenticity. Such music, you could say, chastens the incipient melodrama of the tale, making the film significantly more 'Japanese' than films like *Sansho*, in which the soundtrack uses Western scoring techniques. This may indeed be one of the reasons why the Japanese themselves have always held this film in such high regard – why actually it is, for many of them, Mizoguchi's finest masterpiece.

Approaches to Colour

Right at the end of his career Mizoguchi made two films in colour: *The Empress Yang Kwei Fei* and *Tales of the Taira Clan*, both of them historical costume dramas. For his final movie, *Street of Shame* (of course he did not know it would be his last), he reverted to black-and-white. These brief chromatic excursions possess the beauty of rarity. I think of them in the same way that I think of Eisenstein's adventure with colour on the captured German Agfa stock at the end of *Ivan the Terrible*: an uncovenanted flowering, rather like the revelation at the end of Tarkovsky's *Andrei Roublev*, when the medieval artist's icons suddenly flood the screen in their full vivid glory. Nowadays we take colour for granted, yet it was once absolutely unusual. Of course the monochrome palette, with its shades of grey and silver, had its own beauty, which was recognised. That recognition still stands. Watching the great classics, it is not usual to wish they were 'colourised' or to feel they lack

---

2   From *Dokutan* ('The German Spy'), quoted by Donald Keene, *Dawn to the West: A History of Japanese Literature* (1998), p. 745.

something by *not* being in colour. Nonetheless, we can easily believe that for the early masters, colour excercised a parallel fascination to black-and-white, just as the possibility of sound did, before *its* appropriate technology became available. There was always this underground curiosity: what would it be like if you could use it? How would your films be affected?

Mizoguchi was not immune from these speculations – far from it. In an interview recorded by Matsuo Kishi in 1952 he recalls a period some twenty years earlier when he was working for Nikkatsu, and had fallen into the company of the experimental psychologist Kojiro Naito, evidently something of a guru in the circles Mizoguchi moved in then. This avant-garde group apparently played with ways to introduce smell and tactile sensation into the filmic repertory, along with the more conventionally dreamt-of innovations of colour and sound design. In 1952, when this reminiscence was recorded, Mizoguchi was making preparations for one of his most visually exquisite black-and-white films, *The Life of Oharu*. But colour was on his mind, as it had been throughout his career. The topic had turned up before, for example, in the course of a '*table ronde*' held at the offices of the film magazine *Kinema Jumpo* in 1937, where we find Mizoguchi quoting from memory one of his favourite authors, Kyoka Izumi: 'The image of a woman in kimono doesn't attract me in films, because it lacks that special something that can only be given by the colour of the costume.' Hiroshi Mizutani, Mizoguchi's production designer, used to say that while he himself was always urging the director to hold back until he was 'ready' for colour (or rather, until the technology of colour was ready for *him*), Mizoguchi was eager to experiment:

> Concerning colour, he wanted to get in there from the start. It was I who held him back. I wanted to wait until the technology of colour got better – until we got better too: we had to become *worthy* of colour. Yet [Mizoguchi] was always impatient. He burned to use new techniques as soon as they became available.[3]

By the early 1950s, the industry itself was ready for the change. Internationally, television was poised to make its first great impact on cinema-viewing figures. The industry in turn would fight back with what television could not yet offer, and that, of course, was Technicolor, along with a magnified screen size (the first CinemaScope films made their appearance in 1953–4). Like many others, Mizoguchi sensed which way the wind was blowing. As a senior representative of the Japanese film industry with an important administrative post at the Daiei Studios, he had policy as well as aesthetic considerations to bear in mind. Thus, in the summer of 1954, he accepted an invitation from Hollywood to study the new technology, returning from the trip full of ideas about the future: knowledge he was to put to good use in the next two films under consideration.[4]

---

3 Conversation with Ariane Mnouchkine, *Cahiers du Cinéma* no. 158, August/September 1964 (Author's translation).

4 The trip was made in the company of cameraman Kazuo Miyagawa and producer Masaichi Nagata. In Japan, Nagata had expressed himself dissatisfied with the results obtained from the indigenous Japanese film stock, Fujicolor, used in the two Shochiku films *Carmen Comes Home* and *Natsuko's Adventures* and wanted to look at alternatives. As well as investigating colour production, a main purpose was to look into the new process of VistaVision, which Daiei was thinking of adopting. VistaVision was a non-anamorphic widescreen process that Paramount, alone among the major Hollywood studios, had taken up (Hitchcock used it, for example, for his Paramount-shot films of those years, including *Vertigo* [1958]). Significantly narrower in aspect ratio than its main commercial rival CinemaScope (1.85:1, as opposed to

'Japan' and 'colour' in any case have a certain congruence, it could be argued. In the Izumi quotation, it is interesting that Mizoguchi considers the question of colour in the context of costume. Costume and colour are assumed to go together, and the fascination with look goes right back into Japanese history. Readers of *The Tale of Genji* and of Sei Sonagon's *Pillow Book* cannot help but be struck by the frequency with which colour is singled out, in an almost abstract way, as something to be publicly noticed.

The Lord Vice-Chamberlain came forward (*writes Sei Sonagon in a typically florid passage*) magnificent in his court mantle of a superb shade of cherry, complete with a lining of which the hue and lustre had an incomparable charm. His divided shirt was of the shade of wineberry, very deep, and it was embroidered with branches of wisteria, larger than life. The colour and the brilliance of the scarlet underdress were splendid, and beneath it he had put on other garments of white and light violet, one after another.[5]

Jill Liddell in her excellent history of the kimono tells us that in the Heian period court ladies wore as many as twenty layers of robe (individually known as *uchiki*), each subtly differentiated. Since each layer was slightly shorter and more deeply cut than the one below, the various colours

---

2.35:1), its advantage lay in its crisper photographic resolution and in the enhanced clarity of its depth of field. There is an interesting aesthetic debate behind these distinctions. Visually speaking, the great technical innovations of the 1940s – the last great epoch of black-and-white cinema – were all linked to emphasising images in depth. That was one of the reasons why Bazin admired Welles's cinema so much, and why he spoke so highly of the work that Gregg Toland (Welles's cameraman on *Citizen Kane*) performed for other directors such as John Ford and William Wyler. Mizoguchi met Wyler at Venice in 1953, and was reported (by Yoda) to have said on that occasion that 'he wouldn't be beaten' by this director, an enigmatic remark that might just be taken to mean: I won't let *his* images have greater depth of field than mine have! The new techniques of widescreen cinema, however, opened up new possibilities of visual composition in which depth of field itself wouldn't be nearly so important, because now variety could be introduced laterally *across* the screen rather than (so to speak) *into* it. I take it this is what Miyagawa is driving at when he writes:

> I regret most bitterly that the director's death deprived me of the opportunity to work with Mizoguchi-san on cinemascope. [He uses Scope here to mean widescreen processes in general, not differentiating between CinemaScope and VistaVision.] What if under Mizoguchi's direction several groups were able to perform at the same time on this wider screen? Suppose each of them is acting independently, and Mizoguchi-san says to me: 'Miyagawa-kun, please shoot them all at once.' I am in a happy agony to think which of the groups gathers the audience's gaze the most. If he said: 'You must catch their performances perfectly, without emphasising one more than the other', what should I do? But I am sure that Mizoguchi's direction would rise to this challenge brilliantly.

[From Kazuo Miyagawa, *The Life of a Cameraman* (1985), p. 88. Translation by Kimitoshi Sato.] The favouring of 'juxtaposition' over 'perspective' or 'depth of field' that is involved here takes us back into the realm of specifically Japanese aesthetics – the aesthetics, for example, of the horizontal scroll (*emaki-mono*) and of the elongated palace screen. What is interesting to note, in general, is how completely the depth-of-field debate disappears with the conversion of mainstream cinema to colour, as if its pertinence had depended absolutely on the specifics of black-and-white photography.

5   Quoted by George Sansom in volume one of his *A History of Japan* (1958). The entire chapter ('The Rule of Taste', pp. 178–96) is of great interest in the context of this discussion.

showed at the neckline, cuffs and hems, graduating from pale on top to dark further down. Getting these stripes 'just so' was evidently extremely important, as illustrated by an anecdote from *The Tale of Genji* in which a lady-in-waiting is taken to task by a court official for allowing the colour of her robes to be 'a shade too pale at the opening of the sleeve'. We are not told whether this was a punishable offence, but we are left in no doubt that it was an unspeakable error of taste. All this, to the modern consciousness, seems fantastic: a kind of parody of neurotic fashion madness (though to mention fashion at all is to be reminded that such distinctions – of hem and colour and cut – are scarcely redundant, even today). The main point of these reflections is the evidence that Japan has always been highly colour-conscious. So maybe it is scarcely surprising that, when the time was ripe, such a passion would move into cinema. For it is indisputable that, after initial experiments and setbacks, the 'palette' of Japanese films in the 1950s and 60s became among the most beautiful in the whole of the art form. Many examples could be cited, though one film above all others stands out: Teinosuke Kinugasa's *Gate of Hell* (a Daiei production from 1953, thus preceding *The Empress Yang Kwei Fei* by two years: it won the Palme d'Or at Cannes in 1954). Anyone who has seen this movie will remember the film's astonishingly vibrant and harmonious colour schemes. (The stock used, incidentally, was Eastmancolor.) I can still summon up in my mind's eye the red of Machiko Kyo's robes when we first see her fleeing the palace rebellion in her covered palanquin; later, the same actress is swathed in orange and gold in some magnificent interior scenes; finally (in the film's great climax when Kazuo Hasegawa arrives to wrest his mistress forcibly from her husband) the apparition of Kyo's shimmering pink kimono decorated with patterns of pawlonia leaves, its lining a wonderful rich mauve.[6]

The Empress Yang Kwei Fei/Yokihi (1955)

Because *The Empress Yang Kwei Fei*, as we shall see, is set in China, its colour scheme is Chinese rather than Japanese, pitched in China's traditional pastel keys. Lemons, pale purples and soft violets predominate, along with that uniquely Chinese shade of matte porphyry that is used to decorate woodwork. Extraordinary efforts were taken to get the decors right. Here are some extracts from the production designer Mizutani's account of the film's genesis:

> We had to recreate the atmosphere of the times, based on evidence from the recorded documents. And at the same time we had to allow for a certain artistic deformation, or 'supplement', from the

6   This brilliance of colour in recent years has also been a hallmark of Chinese cinema. Zhang Yimou, Chen Kaige and Wong Kar-wai display notably rich and vibrant palettes. (One of Zhang's films – *Ju Dou* [1990] – is set in a dye factory.) It is hard to get away from the feeling that colour is part of the essence of our deepest apprehensions about cinema. It's one of the strongest elements of film that I personally recall from numerous childhood visits to the local picture palace: I mean something like the strange pale blue of the outfit worn by the Lone Ranger; or else, in another context entirely, the magical scarlet of Moira Shearer's dancing pumps in Powell and Pressburger's famous ballet film *The Red Shoes*. Epics, too (*Spartacus, The Ten Commandments, Ben Hur*), had their own lurid hues of desert and blood that have lodged themselves in the childish memory bank. The phenomenology in question extended itself, in fact, to all aspects of the filmgoing experience. In those days (the 1950s) you could buy – or persuade your parents to buy – souvenir programme booklets whose production stills were reproduced with a kind of sombre golden varnish which even today convinces me as being the very colour of the ancient world itself.

aesthetic point of view . . . I began my research in the middle of December 1954 by travelling to Hong Kong together with Mizoguchi, Kawaguchi (scriptwriter) and the producer Masaichi Nagata. [The film was to be a co-production with the Shaw Brothers, a successful Chinese film company based in the then-British colony: Shaw Brothers put up thirty per cent of the costs.] On arrival, I was disappointed, for I failed to discover any of the small historical items necessary for the film . . . In Hong Kong, there was no trace of the Chinese continent! I requested that I might employ some Chinese artists a bit familiar with stage work to come to Japan, to see what we could do back home. In response, Lu Soho, plus a tailor and an expert on small art items agreed to visit us. Meanwhile, during the five-day stay in Hong Kong, Lu guided us to four or five big stores, where we ordered about thirty costumes, and some dozens of bales of precious embroidered materials. We also saw wigs and artcraft made by Lu for a previous Hong Kong Yokihi movie, but I found them a bit cheap and useless. I told myself then: 'Well, we'll really have to make everything from scratch.' Lu's designs were too stereotyped – they weren't faithful to historical truth, I thought . . . Back in Japan, we made a dossier about 150 pages long concerning the epoch. Our first necessity was to procure a map of T'ang China. It turned out the T'ang capital was nothing other than Kyoto on a bigger scale! . . . For ten absorbing days we made an investigation of historical aspects of the story, starting by visiting Professor Yoshikawa, an expert on Chinese literature at Kyoto University. We frequented the Kyoto Museum. We made many photocopies, and gathered relevant literature from antiquarian bookstores. The books we gathered were not only in Japanese but also in English, French and German. Actually, we obtained most of what we wanted, to the surprise of our friends the professors. (Our purchases resulted in a sudden price-hike for books in Japan concerning T'ang China!) . . . At the end of December, we engaged several art students to begin copying slates, furniture, clay dolls, along with sacred and secular paintings of the epoch. Next, we decided to make a test set: the Chinko chamber, reconstructed under the auspices of Professor Murata of Kyoto University. For two days, we bombarded him with questions concerning building details, using as our guide, open in front of us, photographs of the chamber provided by the Department of Oriental Studies in the Boston Museum of Fine Arts. Murata taught us what the T'ang Palace buildings looked like: actually not so decorative as one might imagine – in fact, a bit like the Toshodaiji temple in Japan. On December 26th and 27th, we went to the Hakutsuru Museum to see handicraft of the period made in China. We borrowed about 50 vessels, 16 books, and 1600 cuts of conservation film. At the same time we took about 120 photos. We asked about the costumes of the period, and were introduced to Professor Harada of the National Museum of Tokyo . . . During the first few days of January 1955, we meticulously prepared the set design of the chamber, and re-read our books about costume in order to prepare for a question-and-answer session with Professor Harada. There were many others enquiries, which I haven't itemised here. Why, you may ask, did we do all this? Let me answer this. Because we were abiding by Mizoguchi's sacred principle: only after we gain sound knowledge are we able or permitted to 'lie' or to fabricate our decors![7]

It seems that in the wake of a number of recent box-office successes, Daiei was aiming for a film that could be exportable in the expanding Asian markets, notably in Hong Kong and Taiwan. The fey, ethereal story alighted upon fitted the bill admirably, in that while the subject matter was

---

7   Quoted from Kaneto Shindo and Yoshikazu Hayashi (eds), *Creativity in Hiroshi Mizutani's Cinematic Art* (1973). Translation by Kimitoshi Sato.

Chinese (and therefore suitable for these new markets), this particular tale of a T'ang dynasty concubine who sacrifices herself for her lord had long since entered into Japanese culture, becoming one of its own treasured legends. *The Empress Yang Kwei Fei* is the most remote historically of all Mizoguchi's costume dramas, set as it is in the late eighth century, the epoch when the cultural fusion between China and Japan was at its most vigorous. This cultural traffic was mainly one way: without actually invading her neighbour, China grafted onto the Japanese psyche modes of thought and ways of looking at the world – particularly in the realm of aesthetics – that were henceforth to be part of the younger nation's deepest identity. Poetry was one of these gifts, perhaps, in the early period, the greatest of them. And among works that found immediate resonance in the hearts of medieval Japanese scholars and connoisseurs was a 120-line lament known as 'The Song of Unending Sorrow', composed by one of China's foremost poets, Po Chü-i (772–846). Here, then, is the first evidence in literature of the semi-historical, semi-legendary events on which the movie is based:

> The lonely, jadelike face, stained with tears,
> Like rain in spring on the blossom of a pear . . .
> His majesty, covering his face, could not save her.
> He turned to look back, his face streaming with blood and tears
> Under Mount O-Mei, a scattering of marching men,
> Flags and banners colourless in the fading sun.[8]

Some 650 years later, after various literary vicissitudes, the story was revisited in one of the best known of all surviving Noh dramas, *Yokihi*, by Kamparu Zenchiku (1405–70). The play (edited and translated into English by Donald Keene) is thought by the Japanese to be extremely beautiful, informed throughout by a kind of wistful yearning described by the special word *yugen*. Maybe in fact it's worth pausing to attempt to define this concept a little more closely, since one of the ways of evaluating Mizoguchi's film is to ask, precisely, whether and how it 'shows *yugen*'.

---

8   Translation by Witter Bynner, in *Anthology of Chinese Literature*, vol. 1, *From Early Times to the Fourteenth Century* (comp. and ed. Cyril Birch, New York: Grove Press, 1965), p. 266. Arthur Waley, in his *Life and Times of Po Chü-I* (London, 1949), summarises the poem in the following way:

> 'The Song of Unending Sorrow' is a narrative poem of 120 lines in seven-syllable verse. It tells the story of the infatuation of Emperor Hsüan Tsung (684–762) for Yang Kwei Fei (718–56). When the An Lu Shan revolution forced the emperor to flee from Ch'ang-an (the then capital of China) the soldiers of the bodyguard refused to march unless Yang Kwei Fei was executed. The emperor was obliged to consent; but during his exile in Szechwan and after his abdication and subsequent return to the capital, he was haunted by her memory and fell under the influence of a Taoist magician who claimed that he could get into communication with the dead. The wizard ransacked the universe and in the end found Yang Kwei Fei's soul in one of the Taoist paradises. She gave him 'certain keepsakes', tokens of their deep love, a blue enamelled box and a gold hairpin to take back with him to the world of men.

According to Waley:

> The poem had an immense success. Po tells us that when a certain General Kao Hsia-yu (772–826) wanted to hire a singing girl, she said to him: 'You must not think I am an ordinary girl: I can sing the "Unending Sorrow"; and she put up her price accordingly.

'Mystery, longing, depth, elegance . . . qualities that make up the Japanese conception of *yugen*'

Japanese *chinoiserie*: Hiroshi Mizotuni's set designs for *The Empress Yang Kwei Fei* (above and opposite)

Le château de rêve

'Lemons, pale purples and soft violets predominate' (*The Empress Yang Kwei Fei*)

The vibrant and harmonious
colour schemes of *Tales of the
Taira Clan*

A melancholy vehemence:
Kiyomori (Riaza Ichikawa) in
Tales of the Taira Clan

Japanese posters for two of Mizoguchi's films. (left) The lost 'tendency film' *Metropolitan Symphony* (1929). Note the raised hammer hovering over images of pleasurable urban decadence. (above) *The Life of Oharu* (1952)

'Thinking of such things [i.e. sex], get well soon.' Letter in Chinese calligraphy sent by friends to Mizoguchi after he was hospitalised, 29 May 1956. Identified by their caricatures, the authors of the letter are (from right to left): director Yasujiro Ozu, novelist Ton Satomi, screenwriter Kogo Noda, film critic Matsuo Kishi and cartoonist Ryosuke Nasu. The letter was written in the Takefu Restaurant, run by Mizoguchi's close friend the actress Chieko Naniwa. Mizoguchi's face appears in the top panel to the left of the bamboo tree ("take" in takefu=bamboo) next to the devil-like virus he is suffering from (far right image of the second panel). Ozu has added a pubic bush to the naked lady drawn by Nasu

Mizoguchi's office and writing table

Everyday requirements on set: briefcase, gloves, watch, stopwatch, light meter

Mood and *Stimmung*

The word has a long history, with many mutations. Thus the great Kodansha encyclopedia informs us that the poet Kamo no Chomei (1156–1215) first explained *yugen* as 'a sentiment unexpressed in words, a vision invisible in form', before going on to liken it to the sight of a lovely woman silently grieving in the gathering dusk. In the same generation, Fujiwara no Shunzei ('the foremost exponent of *yugen* in his day') cited a poem on the autumn moon that made the reader hear *a deer's cry not described therein*. In the thirteenth century, Shunzei's son, Fujiwara no Teika, explained *yugen* by recounting a story of an ancient Chinese emperor who had a brief romance with a heavenly goddess. The beautiful goddess, before her final return to heaven, told the grief-stricken emperor to watch the moving clouds hanging over a certain mountain whenever he longed for her: *that* was *yugen*. And so on. Zeami (1363–1443), Zenchiku's father-in-law and the founder of classic Noh drama, argued that all styles of Noh acting possessed *yugen* 'latently'. His own preferred simile for the concept was 'a white bird with a flower in its mouth', while Zenchiku himself fixed on monochrome imagery such as pampas grass on a withered moor, or a wan moon in a dawning sky. Gathering all these indications together and extrapolating from them, we may say we expect to encounter in any work expressing *yugen* all or some of the following attributes: mystery, longing, depth, elegance, ambiguity, calm, sadness.

With this in mind, let us briefly turn to the events of the movie.

The first wife of the Emperor Hsüan Tsung has died long ago. The widower (Masayuki Mori) sits alone in the court devoting his life to the composition of music. Courtiers from the Yang family, in league with the Turkic general An Lu-Shan, are attempting to find a new wife for him from their own camp in order to further their political ambitions. It is the ruffianly red-haired general An (So Yamamura) who spots that Yu-Huan (Machiki Kyo), a lowly Yang relative working in the kitchens, bears a striking physical resemblance to the emperor's deceased wife, and arranges for her in due course to be placed in the imperial suite.

The ruse works; the emperor meets and falls in love with the girl. Under a new name, Yang Kwei Fei ('Yokihi'), the innocent maiden finds herself elevated to the position of official first concubine. However, by this time, the Yangs have become unpopular, having fallen out (in particular) with An Lu-Shan. Soon the country is in turmoil – invaded from the north by An Lu-Shan's forces, and undermined, in the imperial capital, by the unfettered wrath of the populace. Only one thing can save the empire: the sacrifice of the woman who, rightly or wrongly, has come to symbolise in the public imagination the hated ambition of the Yangs.

That is the plot in a nutshell. Appropriately enough for a Chinese subject the metaphor that serves best to describe the film's machinations comes from the traditional puppet theatre. Yokihi is a puppet in the political ambitions of the Yang family; but the emperor himself, smothered in protocol and locked up in a dream world of art and memory, is no less limited in his freedom of movement – he is no less a puppet in that sense than she is. In the midst of this given determinism, the film seeks to evoke a 'margin of freedom' whereby each of the two principal characters may escape from his or her respective imprisonment. Such a margin comes to be represented by the possibility of love, freely and mutually entered into. But how to be sure of it, when each knows, precisely, that he/she is being edged towards a politically useful outcome? How can each be certain that the other is honourable in his or her intentions?

In Mizoguchi's schema, the key to their happiness turns out to hinge on the notion of sincerity – channelled or mediated by the emperor's devotion to music. Thus the revelation to Yokihi that the emperor is an honest man and someone to whom she may safely entrust her heart comes when she overhears him playing one of his compositions on the lute. The beauty of the melody enters her soul and gives birth to a genuine longing, so that when, a short while later, the emperor overhears her playing the same composition (in the same plum grove in which it was composed) the music in turn becomes proof of the purity of *her* intentions – for the fact that she plays it so well, with true sincerity and understanding – singles her out, despite her low status, as a spiritual soulmate, with no hidden agenda or dissembled ambition.

Sacrifice and Self-sacrifice

The Empress Yang Kwei Fei is unusual in the Mizoguchi canon in the way that (in contrast to *Chikamatsu Monogatari*) it seems to hold back from physical expressiveness. It aims for a kind of serenity: the serenity, perhaps, of old age and of accounts settled. What kind of object is it exactly, in the Aristotelian sense? It is a mixture of many things: a chamberwork; a ghost story; a fairy tale (with 'Cinderella' elements); a kind of 'ballet' or mime; even in the end an imperial tragedy: the tragedy of Yang Kwei Fei's sacrifice. The weight, meaning and poignancy of this act is after all what gives rise to the story, and what (if anything) unites it to the thematic charge of Mizoguchi's numerous other movies on the same subject. If the idea of sacrifice is crucial to Mizoguchi's worldview, it is pointless to deny that it is also, at times, the biggest stumbling block even for a sympathetic modern viewer. For who now 'believes in' sacrifice, or can claim to understand its otherworldly mechanics? A secular rationalist or feminist might decline to accept the 'pathos' of this film at face value, asking why it should always have to be a *woman* who is sacrificing herself for a man. Does not the very notion of sacrifice involve an outdated emphasis on docility, even cowardice? On the other hand, the question of sacrifice has its own resonance for Western audiences, whose system of morals still owes something (if only vestigially) to Christianity, at whose ethical centre, of course, the mystery of sacrifice is enshrined. In Japanese culture too, sacrifice has its grave and beautiful specificity, a specificity that only becomes 'controversial' (and difficult to go along with) when the demand for the deed issues from the lips of an emperor. Obviously *The Empress Yang Kwei Fei* is not (and was not designed to be) a political parable: it resists a politicised reading. Still, we do not need to be reminded that it was in the emperor's name that, during the war, the Japanese pledged their fatal allegiance to militarism, just as, after the war, it was the very fact that it was Hirohito alone, of all the war leaders, who remained unpunished which began to 'show up' the notion of sacrifice, to many Japanese, in such a retrospectively sardonic, bitter light.

In *The Empress Yang Kwei Fei*, the idea is that the emperor is above the mêlée – he is a puppet around whom events take place, rather than the initiator of those events. When at the end of the film, Hsüan Tsung, gazing on the body of his martyred beloved, murmurs 'Will this bring peace to my country?', the viewer is caught between wondering whether the question is evidence of a cruel self-delusion, or whether it is literally true, that our hero *has* no ultimate say in the matter. Maybe Hsüan Tsung, in short, has 'thrown Yokihi to the dogs'; or maybe (as the film argues) there is a finer logic operating that yokes together the twin destinies of the lovers into an ultimately joyful complicity. It is the artistic question, not the moral or social one, that is our concern here. The death scene is one of the most famous in Mizoguchi's oeuvre; it joins Anju's sacrifice scene in *Sansho* in being the most *explicit* instance of female self-sacrifice in Mizoguchi's cinema. Like Anju's self-annihilation, it gains whatever poignancy it possesses through the sense, conveyed unambiguously, that the sacrifice is above all *self-chosen*.

Let us recapitulate: the mob, in these late scenes, is baying for the blood of the Yangs, and we see the emperor pondering, with horror, the implication of the demand that Yokihi should be delivered up to them. Meanwhile, unobserved by her consort, Yokihi looks on at the scene from the shadows and quietly makes her fateful decision. Taking leave of her kneeling, weeping maid-servants, she asks them to pray for future peace in the land. To one of them she entrusts her golden hairpin, requesting that it be delivered as a memento to the emperor with her blessing. Then, taking up her silken scarf that has been hanging over the mirror, she accompanies the waiting soldiers to the dimly lit execution site. A gallows has been hastily constructed from a spindly tree outside a ruined cottage, and a few metres in front of this device Yokihi pauses. The silken scarf she gives to a soldier, who substitutes it for the coarse hemp that is hanging over the gallows' cross-bar. She kneels down and says a final prayer before unclasping her embroidered *haori* and letting it drop gracefully from her shoulders.

The execution itself is not seen: instead there is a beautiful ellipsis. As she moves towards the gallows, the camera follows not Yokihi but the hem of her gown in close-up, sweeping over her tufted,

bejewelled slippers. At the foot of the tree the camera halts, while onto the bare patch of ground we see falling the brooch and earrings which Yokihi casts off in a last gesture of queenly renunciation.

Does the film, then, possess *yugen* – glossed here as longing, depth, poetry? Or are critics right in their suspicion that it lacks some of that moral vigour and gracefulness which render Mizoguchi, when he is 'on form', unsurpassable? Is it delicacy the film shows, or lassitude? Individual moments (such as the execution scene just described) may indeed stand out; but does the drama as a whole cohere? In short, does *The Empress Yang Kwei Fei* belong among the ranks of Mizoguchi's masterpieces? We know, from the reminiscences of Machiki Kyo among others, that the making of it was not a happy experience for many of the principals. Constrained in a leg brace for a year after a fall on the set of *The Woman of Rumour*, Mizoguchi was more than usually irritable and wayward. (He may already have been suffering from the leukemia that killed him less than a year and a half later.) Still, all films, more or less, are difficult to make; and, curiously, there is no necessary correlation between happiness on set and a perceived happiness (or unhappiness) in artistic outcome. Critics of the film, such as Tadao Sato, complain about its lack of passion, its failure of 'emotional electricity'; and it is true that the acting is at times slow, even stilted, rather as if the constraint of adapting to foreign protocols – the actors navigating their way through a Chinese set that includes (as Japanese settings do not) tables and chairs and other upright furnishings – seems to introduce an awkwardness into the playing, over and above the awkwardness (or shyness or modesty) that is inherent in the story.

Such reservations are ultimately matters of individual taste. Yet it is interesting how often *The Empress Yang Kwei Fei* has been mentioned in polls of viewers' favourite movies. The Portuguese director Manoel de Oliviera cites it as one of Mizoguchi's supreme achievements. For me the film finally does work. Perhaps because it operates in such an exceptionally closed artistic universe – throughout the movie we scarcely see sky or landscape – its flavour lingers insidiously, like the aftermath of a luxurious dream. In the right mood, Yokihi's colour, rhythm, and even 'staginess', are all captivating.

Tales of the Taira Clan/Shinheike Monogatari (1955)

I have alluded several times to aspects of Mizoguchi's films that – in their very 'Japaneseness' – are unavoidably strange, even off-putting, to the Western viewer. Sometimes that Otherness of Japanese cinema recedes, and one feels there is no problem at all – the plotline is clear, the morality lucid, the acting vivid and engaging. At other times one can feel that the action belongs to a universe that is somehow inherently incommunicable to us. In *The Loyal 47 Ronin* both the initial insult and the extraordinary punishment that follows seem part of this puzzling moral universe, although it is useful to remind ourselves that there are at least equivalent opacities in Western culture: aristocratic codes like duelling, for instance, that were once common currency but have long since fallen into desuetude. Yet such codes are alive to the historical imagination; they are not in any absolute sense beyond us, and maybe their mysteries can be exaggerated. Thus if *Tales of the Taira Clan* is, like *The Loyal 47 Ronin*, is a mysterious and complicated film on the surface, it is also very beautiful, and one can feel the desire to understand it properly even in the midst of being frustratingly puzzled by it. Such puzzlement can take various forms, and differs from person to person. For instance, I was confused when I first saw the film by a scene three quarters of the way through in which the hero's venerable father Tadamori is slapped by a man who appears to be the ex-Emperor Shirakawa, to whom he is the most faithful of servants. What has he done to deserve this rebuke? Why does he take it so humbly? Why doesn't his son, Kiyomori (the film's hero), who is present, leap up to defend his father? The confusion vanished when it dawned on me that this was not the ex-emperor at all, but an arrogant Minister of the Left. The problem was simply that the two actors are the spitting images of each other – or at least seemed to be so, to my not-yet-acclimatised vision.[9]

Complexity of Plot as an Aesthetic Problem

The son Kiyomori's passivity, and the explanation for it, will be discussed later. There are feudal restraints in operation that could plausibly be understood to curb the filial chivalry of someone even as passionate and ingenuous as our hero is portrayed. And besides, Kiyomori's relationship with his father is, at this stage of the intrigue, nothing if not psychologically 'fraught'. A larger and more pressing obstacle to the viewer's patience is the inordinately elaborate system of government that forms the background to the story, and that needs to be understood, at least in outline, if we are fully to grasp the finer details of the film. The chief cause of confusion is the system of the twin courts: the imperial court, presided over by a currently reigning emperor, and the cloister court, presided over by an ex-emperor who has retired and become a monk, but who seems still to wield a certain degree of power and patronage. Why are there two courts, and what is the relation between them? The system goes back historically to the influence of the Fujiwara Regents who, through their grip on the imperial household (a grip artfully enforced by dynastic marriage), effectively ruled Heian Japan for about 120 years from the middle of the tenth century. Towards the end of the eleventh century, however, the emperors began to reassert their power by abdicating, abandoning the court and their Fujiwara parasites, and setting up their own base of operations elsewhere (though still in the capital city Kyoto). In his succinct introductory survey, *Japan: A Short Cultural History*, Sir George Sansom summarises this baroque system – surely one of the most extraordinary in the annals of government – as follows:

> From 1073, for more than half a century, there sat on the throne titular emperors, with titular regents, chancellors and ministers; while during each reign, not far away, in a palace of his own, keeping imperial state and assisted by his own officers, was an abdicated emperor in holy orders who, in name a monk, was in fact a ruler. It was his edict, and not those of the titular emperor, that was valid, in so far as any order of the court in those days was obeyed. The government, therefore, appeared to consist of an emperor, delegating his authority to a regent [always a senior member of the Fujiwara clan] who controlled a council of state and the ministerial boards; and of an ex-emperor, in tonsure, whose commands overrode those of the occupant of the throne.

---

9   Donald Richie tells me of a similar confusion that occurred when, as a young would-be subtitler, he was first exposed to this movie. 'What is all the business about lavatories?', he asked a Japanese companion in a puzzled tone when coming out of the theatre. It turns out that the word 'denjo', which comes up frequently in the movie, is old Japanese for a palace. Richie, mistakenly, had heard it throughout as 'benjo', which would have to be translated as the smallest room in such an establishment!

As Sansom remarks sardonically: 'It is obvious that such a complicated machine could only exist as long as it did not have to function effectively.'

Tales of the Taira Clan is set in the year 1137, when the system was decadent but still operative (it ran for another twenty or so years). The complicating factor for the audience is that, although Tadamori, his son Kiyomori[10] and their Taira kin owe their allegiance to the cloister (i.e. the seat of the ex-emperor), there are still occasions when they need to be in contact with the *other* court. Since the functionaries in either establishment dress in a similar way and conduct themselves with a similarly restrained formality, against backgrounds and furniture that are largely indistinguishable one from the other, it is often quite difficult for the viewer to know exactly where he or she is. Captions are out of the question: it is simply not that kind of movie. A brief written scroll prefacing the credits gives some of the main historical facts; otherwise, in order to position himself, the viewer has to rely on the odd moment of expository dialogue – as for example during the film's virtuoso opening sequence, an extended crane movement that slides down onto the Kyoto marketplace, picking up in the space of less than two minutes fragments of conversation from no fewer than five separate sets of passersby. Scene-setting like this could sometimes be criticised as a scripting fault; but here the viewer is grateful.

To complicate matters further: the rival courts are not the only powers in the land. One of the issues that affects both the cloister court and the reigning emperor – and which involves therefore this slightly confusing to-ing and fro-ing between locales – is the behaviour of the monks from the neighbouring monastery on Mount Hiei, whom we first meet in the opening sequence. A band of them swagger down the main street in front of a procession of palanquins, demanding that all who come before them (including the Taira warriors, returning from a hard-fought campaign in the west of the country) should bow down and offer them homage. Once again, the details appear to be historically accurate: during the eleventh and twelfth centuries, the great temples, far from being havens of peace, were active forces of disruption in the land. Conflict between church and

---

10   Taira no Kiyomori (1118–81) was an important historical figure whose career coincided with the ascendancy of the Heike (= Taira) clan over their traditional rivals the Minamotos during Japan's turbulent twelfth-century political in-fighting. On the one hand stubborn, strong-willed and short-tempered, he was at other times tactful, considerate and gentle: in short, a complicated and intriguing character, who may or may not have been corrupted by the power that became his through conquest from the late 1150s onwards. Sansom comments (ironically, in the light of the way Kiyomori is portrayed in Mizoguchi's film): '[Kiyomori] became a conservative, instead of making or introducing a new age, as he was fitted to do by his unusual gifts.' More damagingly:

> It's probable that Kiyomori really wished to do away with the system of cloister government and restore a limited authority to the reigning monarch, since he could then revert to a dictatorship like that of the [eleventh-century] Fujiwara regents.

The events of the epoch which Kiyomori dominated are recorded in the classic fifteenth-century text *The Tale of the Heike* (a new English translation by Helen Craig McCullough appeared in 1994). Mizoguchi's source, however, was a modern 'potboiler' version of the tales by the popular novelist Eiji Yoshikawa (1892–1962). It's important to note (and this too has some bearing on the film's obscurity) that Mizoguchi's film only dips into Yoshikawa's novel: two further films – by Teinosuke Kinugasa and Koji Shima (both released by Daiei in 1956) – consider later aspects of these complicated and fascinating clan rivalries. Maybe it is also worth adding that Kobayashi's famous film *Kwaidan* (1964) shows (in magnificently stylised form) the spectacular battle of Dannoura that ended the hegemony of the Tairas.

state of course has parallels in European history – though what I suppose is unusual here is to see men of the cloth portrayed so unambiguously as ruffians. In Japan, the issue at stake was not, as it was at least partially in eleventh-century Europe, theological; it was a mainly secular power struggle centred on the monks' demand that their estates should be exempt from imperial taxation. Their method of enforcing such demands involved, besides an unbridled recourse to armed retainers, a reliance on the blackmailing properties of the Buddhist relics they possessed, housed in elaborate palanquins that were carried by the monks into the streets on their frequent martial sorties. (Nobody will dare to attack them if they are carrying these objects in their retinue.) In the film, lands belonging to one of these monasteries are eventually ceded to the Taira clan as a long-delayed reward for their military services; and while there is a claim put forward on the monks' behalf that the peasants who cultivate these lands would be 'happier' under monastic rule, it is made pretty clear, at key moments in the narrative, that such arguments are only self-serving. In short, the moral stance that we are asked to identify with is that of the Taira clan, Kiyomori pre-eminently, in whose eyes there is nothing to choose between the superstitious cynicism of the monks and the no less offensive decadence of the imperial nobles – two groups in society whose privileges must be overcome if Japan is to have any future.

Kiyomori's Parentage

Kiyomori's 'radicalism' (his intention, stated explicitly at the film's climax, to sweep away the corruption of the past) is unambiguous, as far as it goes. There is little difficulty, on the face of it, in linking Kiyomori's vow to cleanse the society of his day to the liberal, democratic, anti-feudal stance that we might expect from films of this epoch. Still, in so far as the film has an unresolved opacity about it, even at its ending, the *central* problem relates, surely, to the character and actions of Kiyomori. The puzzle surrounding him is posed by the film in a frankly Oedipal way. Who exactly is he? More importantly, who is his father? His nominal father, as we know, is the samurai Tadamori, who is loyal to the cloister. But, in the course of two separate, extended flashbacks early on in the film, doubt is cast over Kiyomori's paternity. His mother we know: she is a mysterious noblewoman known as Lady Gion, married for twenty years to Tadamori but, from our first glimpse of her, no longer happy – in fact estranged (she refuses to take part in the celebrations to welcome Tadamori and Kiyomori back from their campaign in western Japan). From the first flashback, which begins with Kiyomori hearing a story recounted to him in a tavern, we learn that years ago she had been concubine to the then emperor Shirakawa. Shirakawa had *given* her as a gift to Tadamori one dark night when, as his trusted bodyguard, the latter had shown bravery in protecting him; seven months later, after the wedding had been solemnised, Kiyomori was born: a little early perhaps! At any rate, this first glimpse of his possible royal paternity comes to Kiyomori as a profoundly disturbing revelation. There is still more to come, however. A second flashback takes us deeper into the events surrounding his conception. Thus, coming to visit his mistress one night – just before or just after the above incident (it is not made clear, and it does not matter) – Shirakawa surprises a hooded figure escaping from Lady Gion's bedroom. Apprehended, the fleeing lover turns out to be a handsome, youthful cleric. So now there is a double possibility for Kiyomori to torment himself over: he may be the son of an ex-emperor; alternatively, he may even be the offspring of one of the hated tribe of monks.

Finely dramatised by the actor Raizo Ichikawa, Kiyomori's moral ferocity, already alluded to, is his single most defining trait. His melancholy vehemence is best understood perhaps in terms of a kind of classical class *ressentiment*. He belongs, by situation and upbringing, to the nascent samurai class, looked down upon or condescended to by the nobles. Constrained to sell his horse to provide money for a feast to reward his kinsmen, he consoles himself that the time of the Tairas will come. 'We are grass seed,' he tells them: 'It's winter, but it will be spring!' In such circumstances, finding out that he is, or might be, the son of an emperor, comes as an almost insurmountable blow to his *amour-propre*. For should he want to be, or *not* want to be, of royal birth? His own moral logic would lead him to treat the confirmation of such news with repugnance. And yet, in some complicated way, the possibility of imperial paternity feeds into his sense of being chosen, singled out – endowed with an historical destiny. The psychological confusion issuing from his impasse is reminiscent in some ways of Hamlet's. (It could be expressed by the question: Is Shirakawa like the Danish prince's *father*? Or is he on the contrary like Claudius? And Lady Gion: isn't *she*, by the same token, Gertrude?).

The point of such a comparison is not to suggest that Mizoguchi and his collaborators had Shakespeare's great play in mind when they adapted their script from the best-selling novel by Yoshikawa. On the face of it that would be unlikely. The comparison works, if it works at all, on a more abstract level of speculation: that there is a sort of incestuous Oedipal groundswell – a psychological field-force – operating in the film that the viewer feels aware of without necessarily being able to identify. Freud, notoriously, linked *all* great drama to the ur-drama of birth and to the mystery of our origins; and though rather few people these days, I suppose, admit to being unreconstructed psychoanalytic believers, that part at least of his theory continues to be persuasive. Wonderfully suggestive, in this respect, are Lady Gion's fleeting appearances during and just after the two flashback scenes, where she is glimpsed overhearing – secretly and unknown to Kiyomori – the various revelations about his paternity as they emerge. The motif of watching and spying (the hidden 'scopic curiosity' which Freud analyses as being central to the Oedipal drama) enlivens this part of the intrigue, and makes it further of *Hamlet*.

Comparison with *Sansho the Bailiff*

The doubt surrounding Kiyomori's paternity is cleared up after all – but only after Tadamori's death. The royal fan found clutched in the old warrior's hand bears a cryptic two lines of dialogue which, when deciphered by Lady Gion, convince Kiyomori that he is indeed the son of Shirakawa, and not of Tadamori or the monk. Actually, this is one place in the film where the exposition is just a little *too* explicit: the delicately ambiguous words – 'Thy offspring flourishes, oh begetter!' 'Pray keep it [the fan]/him [Kiyomori] with my blessing, dear guardian!' – don't need the verbal underlining which the dialogue provides at this point. In any event, the confirmation releases Kiyomori from his torment. Now that his paternity is known for certain, he can, as it were, place it safely behind him, and move into his own adult identity. His emergence at the end as an autonomous moral agent is similar to the transformation that affects Zushio in *Sansho the Bailiff* when his petition is

An Oedipal groundswell: Kiyomori (Raizo Ichikawa) berates his mother the Lady Gion (Michiyo Kogure) for her sexual misdeeds in *Tales of the Taira Clan* (1955)

accepted by the court in Kyoto, proving to the world *his* erstwhile noble origins. In both cases, an exceptionally motivated energy enters into the make-up of the protagonists to speed each film towards its respective powerful climax. Thus, the fierce and lively scenes in *Sansho* where we see Zushio enforcing, or attempting to enforce, the imperial decree against slavery on the manorial estates find their equivalent here in the marvellous sequence in which Kiyomori settles his accounts with Mount Hiei monks by ambushing their procession, and firing his arrows into the massed assembled palanquins.[11] Both films paint civil unrest vigorously: cadres on the move, proclamations made and overturned, rebellion faced down by decisive moral authority. And in both, the strength to rout superstition and bad government seems to issue from a return to simple, private piety. Thus before setting out, Zushio says prayers at the grave of his father; while Kiyomori, indifferent at last to the lure of imperial glamour, brings sacred offerings, and apologies, to the tomb of the old warrior Tadamori.

Yet in other ways, the endings of the two films are significantly different. Thus Zushio's acts of political will are seen to be the preface to a sublime act of renunciation whereby he casts off his titles and, in the garb of a mendicant, sets out to find his blind mother. It is a film about mercy and forgiveness: perhaps *the* film about mercy and forgiveness in the repertory. *Tales of the Taira Clan* also ends with an encounter between son and mother; but the moral and emotional temperature here, is quite the opposite of that in *Sansho*. The scene opens with a panorama of a magnificent picnic in the countryside with Kiyomori watching from a distance, uninvited. Colour and costumes are at their most splendid. The courtly dance in progress is beautiful. Yet there is something decadent about this idyll, apparent from the gestures of the participants. At the centre of the gathering, tipsy and flirtatious, is Lady Gion who has abandoned the Taira household and gone back to her old Fujiwara associates. 'She has refound her old profession. I suppose she is happy again!', Kiyomori remarks to his companions, with unfilial bitterness. (Hamlet again: unwilling to forgive Gertrude.) A party of guards march over to tell him that he and his entourage are unwelcome. The guards go, and Kiyomori surveys the scene calmly for a moment, then steps forward. The film ends with his dark fierce words: 'Dance, my lords, dance. Your end is near. Tomorrow will be ours!'

'Tomorrow will be ours!' A threat or a promise? A threat *and* a promise! The speech has a fine chilling scorn to it. But the prophecy itself is interesting. The Taira or Heike clan (of which Kiyomori was probably the most famous historical representative) perished to a man at the naval battle of Dannoura in 1185, a watershed in Japanese history. Yet in another sense, that epic engagement confirmed, in the victory of the rival Minamota clan, the hegemony of the samurai class to which Kiyomori belonged: a class that was destined to stay in power until the nineteenth-century Resto-

---

11 A Japanese friend tells me that this scene – the climax of the film – has a remarkable resonance for the ordinary Japanese viewer. There is a sort of audacity about it that we in the West fail to appreciate unless we are attuned to what my friend calls the 'heroic blasphemy' that is involved in shooting arrows into the most sacred of holy places. (Shinto *and* Buddhist pieties are both at stake here. Incidentally, the film is known in France under the title *Le Héros sacrilège*.) Mizoguchi was typically anxious (some would say cowardly) about the consequences of his boldness, summoning Yoda to the set in front of the assembled crowd of extras. 'You wrote this, didn't you?' (conveniently forgetting that if Yoda had written it, Mizoguchi had passed it at the script stage). 'I want *you* to take responsibility if we're criticised or attacked by right-wing vigilantes.' Only when Yoda promised to bear whatever consequences occurred (there were none in fact) could filming of the scene in question resume.

ration and beyond. Samurai rule under the Kamakura shoguns (1185–1392) was indeed modernising and progressive, in the sense that it swept away old imperial privilege – in fact, it swept away the imperial institution itself, leaving behind a purely decorative residue. But as all Japanese know, it did so at the cost of installing a feudal military system which – notoriously – presided over four centuries of intense internecine warfare. In one sense therefore Kiyomori's declamation can be understood as fierce, noble and fuelled by fine democratic anger. But in another sense it is harshly sectarian (and 'samurai-protective'). This ambivalence about the *beneficence* of Kiyomori is one of the things that makes this film so fascinating. We can say this at any event: the hostile contempt with which Kiyomori faces down his mother and her retinue could not be further, morally speaking, from the sublime and tragic serenity which (only a year earlier, in 1954) brought *Sansho the Bailiff* to its extraordinary Shakespearean conclusion.

7 | Respectable Women

The world of geishadom and prostitution – a milieu which Mizoguchi, despite his critique, was constantly drawn to and dwelled upon in his art – was governed, at bottom, by harsh laws of poverty and constraint. Yet the question of women's dependence, or otherwise, on men is one that arises at all levels of society, even the highest – no matter that the harsher manifestations of such bondage are disguised, at the higher levels, by layers of decorum and civility. In a series of films that came out at the beginning of the 1950s, Mizoguchi took time to explore certain aspects of high bourgeois and aristocratic society, at the very moment at which (thanks to stringent fiscal measures introduced in the new post-war Japanese democracy) the upper classes found themselves threatened with extinction. The films in question – *A Picture of Madame Yuki/Yuki Fujin Ezu* (1950), *Miss Oyu/Oyusama* (1951) and *The Lady from Musashino/Musashino Fujin* (also 1951) – are based, as usual, on literary originals, adapted in each case by Yoda. They form an obviously self-contained group – another of those fascinating trilogies that we keep coming across. Like *Gion Festival Music* and *The Woman of Rumour* they are bound to be considered minor films, although they have their admirers, myself among them (with qualifications discussed presently). The trio of heroines – two of them played by the same actress, Kinuyo Tanaka – are united both by their feminine gentleness and their profound melancholy. The films are in one way psychological case studies – studies in neurosis, defined, as in Freud, by a sort of blockage of the will, or moral paralysis. Something is wrong with the souls of these women; but what? In the more successful of the three adaptations (*A Picture of Madame Yuki* and *The Lady from Musashino*), the mystery is rich and intriguing. *Miss Oyu* is less interesting psychologically, although it has some striking scenes, and is not without merit.

Before this, in the late 1940s, Mizoguchi had made two other films with intriguing heroines far removed from the world of geisha and prostitution – at least, they appear to be so on the surface. Whether the women in question (both based on real-life characters and played in each case by the same actress, Tanaka) would have been considered 'respectable' by their contemporaries is another matter. For one is a path-breaking actress, the other a pioneer feminist. Simply by adhering to their chosen roles, both break the rules of society, and end up being punished for doing so. The films in question (masterpieces in my judgment, though not often spoken of as such) are *The Love of Sumako the Actress/Joyu Sumako no Koi* (1947) and *My Love Has Been Burning/Waga Koi Wa Moenu* (1949). If 'neurosis' comes into the psychology of their main characters (and it surely does, especially in *The Love of Sumako the Actress*) it is not of the variety that paralyses the will and pushes the victim into solipsism. These women are no shrinking violets. On the contrary: both Sumako and Eiko (the heroine of *My Love Has Been Burning*) are extraordinarily strong personalities in their own right, ready to endure the ostracism of society.

Their deepest energies turned inward: Kinuyo Tanaka in *Miss Oyu* (1951)

An Actress's Challenge to the Establishment

The Love of Sumako the Actress is set in the early years of the twentieth century, at the time of the budding *shingeki* movement, when Western drama for the first time was being translated into Japanese. At first, these translations of Shakespeare, Chekhov and Ibsen were simply published in literary magazines, but the question arose, inevitably, as to whether they could be staged, and how best to do it. Shoyo Tsubouchi, the professor at Waseda University whose distinguished renderings of Shakespeare and Ibsen made him a key figure in the popularisation of such dramatists, was convinced that the traditions of kabuki (even a reformed kabuki) were unsuitable for the task at hand. So, in an epoch-making decision, taken in consultation with his protégé Hogetsu Shimamura (another professor at the university who was also a writer and critic), he determined to recruit and train amateur male actors from within the circle of his own students, supplemented by actresses, again amateur, drawn in the main from Japan's newly established and popular women's colleges.

Enter Sumako Matsui. Sumako, whose real name was Masako Kobayashi, was born in 1886, the eighth child, and fifth daughter, of a businessman of samurai origins from Shinshu province. By all accounts there was nothing particularly brilliant about her early years. She was lazy and rather ugly (she had a snub nose, later corrected by plastic surgery, and a large, 'masculine' body). She married young and the marriage failed. A second marriage, in 1908, drew her (she had always been bookish) into literary circles where a group of traditional storytellers were experimenting with dramatisations of children's tales. She seems to have had an extraordinary access of will-power at this point in her life. From the moment she saw the first of these adaptations staged in a theatre she became determined to become an actress herself. Brooking no discouragement from her conservative-minded second husband, she got herself introduced to Hogetsu and taken on as a trainee in his new troupe of university players. It was two years before the Bungei Kyokai (Literary Arts Association: the name that the group was known by) put on their first play in public. The choice was *Hamlet* and Sumako's Ophelia was an immediate sensation. Even more notable (for a start, the role was much larger) was her Nora in Ibsen's *The Doll's House*, performed at the Imperial Theatre a few months later, in November 1911. Here on stage for the first time was an interpretation of the 'new woman' – diametrically opposed in every imaginable way to the traditional Japanese ideal of *ryosai kenbo* ('good wife and good mother'). (So radical was Ibsen's conception of feminism to Japanese eyes, that there was a genuine problem of comprehension in some quarters: what on earth was the play *about*? Didn't the average Japanese woman precisely *want* to live in a doll's house? Why was Nora so keen to knock the doors down? And so on.) More controversy in a similar vein ensued the following year when Sudermann's *Heimat*, in which Sumako had the lead role of Magda, was closed down by government order as an affront to public morality, and only re-opened when Hogetsu agreed to rewrite the ending to fit in with the social doctrines embodied in the emperor's 1890 Rescript on Education.

By now Hogetsu and Sumako had become lovers. The professor threatened to leave his wife and move in with the actress, which raised all sorts of problems, not least within the company itself because Tsubouchi, the founder and inspiration of the troupe, was something of a puritan in sexual matters: strict regulations existed governing the comportment of men and women under his tutelage. (Even sharing an umbrella on a rainy day was forbidden!) Out of an original complement of eighty players, twenty had already been given their marching orders for romantic misdemeanours.

Now his friend and major protégé had become embroiled in an unseemly affair. The Bungei Kyokai broke up amidst recriminations, though not before Hogetsu had managed to found another company, the Geijutsuza ('Arts Theatre') whose productions would keep his lover's talents in the public eye.

Sumako's historical fame apparently reached its zenith in the early years of Geijutsuza. In particular, her role as the prostitute Katusha in the stage version of Tolstoy's *Resurrection* (1914) touched a popular, sentimental chord hitherto untapped in previous roles (a famous song from the adaptation was important in broadcasting her fame). Yet with her rising celebrity came an increasing wilfulness and unhappiness. She quarrelled with her colleagues and with Hogetsu. Artistic standards declined in the wake of the company's urge to stay solvent at all costs. Hogetsu died prematurely, a victim of the pandemic of influenza that swept the world in the wake of World War I. Although the couple quarrelled bitterly towards the end, Sumako found herself bereft. On 5 January 1919, two months to the day after her lover's death (so Brian Powell informs us, in an admirable article about the actress),[1] Sumako committed suicide by hanging herself.

This is the bare outline of the life from which Mizoguchi and Yoda planned to make their new movie: an interpretation, of course, since a work of art, even when it is based on true facts, inevitably highlights certain features over others for the purpose of internal harmony and overall dramatic intensity.[2] It seems that Shochiku, Mizoguchi's production company (aware that a rival company, Toho, was also on Sumako's trail), was looking for a script that would emphasise the sensational aspects of the legendary actress's life, the scandalous events (the elopements, the bust-ups) that made her notorious among her contemporaries. Mizoguchi's notes to Yoda written during the construction of the screenplay exist *in extenso* (a selection is quoted in the scenarist's memoir), and immediately it is

---

1   Brian Powell, 'Matsui Sumako: Actress and Woman', in W. G. Beasley (ed.), *Modern Japan: Aspects of History, Literature and Society* (1975). For a recent reflection on Sumako's career, see Ayako Kano, *Acting Like a Woman in Modern Japan: Theatre, Gender and Nationalism* (2001).

2   In my short sketch of Sumako's career, I have not gone into the question of the novelty, in Japan, of there being actresses in the first place. On the kabuki stage, by time-honoured tradition, female roles were taken by specially trained male actors called *onnagata*, a practice that continues to this day (see my comments in the following chapter on *The Story of Late Chrysanthemums*). The female roles in *shimpa* were also taken by *onnagata*, as indeed were the first female roles in the movies, a custom which only stopped in the 1920s, at roughly the time when Mizoguchi was starting his career (in fact Mizoguchi was one of the directors who campaigned most vociferously against the tradition). *Shingeki* – Sumako's style of theatre – was different, founded as it was on the premise of Western naturalism. Yet it is important to remember that there had always been actresses in one form or another. Lesley Downer, in her book about geisha (2001), reminds us that 'Geishas and courtesans were, as it were, "parlour actresses", performing on a small stage to a select audience, and just as famous and celebrated as if they had performed on the public stage.' She brings up the case of the famous ex-geisha Sadayakko, mistress of Prime Minister Ito, who toured America at the end of the 1890s playing kabuki roles. Downer writes:

> Abroad Sada played a geisha or a courtesan in productions especially tailored to suit Western taste. But at home, along with [husband and impresario] Otojiro Kawakami, she was instrumental in introducing Shakespeare to the Japanese public. She played Ophelia, Portia and Desdemona, among other roles, and founded a school for actresses. (pp. 152–9)

(Downer has written a full-length study of this intriguing personality: *Madame Sadayakko: The Geisha Who Bewitched the West* [2003].)

apparent that the aspects of Sumako's life that attracted the production company did not particularly interest the director. On the contrary, his instructions to Yoda are all directed at making the fic-
tional Sumako complex, thoughtful and attractive. 'Sketch me an interesting portrait of a woman,'
he writes. 'Sumako's personality bristles with rich possibilities.' Another note elaborates:

> You have to give Sumako 'character', without making her wild and 'idiotic'. Try to paint me the portrait
> of a 30-year-old woman, possessed of a strong will and a certain vehemence, but above all *feminine*
> and *sympathetic*.

Since the film was to be a portrait of Sumako, it would inevitably offer a joint-portrait, too, of the
lover Hogetsu. The aim (says Mizoguchi) should be to dwell not just on his 'sufferings' but 'his
hopes, his ambitions, his sense of beauty and possibility'. Sensationalism was to be avoided at all
costs. Yoda, as usual, was self-ironic about his success in achieving these unexceptional artistic
aims (he believed to the end that his sketch of Hogetsu was too 'shadowy' to be interesting). Yet
it seems to me that, contrary to what the scriptwriter implies (and fears), the film works on all the
essential levels.

Take, for example, the business of Sumako's 'complexity'. She could have been portrayed as a
grasping woman, ruthless in her pursuit of artistic fame, but the combination of Yoda's script and
Tanaka's acting fills the role with scruple and nuance. Particularly effective, for me, are the swings
of mood from gaiety to seriousness and back again, as in the scene where Sumako answers
Hogetsu's declaration of love with a maturity and delicate reticence that cast off any suspicion of
'gold-digging'. Later, after the die is cast, her true vehemence emerges. There are a number of
scenes where the governing emotions are bitterness and a sense of failure; but throughout them
the actress succeeds in communicating a crucial vulnerability – a crucial *self-awareness* – which I
believe was central to Mizoguchi's conception of her character.

The story is unusual enough as it is: the pathos is implicit in what happened, and does not need
to be artificially elaborated. After the initial lightning strike of passion comes a long 'neutral' period
of cooling-off that the film dwells upon at length. So the aftermath of the love affair (in all its naturalistic misery) is given as much weight as the happiness of the initial romance. Gratefully or
ungratefully – we are never quite sure which – Sumako becomes independent of her mentor. Yet
this independence in the end is deceptive. For when the test comes, and Hogetsu is stricken with
paralysis, she is literally unable to live without him. Love, which was thought extinct, flares up again,
only to be extinguished by the grave. In one way, it is the most romantic scenario imaginable. On
the other hand, the facts of the case allow us to believe that this is a portrait of tragic
neurosis. Parallel to the surface charm of the love affair runs a fascinating sociological case history,
premised on the inability of a particular woman during a particular epoch to divide her life up into
the separate compartments of love and career. Men can usually do this and thus survive better. The
problem for women of Sumako's epoch, was *having* a career in the first place. The actress is making
her way in the world and it is as if, in spite of her astounding personal *éclat*, she hasn't yet learned

Running towards death: Sumako (Kinuyo Tanaka) as Carmen in Mizoguchi's penetrating exploration of the
shingeki theatre, *The Love of Sumako the Actress* (1947)

the requisite ruses for survival (the kind of ruses, you could say, that were second nature to Mizoguchi and all successful, hard-working male directors like him). Words like 'weakness', on the other hand, unless they are inflected with a special spiritual significance, do not begin to describe Sumako's true position, or hint at her beautiful lucidity, since she can see more clearly than anyone else that life and art *are* part of the same continuum, and that their enforced segregation is a tragic deformation of life's richness. There is, in this film, something indefinably gallant and moving in the way that Sumako runs towards death. Everything depends on Tanaka's sure-footed, tactful interpretation of the part. In one of the film's finest sequences, Sumako rehearses the play *Carmen* (Merimée's stage version, not the Bizet opera). The extract is the climax, when, goaded beyond endurance, Don José stabs the errant gypsy for her infidelity. Somehow, the rehearsal is not going to plan. The actor playing the Spaniard seems intimidated, unable to recite his lines with conviction. With daring mockery and recklessness, Sumako taunts her leading man about his failure. 'Put some "oomph" into it,' she demands of him, 'make the audience believe that you really *can* kill me!'

Yet nothing, it seems, can meet her demands – unless it is the real thing itself. On stage she rehearses her future self-immolation, with wit and bitterness and high dramatic style – and also with that *audacity* that must have drawn Hogetsu to her talents in the first place.

My Love Has Been Burning

My Love Has Been Burning/Waga Koi Wa Moenu is separated from *Sumako the Actress* by a gap of two years. The intervening year, 1948, had seen the preparation and release of *Women of the Night*, one of Mizoguchi's most outspokenly engaged denunciations of the oppression of women in society, a 'political' film if ever there was one. The film that came out in 1949, equally political in its way, is based on a story by Kogo Noda that in turn was taken from the memoirs of a pioneer feminist of the Meiji era named Hideko Kageyama. In the film Kageyama's name is changed to Eiko Hirayama, and she is incarnated, with extraordinary force and sincerity, by Kinuyo Tanaka, in what must surely be one of the finest performances in this marvellous actress's career.

The story begins on the island of Okayama in 1884, where Eiko, a young, idealistic schoolteacher, is living, unmarried, with her parents. Excitement awakes in this sleepy location when it is visited by a famous radical named Mrs Kishida (colourfully described in the film's subtitles as a 'female bravo') who is plainly not welcome to the authorities. In a wonderfully shot waterborne sequence (boats, lanterns, crowds of supporters), Eiko listens to the politician's message and finds her life beginning to alter. Pinning her colours to Mrs Kishida's mast, she determines to devote her energies to 'changing the world for the better': a wish that means travelling to Tokyo, where the Jiyu-to political grouping to which Mrs Kishida belongs is attempting to find shape and legitimacy as a nascent parliamentary party.

A male friend and fellow islander, Hayase (similarly disgusted with the status quo), will provide Eiko's practical entrée into these circles; yet when she eventually arrives at his Tokyo lodgings, she discovers that this dour young man's manner has changed towards her. The fact that she is a woman seems now to stir his resentment. He is cold and inhospitable, and tells her, in so many words that she is a burden to him. His manner profoundly shocks her, because her offer of service has been so innocent. Here, then, is the first of two major betrayals that will scar her soul and qualify – in fundamental ways – her commitment to politics.

Betrayer number two now arrives on the scene and seems at first to be a much more engaging figure. He is Kentaro Oe (played by Ichiro Sugai), a rising star in the political firmament who takes Eiko under his wing by offering her a job on the party newspaper. As politicians – or future politicians – go (it is obviously a murky world), he is clever and honest and attractive. One of his first actions after their acquaintance is to expose Hayase in front of his new friend as a paid-up government agent. And so it goes on: while others in his party succumb to bribery and defeatism in the face of mounting governmental pressure, Kentaro sticks to his ideals, even to the extent of suffering imprisonment (for four years) for the part he plays – an absolutely honourable part – in attempting to address the grievances of the poor silk farmers in Chichibu whose cause he has taken up and championed. Probity like this stands him in good stead to take up the leadership of the party on his eventual release from jail, and to steer it towards its most triumphant historical accomplishment: the introduction, in 1889, of a written constitution as a guarantee of parliamentary freedom.

This is the apogee too, therefore, of Eiko's happiness – or rather, it ought to be. Throughout Kentaro's trials she has stuck by his side, suffering imprisonment like him in the wake of the farmers' riots. Kentaro has long since declared his hand to her, and now, in their new-found freedom, the world sees them living together happily as man and wife. There is only one problem with the arrangement: almost as soon as they have installed themselves in the marital home, Kentaro secretly takes a mistress. It doesn't help that the woman he chooses is an acquaintance of Eiko's from Okayama whom she befriended years ago, and whom she has helped ever since the girl was first sold into servitude by her parents.

This second betrayal by a man she thought she loved (it is shot by Mizoguchi in a way that is visually reminiscent of Hayase's exposure as a spy in the newspaper office) is a decisive moment in her coming to consciousness. She realises with the force of revelation that political reform is a secondary or even irrelevant cause, compared to the much greater need for reform in the way that men and women customarily treat each other. Until *that* is put right, no amount of parliamentary freedoms or extensions of the franchise will make much difference, for the higher and more fundamental ideal is social and moral. And thus, at the very moment of the Jiyu-to Party's triumph (Kentaro has never been more popular), she pens her lover a dignified letter of farewell that spells out her new position explicitly: 'While man does not recognise woman as another human being, and continues to consider woman as a mere tool of the family, there's no freedom, no true human rights. These are my parting words to you.' And back she goes to Okayama, to found a school where these radical ideas of hers will be put into practice.

Is this, then, the film's parting 'message'? Are these Mizoguchi's private feelings on the matter, brought forward, as it were, from the obscurity of the Meiji era into the light of the post-war epoch, where they may still be as relevant as ever? Everything we know about Mizoguchi's personal convictions gives one reason to think so, but of course there is still the question of *how* the message is put across, and whether its explicitness (on the level of social propaganda) interferes with – or even overrides – the movie's efficacy as a work of art.

Before we attend to this question, we need to look a bit more closely at the film's other main plot strand which involves, precisely, the long-standing relationship between Eiko and her husband's mistress, the servant girl Chiyo (played beautifully by Mitsuko Mito). The acquaintance between the two women started in Okayama at the time of Mrs Kishida's epoch-making visit.

While crowds mingle on the foreshore, Eiko spots the girl weeping and on further enquiry finds out the reason for her unhappiness: Chiyo has just been sold (for thirty yen) into the hands of a rough-looking fellow who will take her away with him to Tokyo. Eiko's remonstrations with her parents (her own parents, not Chiyo's) fail to elicit any sympathy: 'If she doesn't go, the family starves,' says her father, brutally. And that is the end of the matter. Yet when Eiko visits Chichibu province along with Kentaro to address the grievances of the silk farmers, it turns out that one of the exploited mill-workers is this same old acquaintance of hers, freshly arrived in the region after who knows what perils and misadventures.

The scenes that follow their re-acquaintance form the movie's central block of action. They are incredibly exciting, full of waving banners and massed crowd movements. The mill-workers are held in virtual imprisonment, and with her own eyes Eiko witnesses Chiyo, along with a number of other women, being beaten and raped by men in the pay of the mill-owners. This interior sequence is one of appalling violence – one of the most violent, perhaps, in the whole of Mizoguchi's cinema. (The women are wrapped in carpets and strappadoed relentlessly with long wooden poles.) Eiko witnesses, too, Chiyo's response to her violation, which is to grab a lantern that has been left within her reach, and in smashing it, set fire to the building. In the ensuing chaos both Eiko and Chiyo are arrested. By refusing an offer of government clemency (relayed through the hand of the renegade Hayase), Eiko finds herself sharing a jail sentence in the same prison as the recaptured and not-yet-chastened Chiyo.

The relationship between the two women, which up till now has been casual and adventitious, becomes at this stage of the film closer and more intimate. In the jail, Chiyo finds herself once more tormented by the predatory attentions of her captors. Eiko is witness to an episode in which Chiyo offers her body to one of the warders in exchange for the promise of freedom, only to find herself tricked and soundly thrashed for her pains. In the prison hospital we learn that the baby Chiyo has been carrying has died from the force of the assault, and although the baby's father – the same ruffian who had purchased her from her parents – has abandoned her, she still loves him. Now, however, what she most wants to do is die. Eiko takes her in her arms and profoundly embraces her, establishing an unbreakable bond between the two women, so that when they are released from jail it is natural for Eiko to take Chiyo into her service – unwittingly setting up the opportunity for seduction of which her husband will unscrupulously avail himself.

In providing these two intertwined plot strands, it is easy to see that the film offers a dual indictment of the historical condition of women in Japanese society. On the one hand, there are what might be called the 'middle-class indignities' suffered by Eiko and women of her background: the fact (for example) that a woman's public engagement in politics can never be on equal terms with a man's. Then there is the injustice suffered in her private life that Eiko, and thousands like her, must put up with a husband's philandering and the grotesque double standards that go with this. (Almost as shocking as the fact that Kentaro has seduced Chiyo is the crude manner in which he refers to her in Eiko's presence: 'She's just a vile woman, a mistress,' he says to her, appearing to believe that such an open display of contempt aids his cause. But in any case, he is secretly unrepentant: 'What's wrong with having two women?' he has asked, moments prior to this. And Kentaro is not even a villain!)

On the other hand, there is the trajectory of 'women of the people' like Chiyo, who are (or were) sold into slavery in their thousands, and thereafter routinely brutalised. Mizoguchi's indignation has not lost its power or its relevance (prostitution and trafficking are probably as rife in our own time, at the beginning of the twenty-first century, as they have been at any time in history). This dual focus of the film makes it one of the most obviously 'feminist' documents in the Mizoguchi canon: feminist before feminism, so to speak. No other movies like this, I think it is true to say, were being contemplated or made at the time anywhere else in the world. Mizoguchi's directness, sincerity and crusading spirit cannot be doubted. Yet what about the artistry? Are artistry and earnestness compatible? *My Love Has Been Burning* seems to have a wonderful stylistic confidence, an organic unity hard to describe (though easy enough to feel). It is partly a matter of timing, and of Mizoguchi's giving the right weight and depth to particular key moments in the drama. As always, his technique of preference is the extended take or *plan séquence*, used here with particular deftness in a series of marvellous interview scenes at the core of the movie: Hayase at the prison offering Eiko a 'way out' if she will only listen to him; or the beautiful passages of dialogue between Eiko and Chiyo in the prison hospital after Chiyo has lost her baby (ending with Eiko, overcome with compassion, gathering the younger woman into her arms); or the scene in the newspaper office when Chiyo's original lover bursts in to tell the assembled journalists that 'his' woman is now living with Kentaro (Eiko observes this scene calmly, herself unobserved on the sidelines). Episodes like these – taking up to four minutes of screen time without a single camera cut – have an extraordinary intensity. Their intrinsic emotion communicates itself, without any false rhetoric or melodrama. Mizoguchi's camera can be so extraordinarily 'cool' and reticent at times! Take, for example, the justly famous sequence where the renegade Hayase comes to visit Eiko in her lodgings in order to ask her to marry him. He is drunk; but even if he wasn't, any feelings of respect she may once have entertained for the man have long since vanished in the wake of the revelation that he is nothing but a wretched government spy. Eiko greets him politely, however, and asks him to be seated. In the course of putting his case to her, he makes a sudden, lustful lunge towards her body. The camera, which up until now has been motionlessly fixed on the pair, at this point very, very slightly tilts downwards in order to 'catch' the couple in the viewfinder as they fall entwined on the floor. That is the only movement Mizoguchi allows it, however! As the skirmish moves off screen, to the left, the camera remains where it is, rooted to the spot, trained on the empty space of the tatami mat, onto which, moments later, a crashing screen hurtles, brought down by the writhings of the unseen combatants. Several seconds of empty screen time now pass before a flustered Eiko emerges into view, walking diagonally across screen to the door on the far right hand of the picture where she pauses and, before exiting, turns to look back scornfully at the still-invisible Hayase. Again, the screen is empty for an extraordinary length of time, during which the audience is left on its own, as it were, to imagine the emotions which are running through the minds of each character. The whole compelling sequence is brought to an end when the drunken, defeated Hayase limps out of the depths of the hidden, off-screen space and wanly surveys the brutal consequences of his recklessness.

What has happened? Everything and nothing! As so often in Mizoguchi, it is as if the more charged and violent the action is, the more distant, discreet and 'invisible' is the camera recording it. This is the paradox buried at the heart of Mizoguchi's best cinema: that it is passionately committed and rigorously disengaged at one and the same time – simultaneously piti*less* and piti-*laden*, so to speak. The engagement is obvious to all, and present in this particular film's title (one of the most beautiful titles in Mizoguchi's oeuvre, I always think): *Waga Koi Wa Moenu*, literally 'My love burns', rendered in most English-language filmographies of the director by the perfect continuous tense: 'My love has been burning' – in any case: mine, and 'burning' and *still* burning! The passion is given upfront: it is hard to imagine a more direct and vividly poetic title. But it is interesting to ask what kind of love it is that Mizoguchi is talking about. Various interpretations seem possible. In the first instance, perhaps, it is the pure flame of sexual desire. Eiko loves her husband Kentaro, just as Chiyo is in love with *her* man (even if, as events turn out, both of them prove to be worthless). Sex is one of the most powerful governing forces in life. At the same time its dominance, in a way, is just what the movie is challenging right from its idealistic opening caption, which tells us that the film we are about to see is 'an appeal to the world for truly free women'. What can 'truly free' mean here *except* free from the dominion of men? Men (at least for the time being) can never be wholly out of the picture, or the species would come to a halt. The point is that men and women should be equal, and that from such equality springs happiness. So the 'burning love' of the title may be a burning love for mankind, for humanity. It is a sublimated, distilled and (in the highest sense of the word) unworldly passion. Hideko Kageyama's book of memoirs on which the movie was based is called *Half a Lifetime as a Mistress*, but there is surprisingly little trace of bitterness in Mizoguchi's film. (For example, it is not called, as it might have been, *My Anger Has Been Burning*.) If it *is* caustic in places, the irony involved is a cleansing one, for what the audience is finally left with is the calm serenity with which Eiko faces her fortune. She will return to the place of her birth, Okayama, and will set up a school specialising in girls' and women's education. In the second-class compartment on the ferry returning to the island, Chiyo catches up with her. With a gesture of forgiveness – that is at the same time a gesture of victory – the older woman welcomes the younger one under the shelter of her capacious white shawl. It is one of the loveliest and most satisfying closing images in the whole of Mizoguchi's cinema.

Aristocratic Interludes: A Picture of Madame Yuki, Miss Oyu and The Lady from Musashino

In the light of these twin masterpieces of the late 1940s, the three films mentioned at the beginning of this chapter must be considered, I suppose, minor work. Yet, though conceived on a smaller scale, they are far from being negligible. (Part of their interest lies exactly in how *unpolitical* they are: how distant from the fierce feminist questionings of *The Love of Sumako the Actress* and *My Love Has Been Burning*.) Chronologically, *A Picture of Madame Yuki* is the first, released in October 1950. Made for Shintoho Studios in Tokyo (the first time Mizoguchi had worked for this company) it is an adaptation of a serial of the same name by Seiichi Funabashi that had appeared shortly before in the magazine, *Shosetsu Shincho*. The film tells the story of a woman who, married to a scoundrel, finds suicide is the only way out. Madame Yuki (Michiyo Kogure) comes from an old noble household; her father, a viscount, has just died as the film gets under way, leaving her, once the debts have been settled, in possession of a mansion which she believes could be made to produce rental income if converted into an upper-class hotel. She is hopelessly impractical, however, as well as helpless in the face of her husband's machinations to take over the deeds of the establishment and install there his mistress, Ayako (Yuriko Hamada). In her loneliness, she falls back on the companionship of a koto-playing professor, Masaya, civilised and refined, who in his own quiet way returns her feelings. The question on which her destiny hinges – the 'suspense' of the film in so far as it has any – follows from the existence of this triangle. Why does she not leave her horrible husband, and marry, or move in with, the professor?

The professor's psychology is not examined in any great detail: as played by Ken Uehara, he is a fairly shadowy figure, and it crosses one's mind (whether or not it's supposed to) that, for all his refinement and gallantry, he may in fact be homosexual. On the other side of the equation, occupying centre stage in the drama, are the complicated feelings that Madame Yuki harbours for the husband, Naoyuki (Eijaro Yanagi). Fat, vulgar and cruel, he is as repulsive a figure as any in Mizoguchi's rather large category of unattractive lead male characters. Yet, in some strange way, Yuki is in thrall to him.

Of course it is a fact of life that women do fall for unsuitable men (and vice versa). The waywardness of the human heart is notorious. So, on a certain basic level, there is little problem with psychological plausibility. The husband is a sort of cuckoo in the nest: the adopted son of Yuki's parents whom Yuki has been more or less forced to marry. Plainly he repulses her; yet his repulsiveness has a sort of mastery about it. Possessed, herself, of a powerful, if underground, sex drive, she comes to believe, on the social level, that this impulsion is at the same time destroying her. Each time she gives in to her husband's importunate demands, it confirms – to her – the impotence of her own will and the nullity of her personality. Yet in the bedroom, the expressiveness of sex takes over: not for nothing her husband calls her a 'she-demon'. Yuki, in other words, denies the most forceful thing about her – which gets transformed, in the privacy of her soul, into an unbecoming badge of guilt and shame.

If the social milieu of *A Picture of Madame Yuki* is nothing if not decorous, the subtext, then, is clearly erotic. Civility is being sketched in this film – but also licence. We sense this above all in the principals' freedom of gesture, a sort of drunken liberty of movement – a typically Mizoguchian freedom of falling, touching, caressing, forcibly glimpsed in the scene, for example, when the husband's mistress, Ayako, embraces Yuki in front of him with all the ardour of a lover (it doesn't matter that she is mocking Yuki in doing this). And the erotic element in the scenario is given extra edge and emphasis by the way that Mizoguchi and Yoda contrive to frame the story. For the comings and goings of the triangle of main characters are observed right from the beginning of the tale through the eyes of two outsiders: an innocent country maid, Hamako (Yoshiko Kuga), and an inquisitive male house servant named Seitaro.

Now in Hamako's case (if not in Seitaro's) the watchfulness seems to stem from a sense of moral concern and love for her mistress, and has no explicit element of keyhole-snooping. Still, the care she affords her, while not exactly sinister, becomes voyeuristic in its subliminal effect on the audience. When Yuki gives in to her lust for her husband, it is *Hamako*'s gaze that follows, in horror, the abandoned litter of her mistress's clothing from the threshold of the bedroom to the bed itself, pausing on the way to notice a silken girdle with its cameo of a miniature Noh mask. Voyeuristic or not, such scenes – and there are many of them – imbue the film with a strange element of formal complexity. For, to watch somebody else watching, is to implicate one's *own* watching in that 'economy of the gaze' which is cinema's metaphysical fascination (and which finds its most fully worked-out dialectic in the masterly ambiguities of Hitchcock).

Equally distinctive in this film is the beauty of its visual compositions. These can be sensed even on the disappointingly faded print that is currently all we have to go by. In the interior scenes, the viewer is again and again struck by the wonderfully crowded casualness that is Mizoguchi's inimitable trademark – the 'Bazinian' sense of depth, complexity and bustle which trumps anything so crude or obvious as 'the directing of extras in a scene', since it seems rather to belong to some documentary disposition of life itself, undirected, in free flow, spontaneous. Counterpointing these interior sequences are the film's silent exteriors, where we observe Yuki walking alone and thoughtful in the pleasure grounds by the mist-haunted lake. Japanese, of course, in refinement and imagery (reeds, pine, gradations of grey and silver water), the grave spiritual beauty of these sequences is the single most memorable thing about this film. Unforgettable in this context (since it is one of the most striking examples of *plan séquence* in the whole of Mizoguchi's work) is the tragic conclusion of Yuki's dilemma: the tracking shot in the last reel, in which, from a great panoramic distance, Yuki is seen walking up through a park to the deserted restaurant where she seats herself alone on the verandah and orders tea. Now the camera – all in the same uninterrupted shot – follows the waiter as he walks into the establishment and re-emerges only to discover (as *we* discover) that Yuki has vanished from the scene – and from existence. The gravity of what's happened is instantly clear to us, though the film-maker does not allow us to witness the woman's actual suicide.

Yuki's off-screen death is sensed to be a delivery and a transcendence, but it leaves us asking: How to interpret it? Is her suicide a noble action, or a cowardly one? To the maid, Hamako, who finds the trail of her mistress's clothing, this time leading down to the reed-bordered lake where she has drowned herself, the act is a straightforward betrayal. 'Without faith! – Ah, Madame!' she cries in despair to the empty surroundings. And since these are in effect the final spoken words of the film, one might be tempted to take them to express Mizoguchi's considered position. Such, at any event, is the view of Joan Mellen in her influential pioneer study of Japanese cinema, *The Waves at Genji's Door*, where she writes about the ending of this movie: 'The maid speaks for the angry Mizoguchi, as if he had been finally betrayed by a character so unworthy of his passionate anger over the oppression of Japanese women.' And she adds (looking forward a couple of years): 'The heroine of *The Life of Oharu* will not so disappoint him.'[3] I'm attracted in a way by Mellen's stout criticism, yet it is also unkind to what is beautiful and pitiable about Madame Yuki. Everything, I think, depends on the intensity of the realisation, and Mizoguchi does not let us down here. The scene I have been decribing (the maid following the trail of apparel to the waterside) matches and rhymes with the earlier scene, already mentioned, where Hamako, on the threshold of her mistress's bedroom, spies the line of Yuki's clothes abandoned on the floor, and comes to the conclusion that the poor woman has 'fallen' again. There, the casually dropped garments signalled captivity: their imagery denoted Yuki's sexual thraldom. Here, by contrast, in this final outdoor scene, sex is thrown off, or exchanged, for the merciful embraces of nature. Like many modern critics, Mellen seems to me over-political in her interpretation: there is peace, happiness, release in the scene. The ambiguity of Yuki's act is dramatised by the close-up, in both sequences, of the Noh medallion in the centre of her girdle; impassive as masks are, and enclosing Yuki's destiny in a finally impenetrable enigma.[4]

Oyu-san

The quality that is most striking about *A Picture of Madame Yuki* – psychological verisimilitude embedded in a delicately drawn sexual subtext – is less to the fore in the second film from the 'trilogy', *Miss Oyu*, released eight months after *A Picture of Madame Yuki*, in the middle of 1951. And this failure of psychological realism is all the odder, it might be thought, in view of the provenance of the story, for the movie is an adaptation of a novel by the author of *The Makioka Sisters*,

---

3   Joan Mellen, *The Waves at Genji's Door: Japan through Its Cinema* (1976), p. 259.

4   Fumiko Enchi's beautiful novel *Masks* (1959) is, among other things, an extended discussion of the continued relevance of Noh traditions in contemporary Japan. A long sequence near the beginning of the book (pp. 22 *seq*. in the pocket edition) recounts a visit made by the three main characters to an acquaintance of theirs in order to examine his collection of fine old theatrical masks. From this richly suggestive passage, three dominant characteristics of the mask emerge that are relevant to this movie:1 *Ambiguity*. The artistry of the mask-maker is to permit the same mask to be smiling at one moment, weeping the next. (Smiling and weeping are on the same continuum of human emotion.) 2 *Tranquility*. Mieko, the heroine's teacher and mentor, is said herself to resemble a mask: she possessed, that is to say,

   a deep sort of inner look. 'I think Japanese women long ago must have looked like that. And it seems to me that she must be one of the last women who lives that way – like the masks – with her deepest energies turned inward.'

(How beautifully this passage describes the poise and the gestures of actresses like Kogure and Tanaka.) 3 *Contact with the dead*. In a novel concerned with spiritual survival, this is not the least of the mask's 'magical' properties. 'Noh masks', says Enchi, 'have such symbolic properties that everyone sees in them the faces of their own dead.' In this way, the dead come alive to us.

Junichiro Tanizaki, a writer whom many regard as being the most subtle and surest master, in modern Japanese literature, of the interior life of complicated women.

The tale that the film is based upon is called *Ashikari/Harvest of Reeds* or *The Reed Cutter*) a longish short story (not quite a novella) written by Tanizaki in 1932. It is told through the eyes of a first-person narrator, a rich and unattached writer (maybe partly based on Tanizaki himself) who decides on a whim to make a visit to the old imperial pleasure haunts outside Kyoto. The moon is full and he has a bottle of wine in his pocket. Arriving at his destination, he falls into conversation with a male stranger who starts reminiscing about a fabulous beauty of his youth who lived in these parts, and whom he (the stranger) used to spy upon as she played the koto at a favourite bend on the river.

It turns out she was in fact his aunt, a rich widow named Oyu, who had a small child from a previous marriage. After her first husband's death, the stranger's father, a wealthy merchant, had become enamoured of her but the beautiful woman had spurned his advances. Instead, Oyu had offered him, in compensation as it were, the companionship of her unmarried, younger sister Oshizu, and the bargain had been accepted. It was a somewhat strange bargain, for Oshizu knew who it was that the stranger's father really loved. Oshizu's conditions for accepting the deal were these: first, that it should be a 'white' (i.e. non-sexually consummated) union, not a marriage; second, that they should all three continue to live together.

Time had moved on; the discreet ménage (scandalous to some, but well hidden generally) was a curiously happy one. Then Oyu's child from her first marriage died tragically, releasing her from any residual obligations. Now she could marry the merchant if she wished, but instead of accepting her admirer's renewed offer, she fell in with a libertine, who married her and left her, though once again well provided for. At the same time, the break-up of the triangle released the younger sister Oshizu from her self-imposed vow of chastity, and in due course she conceived a child by the merchant. That child, of course, grew up to be the stranger who is telling the tale to the narrator. Somehow, the ghost of Oyu, and the atmosphere she exhales of melancholy hedonism, still haunts the surroundings. In fact, aren't there ghosts everywhere? For when the narrator looks up from his musings, the stranger himself has vanished: perhaps he too was a spirit! Perhaps the whole encounter was a dream, fuelled by moonlight and alcohol.

Even with this short outline of the original tale's plot, the possibilities for complexity, reflection, and 'multilayeredness' that might have appealed to Mizoguchi can be glimpsed. Part of the tale's enchantment lies in the fact that the events depicted are far away, lost in the mists of time: cut off from the twentieth century, and preserved in a sort of mythical aristocratic amber. What needs explanation is that in preparing their adaptation of the tale, Mizoguchi and Yoda chose first of all to dispense with the story-within-a-story element that makes the tale so subtle. It was their right, of course (the initial step in any filmic adaptation is often simplification), but the danger was that in getting rid of the framing device (the 'relay of narration' whereby the story, as it is passed on from narrator to stranger, becomes progressively more mythical and fabulous), Mizoguchi and Yoda risked interfering with or even destroying the enchantment. For, with the loss of the enchantment comes the loss, too, of the residual psychological complications that gave the original story its odd, special interest.

This thinning out of psychology extends to the framing of all three figures in the triangle but, above all, the younger sister Oshizu (who in this sense shares 'equal billing' as heroine). In the film we find ourselves stranded on the puzzle of what her feelings are when she undertakes her bargain with Shinnosuke (the merchant suitor). It is clear enough that she loves her sister in some way; and that this is her way of continuing to be with her. Yet it is ambiguous whether she is someone who has not yet come into sexuality, an innocent virgin, so to speak; or whether she is someone who *does* entertain sexual desire, but has chosen to be noble and sacrifice herself. For the film to make sense, I think we have to know – otherwise the intrigue is mere formalism. The book is much deeper and more intelligent, for Tanizaki's writing makes clear (in his fascinatingly perverse way) that Oshizu is not only Oyu's sister but her *maidservant*. More than this: that the content of the love she bears her has an intriguingly unspoken lesbian element.

It may seem unfair practice to compare the film to the literary original in this way. What makes the failure of *Miss Oyu* piquant is that Tanizaki is in many ways so close to Mizoguchi: he was one of the director's favourite authors. The two men are alike in their connoisseurship, their fascination with somewhat sophisticated and decadent sexual relationships; also in their shared knowledge of and love for Japan's traditions (traditions which include, of course, a taste for the 'bizarre' and the erotic). Here some external constraint seems to have intervened to tone down the original, and to leave the resulting adaptation with an uncharacteristic coldness or blandness. Even before shooting ended, it is said, Mizoguchi felt the project was slipping away from him. His comments on his films sometimes seem excessively harsh, but here, for once, I am forced to agree with him. 'We weren't able to finish this one without running into a lot of difficulties,' he said (in an interview recorded in 1956). 'I might have been too conscious of the fads and fashions of the time. I didn't do well.'[5]

Mizoguchi and Ooka

In fact Mizoguchi was no less dissatisfied with the final film in our trilogy, *Musashino Fujin/The Lady from Musashino* (released September 1951). He felt that its 'multiplicity of plot strands' didn't 'hang together', and that it therefore lacked one of the requisites of good art, 'formal unity'. Modern independent criticism has not been much kinder: the Andrew brothers for example dismiss the movie as 'insignificant'.[6] I find this a puzzling verdict, for *The Lady from Musashino* has a number of obvious qualities, both aesthetic and sociological. As a snapshot of important strata

---

5   Why wasn't Mizoguchi more engaged by this tale? Donald Keene, in his magisterial four-volume history of Japanese literature (1998), points out that the original novella by Tanizaki is a ghost story linked to the subdivision of Noh drama known as *mugen*. 'In such a play, the ghost appears before the *waki*, relates his life story, then disappears.' Keene's speculation is intriguing and, in view of Mizoguchi's attested interest in these things, leaves one more puzzled as to why the 'Noh content' wasn't brought out in the adaptation. Yoda, in his memoirs, says the pair of them *wanted* to do so but were prevented:

> The construction of the tale included three movements – three returns to the past – which it was necessary to conserve if the film was to keep the dreamlike quality of the original. I therefore insisted on this narrative aspect in order that the film's 'search for lost time' should provide our adaptation with depth and mystery. Alas, my suggested flashbacks were pitilessly refused by Matsutaro Kawaguchi, the director of Daiei's Kyoto studios. He feared they would lead to commercial failure. I still bitterly regret his decision.

  (*Souvenirs de Kenji Mizoguchi*, 1997, p. 98. Author's translation.)

6   D. and P. Andrew (1981), p. 19.

of Japanese society taken at a key moment of its immediate post-war history, the film has, at the very least, a powerful documentary interest. One could go further: the multiplicity of plot strands that Mizoguchi is wary of, in my view, hang together psychologically, giving the film a novelistic 'thickness' – an amplitude, a breadth of canvas – that exceeds that of the two previous films we have been looking at.

The film is adapted from a novel by the distinguished critic and translator of Stendhal, Shohei Ooka (1909–1988) whose most famous work of fiction, *Nobi/Fires on the Plain,* came out the same year that the movie version of *The Lady from Musashino* was released. The milieu is immediate post-war society. Two families live next door to each other on the fertile Musashino plain outside Tokyo. Their background seems to be prosperous. One family has made its living from munitions supply during the war; the head of that household, Eiji (So Yamamura), an entrepreneur, married and with a pre-adolescent daughter, is now in the process of converting his factory to the production of saleable domestic products. The relative prosperity of the house next door comes from more traditional sources: Eiji's cousin, Michiko (Kinuyo Tanaka), the 'lady' of the film's title, is descended from samurai stock and stands to inherit the elegant property from her elderly parents. Her husband Akiyama (Masayuki Mori) comes from a peasant background, though he is now a professor of literature, an expert on Stendhal (as Ooka himself was), whom he teaches to a young, Western-oriented generation of students, glimpsed in the cafés and lecture halls of post-war Tokyo. Onto the fringes of this group, the handsome Tsutomu (Akihiko Katayama), cousin of Michiko, in due course attaches himself. He has returned, disillusioned, from a prisoner-of-war camp and is looking for anchorage. What are his chances in the current situation? What profession should he follow? How should he make sense of the disorientation he feels in the wake of Japan's shameful defeat?

Michiko and Tsutomu are at the centre of the tale. But, in contrast to the two preceding films of the trilogy, the supporting characters in the drama – the professorial husband Akiyama, Eiji's sophisticated and unhappy wife Tomiko (Yukiko Todoroki), the students in Tokyo, even the sweet daughter Yukiko (Minako Nakamura) – all have strong parts to play. They each, as it were, possess their own personal story, circling round and tangentially colliding with the main events of the tale (Mizoguchi's 'multiplicity of plot strands'). The flavour of the film (and the clue to its bitter, almost decadent social unease) is established by the frequent references to Stendhal and to French culture generally, conceived of from a critical, even hostile perspective. In the cafés and lecture halls of post-war Tokyo there is a sense of second-hand or imported existentialism, awkwardly grafted onto the Japanese moral consciousness. In the context of the film, the great nineteenth-century French novelist stands for modern morals, a new or free way with love that proudly contrasts itself with pre-war customs and hierarchies. Yet as the movie progresses, the putting-into-practice of this new morality is judged to be profoundly inauthentic. The characters espousing Stendhalian freedoms (above all the professor and his waiting-to-be-seduced pretty, female students) are pictured, somehow, as forlorn, lost, thrashing around in the void, victims of illusory sophistications. Standing back from the mêlée is the calm and dignified figure of Michiko who, in outlook and morality, embodies, precisely, traditional Japanese reticence and modesty. Thus, the core of the drama revolves around the question of how she *herself* should act when she finds herself falling in love with her fierce youthful cousin Tsutomu, in essence a natural ally and conservative fellow critic.

The moral dilemma is confronted when Tsutomu and Michiko are forced to share a hotel room in the countryside on a storm-ridden evening. Obviously it is a question of now or never – for both of them. There is a dramatic and violent altercation between the pair. In the event, Michiko refuses the younger man, wanting their relationship to remain platonic. The whole incident is dramatised with extraordinary psychological forcefulness. On the surface there is every reason for Michiko to have welcomed this unlooked for opportunity to console herself with the handsome younger man. Her husband has behaved abominably – and paying him back in kind would be no more than long-delayed natural justice. But the fact that he *has* behaved badly is merely the reason, in her opinion, for them to foreswear this consolation. 'Akiyama is a loose man . . . you think we should be loose too? The looser he is, the more we must behave!' she pleads with her ardently importunate lover. He, in reply, offers to grant her 'freedom' from the shackles of an unhappy marriage, but she is adamant in her defence of morality. 'God or freedom? Who decided that people are free?' she hurls at him. Yet in the very act of breathing 'never', she is leaving an option open to the future. She calls this mystical bond their 'promise'. The opaque, symbolic dialogues at this point need to be reproduced verbatim.

MICHIKO: 'Real strength is moral strength. Understand? I love you; but I must do what I think right.'
TSUTOMU: 'You love only yourself!'
MICHIKO: 'That's not true.'
TSUTOMU: 'Then why talk of morals now? It's cowardice.'
MICHIKO: 'There's something higher than morals – a promise. Believe me and promise!'

And the scene ends with her flinging herself forward onto his prone body with a passionately repeated imprecation: 'Promise me! promise me! promise me!'

What, we wonder, can be meant by a promise that is 'higher than morals'? At its most basic level the appeal is surely the traditional one of many women in such circumstances: 'Promise me you'll go on loving me even if we don't consummate the bond between us sexually'; though it could also have the lesser meaning: 'Promise you'll wait – wait until my husband dies!'; or else even 'Wait until the rules of society change' (though in her heart, perhaps, she believes they never will). The power of the scene arises from the inherent contradictoriness of the emotions that have been let loose, the head saying one thing, the body – recalcitrant – demanding another. Denying her lover, she flings herself upon him. For all her 'certainty', she is tormented, guilty, riven by a kind of interior moral panic. Even as she makes the splendidly brave plea to him just quoted she wonders, perhaps, whether her words denote wisdom; or whether they are not, after all, indication merely of her fear of life, fear of her husband, fear of losing face. All this is both known to her (this is what is so subtle about the scene) and *not* known at one and the same moment. Like Madame Yuki's in the earlier film, her sexuality exists as a real force (without it, there would be no interest, no conflict) but in an underground cavern of her consciousness, powerless in the circumstances in which she finds herself to flow into its proper meaning and expressiveness. So, since she is a woman of extreme moral scruples, the dilemma is impossible to resolve, and leads in due course to her suicide.

The Lady from Musashino is not exactly a flawless movie. Its rhythms, particularly at the beginning of the film, are at times awkward and disjointed (Michiko's aged parents, in the prologue, are bundled off screen without ceremony – we feel we need to know more about how their deaths 'hit' Michiko than the movie allows). Yet once the film gets into its stride, it reveals itself as an authentically rich and powerful work: serious and unrhetorical in its depiction of post-war anomie. The relevant European comparisons seem to be with mid-period Rossellini (*Europa 51* [1952], *Paura* [1954]) or with early period Antonioni (*Cronaca di un amore* [1950], *Le Amiche* [1955]). This, too, is a lyrical film, its lyricism evident, for example, in the sweeping camera shots that accompany Michiko and Tsutomu on their walks together in the countryside, through the watery meadows of Musashino. For all the film's focus on city ills, 'nature' plays a prominent, palliative role in the drama, as it does in the other films under discussion (pre-eminently, as I have suggested, in *A Picture of Madame Yuki*). These two films indeed have several resemblances: their heroines, from similar backgrounds, are caught in similar dilemmas (how to deal with wretched husbands seeking to cheat them of their inheritance) solved, in each case, with a similarly drastic finality and pathos. For some reason, an orthodoxy has grown up that Mizoguchi was ill at ease in delineating the psychology of upper-class characters – as if, not coming from that milieu himself, he knew nothing of its pleasures and its sadnesses. Yet the two films in question (and *Miss Oyu* also) go some way, it seems to me, in proving the contrary. A true artist, we might anyway reflect, is devoid of prejudice in class matters. So, in their way, these proud, timid aristocrats we have been talking about come across in the end as authentically 'Mizoguchian': no less so than the feisty, down-to-earth heroines such as Sumako and Eiko whom, elsewhere, he imagines so brilliantly.

8 | Alive or Dead?

Gesture in Japanese Movies

The style of acting in Japanese films is surely one of the strangest in the world. Men and women seem to hurl themselves to the ground at the least provocation, overcome with floods of emotion. These bowings and prostrations carry with them a repertoire of noises from the back of the throat – keenings, groans, strangulated expressions of anguish and solicitation – that is far in excess of any equivalent gestural system in Western acting, whether in the theatre or, as we would like to think of it, in the more naturalistic medium of film. This exaggerated language of the body is particularly visible in period films, but it affects modern-day drama too, making the experience of watching Japanese films difficult at times for the Western viewer – even, for some people, penitential. In period films, the problem has partly to do with the costumes the actors and actresses are encased in, the actresses in particular. The tubular kimono secured at the back by those mounds of intricately wound cloth that make up the obi (or 'bustle') is an incredibly beautiful garment, its invention one of the triumphs of Japanese artistic genius. But the finished result is also, to the foreign onlooker, curiously de-sexing. For one thing: there are no curves visible through its integument: or else the curves are the wrong curves (the obi – a curve of sorts – might be better termed a hump, or inorganic excrescence). It is difficult to walk naturally in such a costume because, in contrast to the Indian sari (for instance), it so constricts the wearer's freedom. The tightness at the knees of the body-length material, coupled to the lack of support at the ankle produced by the strapless sandal or clog, gives rise to the strange, bowing-forwards, shuffling mode of locomotion that can make Japanese actresses in films seem, at times, like creatures from another planet. The 'ordinary Western viewer' who has not visited Japan finds himself in the position of not quite knowing how stylised such a gait is: do all Japanese people walk like this? Or is it merely a filmic/theatrical convention? Such questions lead naturally into the wider and frankly more portentous question of how alive or dead – how genuinely graspable by a Western audience – such movies are. Can they come to dwell in our hearts, as art ought to do? Or is our interest in them always condemned to be *essentially* scholarly and archeological?

Take the example of *chambara*, or sword-action dramas. During the 1920s in Japan, such films were enormously popular. Tadao Sato, in his informative 1988 documentary about the great *chambara* actor Tsumasaburo Bando, tells us that in 1924 no fewer than 850 such *jidai-geki* films were released. In subsequent years, up to the 1960s, this figure settled down to something between 200 and 500, but by any calculation, this is still an astonishing total. What kind of films exactly were

The actors Eizaburo Onoe VI and Kikugoro Onoe VI in the dance drama *Suo Otoshi*, staged at the Kabukiza Theatre in Ginza (Tokyo), May 1903: woodprint by Kochoro Hosai

they? During the silent epoch, such a movie would typically recount the adventures and misadventures of a samurai who had been forced into outlawry by an act of high-handedness committed by some feudal superior. In hiding or disguise he shows himself a friend to the poor (a veritable Eastern Robin Hood) through many light-fingered acts of charity. The climax of the film invariably involves an elaborately staged setpiece battle scene in which our hero – tracked down at last to his lair – takes on literally hundreds of heavily armed opponents, slaughtering all of them, or nearly all of them, before himself being struck down in a martyr's glory, victim of the overwhelming odds against him. I have not seen all that many of these films from the 1920s, but in the few I have the climaxes to the action seem to be carried out at almost superhuman speed: bands of attackers and retainers (often filmed from above in elaborate set patterns) dart backwards and forwards across the screen like swarms of angry wasps. To the modern viewer, it is too mechanical for there to be much feeling or empathy – let alone pathos – attached to these multiple sorties. And yet, so Sato tells us, audiences of the time were both enthralled and devastated. It was common for them to sit in the stalls with tears literally coursing down their cheeks. There was nothing stylised or abstract, for them, in the grimace of pain that signified, in close-up, the hero's prolonged agonised death rictus; it brought out all their deepest feelings about the beauty and unfairness of life. And yet for the modern viewer eighty years on – including, possibly, young Japanese viewers – there is something absurd, exaggerated and maybe even unintentionally comic in the way such death scenes are imagined. Numerous mutations had to take place – numerous developments in both the artistry and technology of the genre had to be negotiated in slow and untraceable ways – before *chambara* turned into what a present-day audience would recognise as a 'living thing'.

The key figure here, I suppose, is Kurosawa, who after the war, succeeded in re-inventing the mechanics of the genre in masterpieces such as *The Seven Samurai* (1954) and *Throne of Blood* (1957). We don't here have the space to go into precise detail concerning what it was that suddenly, and at the same time decisively, gave the genre such renewed depth and verisimilitude – a combination of factors, most likely, among which attention to the soundtrack (the whinnying of horses, the squelching of footfall in mud and rain, the whirring of arrows and the dull thud as they hit home) was evidently among the most important. Neither of the great films just cited, as a matter of fact, is pure *chambara* (any more than *Rashomon* is); yet the innovations in shooting and editing that Kurosawa was responsible for seem to have fed imperturbably into the mainstream popular samurai films that continued to be produced by the industry in large numbers during the 1950s and 60s, transforming these works in due course into some of the most physically refined and exciting action films ever made.[1]

---

1   To gauge the importance for the industry of Kurosawa's innovations, compare two versions of the Musashi Miyamoto cycle, the earlier (pre-Kurosawa) version made for Toho in 1953, the later one for Toei in 1964. Hiroshi Inagaki and Tomu Uchida are the respective directors, both industry veterans. The sword fights in Inagaki's 1953 version (available on DVD in the Criterion collection) are fine as far as they go, whereas the corresponding set-pieces staged by Uchida have a virtuosity and skill that take the breath away. I am sure I am not the only viewer who feels that the moment of truth in *Duel at Ichijoji* – in which, in the heat of battle, Musashi transfixes the young prince to a pine tree (at the same time begging his forgiveness) – possesses an audacity and swiftness that take it (and us) into the sphere of the finest tragic art.

Like creatures from another planet . . . Toshiro Mifune and Kinuyo Tanaka in *The Life of Oharu* (1952)

Mizoguchi's Early Lost Films

It is evident that I believe Mizoguchi's great films – notwithstanding all the problems of interpretation outlined above – to be not only accessible to any sympathetic viewer in the West, but to be 'alive' in the more important sense: that is, able to move and affect us in the manner of great universal art. But is this true of *all* his films, including the very earliest? Or was there also a transformation in Mizoguchi's work, comparable to the transformation that Kurosawa brought to *chambara*? Where do we first find his genius? What percentage of his work remains alive to us?

The passing of the decades performs its own silent winnowing. Compared to the West, the survival rate of Japanese films is exceptionally low: only one hundred Japanese films made before 1930 still exist, and only eleven before 1923.[2] Of the sixty-three films Mizoguchi directed before Japan entered World War II, fifty-two have disappeared from the archives. Among these, how many (if any) are lost masterpieces we can never know. Some of these lost works are more famous than others: we know they were spoken about admiringly by his contemporaries. After an industry apprenticeship lasting three years during which he directed approximately thirty films (all missing except for one, of which more later), Mizoguchi felt that he came into his own with *A Paper Doll's Whisper of Spring/Kaminingyo Haru No Sasayaki*, released in 1926, and starring Yoko Umemura and Tokihiko Okada: a melodrama which, plotwise, seems frustratingly little different from countless other movies produced at the time. Yet Mizoguchi is adamant about its importance in his career. ('It was the first time I felt I had real collaborators,' he says.) A film made later in the same year called *The Passion of a Woman Teacher/Kyoren no Onna Shisho* was one of the first ever Japanese films sold abroad, so it must have had something to recommend it (apparently it made a lot of money for Nikkatsu). Two other films that we can read about from this time also seem tantalising: in both *Metropolitan Symphony/Tokai Kokyogaku* (1929) and *And Yet They Go/Shikamo Karera Wa Yuku* (1931), Mizoguchi deserted the safety of the studio and for the first time made use of genuine locations in the lower reaches of urban Tokyo. This was during the heyday of the so-called 'tendency film', a movement of committed political film-making that flourished briefly at the end of the 1920s before disappearing in the general lurch to the right (and the repression that followed from this) in the wake of the Manchurian Incident. Mizoguchi's political liberalism was, I think, inseparable from his make-up as an artist and visible at every stage of his career: it was never dependent on slogans or didacticism. If he was ever, even embryonically, a 'Marxist' it was because he was naturally drawn to subject matter (like prostitution and geishadom) where injustice and inequality prevailed – his contribution to politics being to look closely, and with compassionate realism, at these kinds of contemporary social deformity. Yoda speaks very highly of *And Yet They Go*, saying it was the first time Mizoguchi made systematic use of the one-scene-one-take method of storytelling, and indeed he dates his own conversion to cinema from seeing it.

Other lost films from the 1930s are similarly intriguing, though for opposite reasons. They hint at a different kind of politics. Thus *The Dawn of Manchuria and Mongolia/Manmo Kenkoku no Reimei* (1932), which starred the then-prominent actress Takako Irie (with whom Mizoguchi was soon to enter a stormy professional relationship), goes into the manoeuvrings for power that

---

2   See Bregtje Lameris, 'Writing the History of Lost Films', in *The Collegium Papers* (2001). The author reminds us that the Nikkatsu company, which Mizoguchi worked for in these years, suffered a double loss, first in 1923, in the great Kanto earthquake, and again during WWII when the studios were bombed by the Allies.

followed the collapse of the Chinese Manchu dynasty in the early years of the twentieth century. From the written description that survives of the film (generically, a melodrama), it is difficult to be sure exactly what 'line' was taken, but the time and the circumstances of the shooting (it was made on location at Mukden, where the Manchurian Incident was sparked off, at the personal request of an army general named Sugiyama) seem to make it unlikely that it dissented in overall sentiment from the prevailing nationalist spirit of the time. Who can tell, however, now that all the prints are lost?

Similar considerations apply to a couple of other films from the 1930s that have disappeared. *The Jinpu Group/Jinpuren* and *The Mountain Pass of Love and Hate/Aizo Toge*, dating from the same year 1934, both have a Meiji period background, as did many films made by Mizoguchi around this time. The first-named of these, adapted from a writer named Gisaburo Juichiya whom Mizoguchi admired, deals with events surrounding the rebellion of the forceful samurai personality Takamori Saigo in 1877; while the second, set in 1883, only a few years later, goes into the background of the Chichibu Incident, which Mizoguchi returned to in his post-war masterpiece, *My Love Has Been Burning* (see Chapter 7). Both are political films, therefore. But from what angle? And with what *conviction*, artistically speaking? Mizoguchi's childhood friend, Matsutaro Kawaguchi, wrote the script of *The Mountain Pass of Love and Hate* which, judging by its plot description, has more than a hint of Tolstoy's *Resurrection* about it. But that is all we can say here, although it is worth mentioning that a clear reason for regretting its extinction is that it is the movie in which Mizoguchi began his collaboration with the great actress, Isuzu Yamada.

The Earliest Extant Movies

Such films are 'dead' in the literal sense. How splendid it would be if some of them, in future years, turned up unexpectedly in the archives! – films not yet mentioned: early experiments like the evocatively named *Foggy Harbour/Kiri no Minato* (1923), which Mizoguchi speaks warmly of; or that pair of works from the early 1940s, *The Woman of Osaka/Naniwa Onna* and *The Life of an Actor/Geido Ichidai Otoko*, both of them set (like *The Story of Late Chrysanthemums/Zangiku Monogatari*) in the world of Meiji theatre? But the more pertinent question is surely: what about the films we *do* possess from this epoch? Are *they* alive to us today? The earliest extant Mizoguchi film dates from 1925. Its title is *The Song of Home/Furusato no Uta*, already the twenty-eighth film the director had signed his name to. (The majority of these films from the 1920s were what we would today call shorts: one- or two-reelers for the most part, conceived of and shot within the timespan of a week or so.) 1925 is also the date of *The Battleship Potemkin*: Mizoguchi and Eisenstein were exact contemporaries, born in the same year 1898. Putting the two films together like this is thus a way of saying that Mizoguchi's filmic genius took longer to develop than Eisenstein's did: unlike the great Russian, he did not arrive on the scene fully fledged. *The Song of Home* does not pretend to be more than it is: a simple tale of country life, neither more, nor less impressive than countless other films being made at the time. Its theme is the importance of the countryside (the movie was in fact sponsored by the Association of Japanese Rice Growers). A young man returns to his home town in the school holidays and meets up with a childhood friend who has not been blessed with the same chances that he has. The narrative goes on to describe a pull between town and country values, with something of an artless predilection towards the latter. But it is not exceptionally ideological: the feeling that emanates from the film is not that of an overt piece of propaganda. None of the characters is demonised, not even (from the point of view of the film's mild nationalism) the 'American professor' – played by a Japanese actor! – whose child is saved from drowning by the prompt action of the hero's uncorrupted young friend. Country values, as I say, are 'upheld'; but town values, equally, aren't anathematised. The fact that the film was made by Mizoguchi – and that it is the first of his works to survive – naturally means that it carries a certain resonance for people lucky enough to have the chance to see it. Yet, the more prosaic truth is that there is little or nothing in the film to suggest what was to come.

The Song of Home is extant, then; but in a way, only just. Like The Straits of Love and Hate, from 1937, it cannot be seen at present outside Japan. The 16mm print of the film that exists in the National Film Center is in fine condition and it would surely be a boon to scholars and collectors to issue a subtitled version of the film on DVD, as has recently happened with Mizoguchi's next surviving movie Tokyo March/Tokyo Koshinkyoku, made four years after The Song of Home, i.e. in 1929. The DVD, issued by a French publisher, has excellent visual quality; yet I am reticent about delivering a critical verdict on the film, because the movie as it stands turns out to be a much-edited version of the original full release print that no longer survives. None of the substantial scenes itemised by the Andrew brothers involving Takako Irie are included. Despite these excisions, the film that remains is readable in its own way, and even intriguing. The milieu is bourgeois Tokyo: two young executives (that is, wealthy young men who have office jobs) compete for the attention of a girl whom they have met while practising tennis. (A passerby not a competitor, she obligingly throws the ball back to them after it has been lobbed over the court's surrounding mesh fencing.) The girl turns out to be a geisha, albeit a reluctant one; she has entered the profession to support an ailing aunt and uncle. Her profession, too, is inherited: her mother was a geisha, and, by coincidence, the abandoned mistress of the father of one of the two young heroes – so that her daughter (the girl who throws the tennis ball) is the half-sister of the young man in question. The film explores the consequences of discovering that the person you are in love with is tragically out of bounds as a future marriage partner, through grounds both of class and consanguinity. Unfortunately for the artistry of the piece, however, the audience foresees the direction events are heading in rather more swiftly than the characters themselves do. This may, of course, be connected to the problem of incompleteness mentioned above. One fascinating thing about the fragment that survives is the plethora of unashamed close-ups in it. Though Mizoguchi may have been on the eve of discovering (or inventing, or appropriating) the famous one-scene-one-take shooting procedure, the editing and camera style, in *this* film, is 'classical' and conventional.

Experiments in Sound

It would not matter much, I suppose, if Tokyo March had not survived as a piece (however small) in the jigsaw puzzle, but this is not the case with Mizoguchi's next still-available film, Home Town/Furusato (1930), which is altogether more interesting and not just because it is his first full experiment with the newly available sound technology. The 'talkies' in Japan had a slightly different history than they did in the West. On the one hand, there had always been sound and dialogues, in the sense that the benshi tradition of accompanied recited commentary had 'taken' in Japan in a way that it never did anywhere else in the world. Introduced early (at the turn of the century), it continued to assert its rights through the 1920s in the face of criticism (from, among others, the youthful Mizoguchi) that its protocols were old-fashioned and inartistic. On the other hand, strange paradox, once the modernists finally succeeded in banishing the *benshi* from the scene, the technology of sound recording took far *longer* to introduce in Japan than it did almost anywhere else. Silent films were being produced with intertitles right up until 1934. (Remember: the world's first sound film, *The Jazz Singer*, came out in 1927.) From Mizoguchi's own filmography, we could cite *The Water Magician/Taki no Shiraito*, released in 1933 without sound; as was another already-mentioned lost film, *The Jinpu Group*, released in early 1934. (In passing, let me add that whatever the reasons for Japan's hesitation in introducing sound – whether the core determinants were cultural, economic or industrial, or some complicated combination of all three – it did manage to give the silent film there a last beautiful flowering.)[3] *Home Town*, to return to the movie we are considering, is interesting primarily because it shows Mizoguchi in unusually populist mood, though at the same time it allows us to see why popular comedy was not his forte. The movie has a very strong musical content, as many of the first experiments in sound did. (And this itself is interesting, in view of Mizoguchi's later distrust of the traditional film score; the effectiveness of mid-1930s masterpieces like *Osaka Elegy* and *Sisters of the Gion* surely has much to do with their rigorous musical asceticism. The previous year's *Tokyo March* had done well at the box office among other reasons because there was a song attached to it. Mizoguchi tells us that he personally distributed gramophone records of this song among the bars and nightclubs of Ginza.) *Home Town* is constructed around a song that went on to become a major national hit. The singer is Fujimura, played by Yoshie Fujiwara, a professional musician in real life – it is his voice we hear on the primitive but serviceable de Forest sound recording apparatus that Mizoguchi utilised, a demonstration of the mechanics of which, in the form of a short lecture to camera, opens the movie in a prologue. The song itself is a simple, sentimental ballad whose local patriotism and direct, unsophisticated emotion are contrasted, in the film's schema, to a sort of false high-art cosmopolitanism (symbolised on the one hand by Western opera, on the other by modern jazz) that temporarily seduces our hero from his path. The genre that the film belongs to is, literally, melodrama, and all the scenes dealing with Fujimura's redemption – through the love of his faithful girlfriend Ayako (Shizue Natsukawa) – are pitched in this conven-

---

3   J. Anderson and D. Richie (1982), p. 76, say that the reason that Japan took so long to switch to sound was because the Japanese film industry could not afford it. The addition of sound in these early years would have tripled a film's budget and – unlike in the United States and Europe – the profit margins of the industry were not geared at the time to accept this kind of burden. Be that as it may, I repeat my observation that the silent film flourished. In October 2001, the annual Giornate del Cinema Muto (Pordenone and Sacile Silent Film Festival) showcased a selection of late Japanese silent films. Among the many masterpieces on display a few may be singled out for particular praise: *Eikan Namida Ari/Tears behind Victory* (Shigeyoshi Suzuki), *Koshiben Ganbare/Flunky, Work Hard!* (Mikio Naruse – his first extant film), *Oatsurae Jirokichi Goshi/The Chivalrous Robber Jirokichi* (Daisuke Ito) (all three from 1931), along with *Kuma no Deru Kaikonchi/The Reclaimed Land Where Bears Live* (Shigeyoshi Suzuki, 1932), *Keisatsukan/Policeman* (Tomu Uchida, 1933) and *Muteki/Foghorn* (Minoru Murata, 1934). (For some reason, Ozu wasn't represented at Pordenone, so let me add his sublime underworld outing, *Hijosen no Onna/Dragnet Girl* (1933), undoubtedly one of the greatest films of the 1930s.) The movies are too various – both aesthetically and ideologically – to be separately analysed in a note such as this. What unites them is a complete mastery of the formal means at the different directors' disposal: editing, visual composition and storytelling are at the highest level. None of these films, in my judgment, suffers in the slightest way from the 'lack' of a soundtrack. All of them may be enjoyed fully by present-day audiences.

tional key. Yet there are comic elements (two fat funny fellows carry important roles in the subplot) and here it can be seen that Mizoguchi's 'touch' is fundamentally less sure in this genre than Ozu's and Naruse's. The lazy, casual charm of these contemporaries, or, say, Lubitsch or Clair (directors whom Mizoguchi admired extravagantly at that time) was simply not within his range, either at this stage of his career, or later on. If you look at a comparable Hollywood musical like *Love Me Tonight* (Rouben Mamoulian, 1932 – Mamoulian and Mizoguchi were exact contemporaries, both born in 1898) you can see that the American film is vastly technically superior. Yet what the film does have is a sort of sociological vibrancy: the soundtrack brings Tokyo to life. There is a fine sense of documentary immediacy. We get to see the interiors of grand hotels and sleazy lodging houses, of record shops and urban dance halls. Miss Omura, Fujimura's 'siren', is fond of sport, so there is a piquant golf scene. Elsewhere, the audience takes in how fashionable Tokyo people dressed, what kind of cars they drove, what kind of ocean liners they sailed on to Europe. Modernity, in short, is broached intriguingly throughout the film – as something to aspire to, as well as to be wary of. As in many films on the cusp of the silent era, sound is used here with an experimental confidence – a verve, a bravura – that was subsequently lost as sound movies 'naturalised' themselves by concentrating merely on registering dialogue clearly. Here the dialogues are sometimes given by intertitle, and sometimes by sound – this variety in fact being a major part of the film's appeal (Ayako, at one stage, goes to work at a printing press; there's an excellent scene where her conversation with the faithful go-between Sankichi – one of the above-mentioned fatties – is totally drowned out by the roar of the compositing machinery. In this scene, *only* intertitles will do). There is no need to push claims for this film further than they will go. 'Much pain, little result', was Mizoguchi's private succinct verdict. It is not a masterpiece: no one (as far as I know) has ever claimed otherwise. But it fits nonetheless into the same category as more famous city chronicles of the time such as Ruttmann's *Berlin – Symphony of a Great City*, or Dziga Vertov's *Man with a Movie Camera*, as an extraordinary sociological document of the times. The charm it communicates is genuine.

The Lure of the Meiji Epoch

There are five more extant films from the 1930s, of varied quality and importance, but linked by a shared subject matter or a shared historical focus: all of them are set in either the Meiji or the early Taisho period. In his memoirs, Yoda, who had writing credits on only one of these films (the last and greatest of them), gently criticises the antiquarianism that underlay this stage of the director's life, and from which the great modern-day features of the mid-1930s (*Osaka Elegy*, *Sisters of the Gion*, *The Straits of Love and Hate*) were to make such a decisive artistic break.

> During the early part of the decade Mizoguchi became consumed by a craze for antiques. He spent his time either putting up stone statues in his garden or collecting old tea services, or trawling the flea-markets in search of fine hand-made garments. Mrs Mizoguchi began to get impatient with these foibles! Scarcely 40 years old, the director seemed deliberately to be cultivating the air of some mandarin connoisseur.[4]

---

4   Yoshikata Yoda, *Souvenirs de Kenji Mizoguchi* (1997), p. 43 (Author's translation).

The films that came out of this interest – *The Water Magician* (1933), *The Downfall of Osen*, *Oyuki Madonna*, *Poppy* (all three from 1935) and *The Story of Late Chrysanthemums* (1939) – are adaptations of works by prominent authors or playwrights who flourished during the period of Mizoguchi's childhood. We should start with *Poppy*, the least interesting of this disparate grouping. Though the film apparently has its admirers (Alain Masson and Antonio Santos among them)[5] *Poppy*, to me, cannot really be described as a living work of art. Adapted from a novel by the most famous of all Meiji novelists, Soseki Natsume (1868–1911), it tells the story of an ambitious young man's betrayal both of his fiancée, and of the trust put in him by the girl's father, a retired schoolteacher who had taken him into his home as a boy. The failure of the film lies, I believe, in its inability to set up any striking or psychologically convincing affinity between the two leading characters (the actors are Ichiro Tsukida and Chiyoko Okura), an affinity, or a compulsion, that would enable the audience to feel that they were truly meant for each other. Isuzu Yamada was going to take the role of the betrayed fiancée, but she was pregnant at the time, and her substitute is unable, for all her efforts, to make the role come alive. One is left imagining what the film might have been like had Yamada been on hand to infuse it with her insolence and dynamism.

There is probably not much mileage any longer, either, to be got out of *Oyuki Madonna/Maria no Oyuki* (1935), an adaptation of Maupassant's 'Boule de suif' transposed into the milieu of the Saigo rebellion: in the chaos of the times, a carriage of mixed social types (among whom, two contrasted geisha/courtesans) flee to a port where they hope to be picked up by a rescue boat. (There are plot similarities with Ford's *Stagecoach*: – Dudley Nichols, who wrote Ford's scenario, and Ernest Haycox, whose short story 'Stage to Lordsburg' the famous Western is based upon, were also evidently fans of the late nineteenth-century French master.) Mizoguchi's first completely sound-dialogued film (*Home Town*, as I have said, is still about fifty per cent intertitled), *Oyuki* suffers from the fact that the single 16mm viewing print in existence is in exceptionally poor condition, almost unviewably dark in certain places, and correspondingly hard to listen to because of a perpetually interfering static on the soundtrack. I think we should pass on this movie, therefore, with the regret registered that Yamada (who *is* in this film as one of the courtesans) is unable, over this distance of time, to communicate with us.

The Downfall of Osen

Four months earlier (in January 1935), Mizoguchi had released another film with an experimental soundtrack, and though the experiment did not work at all levels (for reasons given later), I find the movie itself considerably more accessible than its successor to the sympathetic curiosity of the modern viewer. *The Downfall of Osen/Orizuru Osen* was Mizoguchi's third and final filmic encounter with the *shimpa* playwright and idol of his youth, Kyoka Izumi. (The previous two adaptations are *The Bridge of Nihon/Nihonbashi* (1929), no longer extant, and *The Water Magician* (1933) which we shall come to shortly. 'Accessibility', as always, has to be understood relatively: it is easy enough to enumerate the film's many awkwardnesses, starting with the soundtrack. The dialogue is given by intertitles, just as in silent films, while at the same time the lines are simultaneously read out on the soundtrack by an invisible off-screen narrator who 'covers' for all the voices (female as well as

---

5   Antonio Santos: 'Three Mizoguchi Films', in J. Quandt and G. O'Grady (eds) (1996), pp. 54–5. Alain Masson: 'L'intensité est silencieuse: sur trois films de Mizoguchi', *Positif* no. 396, February 1994, pp. 48–51.

male), much as the *benshi* did in days of old. Dramatically speaking, this hybrid is not very satisfying. Nor is the experiment improved by a rather vapid Western-style musical score, composed of snippets from the orchestral classics (waltzes, Irish airs, extracts from the Brandenburg Concertos) promiscuously mixed together with little or no regard to the dramatic action. The plot itself, based on the machinations of a gang of 'fences' specialising in the disposal of stolen religious artefacts, is difficult to follow, especially in the early parts of the film, where much overheated camerawork (frequent changes of locale signalled by disconcerting zip-pans) disorientates the viewer, preventing him or her from registering the characters as independent dramatic entities. Eventually we do get to know the two lead characters; but here we are met with yet another barrier, not so much technical as cultural, and arising out of the genre of *shimpa* itself: that is, the schematic and radically sentimental nature of the relationship depicted. Sokichi (Dajiru Natsukawa), the hero, a young man with ambitions to become a doctor, is taken up, in the traditional way, by an older fallen woman who offers him protection and an exit from the raffish, criminal underworld into which he has inadvertently fallen. Yet his ambition to become a doctor seems merely 'given': it is not marked by any impelling internal dynamism (as it is, for example, in Kurosawa's *Red Beard*) which could persuade you to become interested in his dilemmas. His main psychological trait is an overwhelming passivity – an anomie that comes across, gesturally, in the frozen immobility of his bodily posture: shoulders hunched, eyes averted, head bowed as if in shame. Rather a miserable specimen, the viewer concludes eventually – and hardly worth wasting pity on.

As *he* is conventionally imagined, so, correspondingly, is *she*. Osen, played by the charming Isuzu Yamada, is the mistress of Kumazawa (Shin Shibata), corrupt leader of the gang of art thieves, but though ensnared in his milieu by circumstance, she is spiritually independent and distanced from it. The film traces the steps by which she comes to take pity on the defenceless young man who has wandered like a lost puppy into this circle of cut-throats. The salvation she offers, in due course, is played out in terms of recognisable *shimpa* female masochism; she scrimps and saves like a good mother to put him through medical school, descending to minor theft when all other resources seem hopeless. Caught and imprisoned, she refuses to go back on her sacrifice, and even in her final bitter madness (graphically depicted, as the film's epilogue) maintains a dogged internal loyalty to the 'one ray of light' who has illuminated her earthly existence. (Men are reviled in her soliloquy, but not *this* man.)

I stress here the conventional aspects of the story and the barriers that have to be overcome in order to get anything out of it. In brief moments, however, the film does come to life, communicating in the process a strange beauty and forcefulness. I am thinking about a couple of crucial scenes in which, contrary to usual *shimpa* practice, Osen's personality becomes imbued by the actress with a strikingly contemporary power and sexuality. The film 'takes off' at these moments, the most important of which occurs about halfway through, when the ex-geisha is seen plotting to escape with Sokichi from the clutches of the art gang. The plan itself is obscure in its details (like so much else in this film) but it appears to involve, among other things, disguising Sokichi as a monk, which has necessitated his head being shaven (we don't in fact see the actual operation). The gang somehow get wind of the ruse, and gather to batter down the walls of the house in which the couple is hiding. Discovered at this crucial instant of her destiny, with the shorn Sokichi in her arms, Osen abandons her usual passive role and turns into a veritable tigress. Her face and

bodily gestures express defiance, not fear. In a marvellous gesture that dares the gang to take her alive, she flips the blade of the razor between her lips, and glares at them like an insolent pirate.

'Taki no Shiraito' and the Triumph of Shimpa

Can a single moment like this redeem a film? How *many* such moments are needed for the audience to feel that the film in question is a real work of art? There was a time in the history of academic film studies (not so long ago, in fact) when it might have seemed that a single flash of truth or of *jouis-sance* was all that it was possible to expect from *any* movie! Fortunately, the aesthetic and ideological puritanism revealed in these strictures no longer prevails. There is no need to make pointlessly elaborate arguments, one way or another, about a movie like *The Downfall of Osen*: it is what it is – a fascinating fragment. It might have stood as confirmation that the *shimpa* genre, in general, is not really conducive to the highest reaches of film art, if there was not a counter-example from within the exact same tradition to suggest a somewhat different conclusion. *The Water Magician* was released in silent format in June 1933, a full year and a half before *The Downfall of Osen*, and it shares a similar literary ancestry, in that it too is an adaptation of a novel-turned-into-a-play by the same iconic *shimpa* writer Kyoka Izumi. Once again, the story involves a 'fallen' woman (a performer this time rather than a prostitute) who takes an interest in a young man from another class, and decides to finance his studies so that he can practise a profession (lawyer, in this case, rather than doctor). The basic conventions, then, are exactly the same as in *The Downfall of Osen*, but *The Water Magician* is much more clearly an original and organic work of art. What is it that gives this film authority – indeed, that makes it a masterpiece (the earliest *obvious* masterpiece in the Mizoguchi canon)? As always in film criticism, a number of different aesthetic considerations might be cited, yet it seems to me that among the most important is the way that right from the beginning – and in contrast both to *Poppy* and to *The Downfall of Osen* – the film makes us believe that the characters are meant for each other. The sentimental evasiveness that mars the genre of *shimpa* in its theatrical incarnation is miraculously absent from this film, and the psychology of the tale becomes correspondingly forthright and convincing.

Part of the story's effectiveness in this regard lies in the fact that, contrary to the usual conventions, the heroine is the same age or even younger than the hero (he is twenty-five when they first meet, she twenty-four), so that the surrogate-maternal feelings which constitute *shimpa*'s emotional stock-in-trade are subtly held back (although they are certainly there, as we shall see). Here at any event, Taki (the wonderful Takako Irie) goes for the young man the moment she first sets eyes on him. Kin-san, the object of her desire (played by Tokihiko Okada), is a handsome fellow and the sort of man any woman might fall for. An initial encounter in a horse-drawn bus (Kin-san is the driver) sets the seal on their subsequent relationship: for when, urged beyond its proper speed by a group of impatient passengers, the contraption breaks down, the daring Taki joins Kin-san against his passengers by fleeing the scene with him on the back of his horse. Arriving at a nearby staging post they collapse in a complicitous heap. We can tell they are lovers, or shortly to become so, by the method Taki takes to revive the young man: stretching out with a sort of humorous laziness, she takes a mouthful of water from a nearby pitcher and sprays it through her teeth over his sleeping features. Will they ever meet again? They do, by accident, in the town of Kanazawa, months later when she is taking a moonlight stroll during a break from performing. He has fallen on hard times and she recognises him. In the beautifully modulated night-time scene that signals this re-encounter (so quiet and delicate and full of subtly conveyed emotion) she asks him straightforwardly to move in with her. Though younger than he, she is more experienced – the experience at issue, we are immediately made to see, being part and parcel of her profession as 'water-artist'. Taki no Shiraito is a juggler and illusionist, and in the great spumes of water that magically spurt up from the fans she holds in her outstretched hands on stage, there are all the signs the audience needs of her having genuine mystique and allure. As with Garance in *Les Enfants du paradis* – first seen in a fairground tent, sitting bolt upright, naked, in a revolving bathtub – the attractiveness of the 'act' is inextricably linked to the attractiveness of the performer (yet also to her distance and disdain). Subject, nightly, to the paid gaze of the multitude, Taki is sexualised from the start, and this makes the film seem exceptionally bold and modern.

Other aspects of the movie might be cited to support this view, all of them harking back in one way or another to its extraordinary lucidity and realism. It is in this film that we recognise (perhaps for the first time from among the surviving works) the authentically Mizoguchian worldview: the sense, above all, that the bonds of society are in the last resort upheld by a kind of pervasive and institutionalised violence. There is a sobriety and seriousness here that is altogether impressive. Out of many possible examples, we could take the passages which deal with Taki's relationship with her professional colleagues. Although she is the star of the show (and consequently a person of stature whose opinion must be deferred to), real power in her milieu lies with two behind-the scenes operators, a knife-thrower called Minami (her immediate boss) and a shadowy figure named Iwabuchi, responsible for the troupe's finances. Neither man, needless to say, is the slightest bit benevolent. During winter, when revenues are low, the pair of them hatch harsh schemes to trim expenses, sacking an actress here, encouraging others to offer their 'services' to clients in lieu of salary. Minami at one stage demands of Taki that she repay him a debt; actually, she happens to have the money in question, or part of it, and in a marvellous scene she tosses the notes at him with a born performer's scorn. (Minami's unimpressed response, after fawning over her: 'It's not enough, but I'll take it!'). Here, at least, the girl gets by. Later on, however, despite her great beauty and intelligence, her luck deserts her. Without going into the precise circumstances of the plot that is contrived against her by the sinister pair, suffice to say it involves their stealing from her some 300 yen that she has earned, in her eyes honestly enough, by sleeping with one of the show's backers. The long and the short of the matter is that Taki is waylaid by anonymous ruffians in the pay of her bosses as she crosses a park and has her purse snatched.

Certain that Iwabuchi is behind the attack, Taki makes her way to his house where, sure enough, the money (she supposes it is the same money) is lying on a sideboard. At first she berates the man furiously, but Iwabuchi responds by going on the offensive. He attacks her physically and drags her by the hair to an adjoining room where he proceeds to lambast her. Goaded beyond endurance, Taki unsheathes a knife on the spur of the moment (it is actually Minami's knife, dropped in her path in the course of the park ambush), and fatally stabs the sleazy financier.

The whole scene is utterly authentic: swift and brutal and exactly as it might happen in life. Its seriousness 'rhymes' with another extraordinary scene of violence from later in the film when Taki is on the run from the police. She is sheltering in a house in the suburbs of Tokyo, her temporary protectors being a couple, Nadeshiko and Shinzo, whom earlier in the story Taki helped abscond from the troupe. The police come round after a tip-off, but (not being able to find Taki) depart without making an arrest. The audience senses, with relief, that the episode is over. Not at all! Seconds later, and without any warning, they are back again, this time in earnest. Taki is seized from the attic where she has been hiding, the police beat her up and drag her off, while for good measure brutally laying into the couple who have been attempting (in their innocence) to aid her.

My point here is not to say that Mizoguchi was unique among his peers in bringing such violence into the register of possible subjects that cinema was permitted to deal with. (On the contrary: whole genres were predicated on violence, as we have seen in the case of chambara.) Nor is it to maintain that the presence of these scenes of violence automatically 'authenticates' the films in question. Everything, naturally, depends on context and tone, and on the presence of an implied moral vision. The Water Magician (unlike The Downfall of Osen) is a completely coherent work of art, in which each part of the drama is assembled with the same care and given the same weight as the other parts – so that in the end even the sections that one might think of as belonging 'merely' to melodrama become imbued, by a kind of artistic osmosis, with grace and gravity.

What, for example, could be more conventional, from the point of view of the film's shimpa origins, than the scene in which we see Taki making a clandestine and unannounced visit to the attic in Tokyo where her protégé, Kin-san, is pursuing his legal studies (studies paid for by her, of course)? The boy is absent and Taki is on the run, so the visit can only be fleeting. Her eyes take in at a glance the shabby room: the threadbare robe hanging on the back of the door, the desk, the inkwell, the candle, the haphazard pile of books. There is even a landlady telling her (without suspecting whom she is talking to) that her hard-working young tenant enjoys the support of a 'sister' living in a far-away city, for whose sake he is endeavouring to excel. All this, as I say, is conventional enough, and yet such is the delicacy with which the scene is handled, the viewer cannot but be moved by it. (There *were* women like that, one finds oneself finally reflecting, Mizoguchi's own sister among them.) Similar considerations to these apply, but on a more abstract scale, to the film's melodramatic conclusion, foreseeable in one sense, yet for all that implacably tragic. For when Taki is eventually captured by the authorities, the prosecuting counsel she comes up against turns out to be her former lover and protégé. Will Kin-san be able to reconcile his duty to the law with the human gratitude he feels towards his former lover and benefactress? And will *she* be able to persuade *him* that, although he may be tempted to waver for human reasons, his duty to his profession is paramount? Such is the dilemma the conclusion hinges on. The logic of the original stabbing is followed through to its harsh conclusion. At the end of a triumphant prosecution, Taki faces the full brunt of the law. The film takes its exit on a haunting and unforgettable image: Kin-san, alone, is standing under the bridge where the couple shared their first moonlit tryst all those years ago. His eyes are wild and he holds a pistol to his head. There is not much doubt that he will shortly squeeze the trigger.

The Story of Late Chrysanthemums

The Water Magician is a great film, but *The Story of Late Chrysanthemums*, Mizoguchi's last film of the 1930s (and the last film we will meet in this book), is a magnificent one. The movie is based on a stage play by Sanichi Iwaya that in turn was adapted from a short novel by a contemporary writer, Shofu Muramatsu. Mizoguchi's old colleague Matsutaro Kawaguchi planned the enterprise in conjunction with the director, and the piquant, searching dialogues of the film were provided by Yoda. The film is what used to be called a biopic: its subject is the early life of the famous kabuki actor Kikugoro Onoe VI (1886–1949). After the excursion into modern drama that marked the middle part of the decade (*Osaka Elegy*, *Sisters of the Gion* etc.), the movie represents in certain clear ways a return to the *shimpa* themes of the early 1930s, for its underlying structure repeats the tropes of female sacrifice and redemption that are the defining characteristics of this genre. In a way, *The Story of Late Chrysanthemums* is even more *shimpa* than some of the earlier works. Otoku, the heroine, is a far meeker and more self-effacing creature than Taki no Shiraito, for example (at least, she is so on the surface). The actress who plays her, Kakuko Mori, has little of Takako Irie's fire and sexuality; her voice, in particular, is high-pitched and plaintive, the human quality it signifies being recognisably one of subservience. In short, there are rather a lot of hostages to sentimentality right from the beginning, if one were approaching the film purely from a thematic point of view.

And yet these observations fail to account for the movie's power and beauty. If I say that this power lies in the film's 'form', I risk giving the impression that I think that form is everything; whereas the exceptional rigour and control of the movie's *mise en scène* is only the precondition for life (poignancy, truth, savour) flooding in here in profusion. The form in question is Mizoguchi's famous 'one-scene-one-take' compositional method. We have already considered the possible origins of this practice, tracing its emergence back to the beginnings of the decade (even to a film that is no longer available); but *The Story of Late Chrysanthemums* was arguably the first film in which this method of composition was rigorously and consistently put into practice right across the board. (Actually, it was used with such consistency in only one subsequent film, *The Loyal 47 Ronin*.) The method was first experimented with and then perfected in *Chrysanthemums*, so Yoda tells us, in response to the practical necessity of shooting the quite sizeable extracts from the kabuki repertoire which form an important element in the scenario. Of course, such scenes might have been cut up and edited together in the conventional way, but Mizoguchi wanted to have them in real time, and he wanted the whole stage to be visible at a glance – he wanted the audience to feel the integrity of the theatrical space as if it were being experienced in a live performance. Established in these scenes, the logic of the wide-angle lens and of enhanced depth of field that Mizoguchi worked out with his cameraman Minoru Miki seems to have moved imperturbably into the other scenes too. As we have observed before, the interesting aesthetic problem with this kind of filming revolves around the question of distance. In order to bind the composition together in a single all-embracing master-take, the camera needs to stand back, and the danger is that, if it stands back too far, the audience will lose contact with the drama. For this reason, *The Story of Late Chrysanthemums* (and films like *The Loyal 47 Ronin* conceived in the same mould) are difficult to watch on television or DVD: the miniaturisation of the characters caused by the long-shot compositions makes large sections of the drama almost invisible.

In the cinema, fortunately, this isn't a problem. The screen is big enough for the audience to take in the characters without having to strain to identify them. And yet, even here, they *are* distant, and this distance inescapably forms part of the film's impact and meaning. In scene after scene, the camera watches from afar as passages of dialogue unfold. The stationary gaze, coupled with the extended length of the take, imparts an extraordinary sense of concentration: one finds oneself watching the characters with a rare intensity. Because they are so far away, one is not quite able to 'read' them. What are they thinking? Why are we interested in what they are thinking? In the words of Bazin quoted at the beginning of this book, 'the entire film is practically pulled out of reach, so that the action becomes surrounded by an aura of inaccessibility'. But 'inaccessibility' here involves a sense of mystery rather than frustration. Exactly as with the complex spatial dynamics of *The Magnificent Ambersons* (the film that was the pretext for Bazin's *aperçu*), the audience is forced to scan the canvas, and in doing so actively to engage in the process of establishing significance. Formulating the experience like this (as a sort of hermeneutic exercise) makes it sound like a penance, whereas in fact it is one of the pleasures of the movie.

'Knowing' and 'Not-knowing' the Characters in a Mizoguchi Film

Take, for example, the scene near the beginning of the movie where guests in a geisha house are awaiting the arrival of the hero Kikunosuke (Shotaro Hanayagi). Assorted geisha, chatting about his reputation, are seated on the balcony of the house's restaurant, but it is night-time, and although we can *hear* the women clearly enough, we can scarcely *see* them in the scene's establishing long shot.

After a bout of desultory repartee, the camera moves into medium shot, but, typically for this film's aesthetics, what remains of the scene is still shot from outside the building, and the single geisha on whom the camera is focused is simultaneously obscured from our sight by an intervening window grill. The effect fractures her body, making it difficult to decipher. Who is she? One of a crowd of extras? Or a character who is going to become important? We wait, intrigued. A cry goes up: Kikunosuke is sighted, but once again, there's a fascinatingly perverse holding-off before the actor arrives within the audience's field of vision. Instead, the camera moves laterally along the bars of the restaurant's balcony in a swift travelling shot, coming to a halt not on Kikunosuke (who invisibly *hors champ*) but on one of the geisha (the same one we have just seen?) who has stood up and strolled over to greet him. Finally, in a cutaway, we do see Kikunosuke, standing in the doorway, looking tired and unhappy. If the scene that now ensues is clearer to make out visually than the scene just described, it is equally hard to interpret – above all because of Mizoguchi's continued fastidious refusal to sort his characters into any kind of conventional dramatic hierarchy. Thus the geisha who approaches Kikunosuke seems to have intimate claims upon him. A girl-friend? Even a fiancée? We're ready to believe either, except that, moments after she has poured the actor saké and scolded him intimately for his tardiness, the partition door is drawn back and *another* geisha appears (like the first one, already slightly tipsy). And the way the newcomer behaves makes it clear that she also has claims on Kikunosuke – claims that may be as well-founded, or as ill-founded, as the first geisha's – we simply don't know. Nobody has been really 'introduced', so that everything remains tentative and open-ended.

The Film's Soundtrack

I do not want to make greater claims for the 'obscurity' of this scene than are plausible or necess-ary. The quarrel that soon ensues between the two geisha has, after all, a conventional enough point, dramatically speaking: it is staged to establish for the audience that Kikunosuke's way of life as an habitué of Yanagibashi houses of pleasure is making him unhappy – and to open up the next stage of the story in which his meeting with the nursemaid Otoku signals a way out of his current crisis. The leisurely and roundabout way of getting to this point seems to be an aspect of the film's extraordinary general artistic confidence. Of course, the viewer not attuned to Mizoguchi's methods is bound to complain about slowness; on the other hand, if you *are* attuned to the direc-tor's intentions, then this slowness becomes a positive advantage. The deliberately spacious rhythms encountered here give the audience time to notice things that are not part and parcel of the ordinary moviegoing experience and which tend to get overlooked in more conventional dram-aturgy. Sensual aspects of the scene, for a start: maybe not scent or touch (although it is scarcely too much to claim, in the scenes just described, that it is almost possible to 'smell' the late summer breezes). Hearing, however, receives an extraordinary emphasis. Throughout *The Story of Late Chrysanthemums*, Mizoguchi devotes the greatest attention to the quality of the soundtrack. Whether it is the cries of the street vendors (a constant reference across the movie) or the hooting of an owl in a deserted sanctuary, or else the clatter of wooden clogs on cobblestones, or the whirring of fans outdoors and indoors (and the sharp clacking noise they make when they're snapped shut), the acoustic element contrives to make this film special.

For example, one of the most beautiful scenes in the movie occurs just after the geisha episode described above: it is the moment when, in an out-of-doors conversation at night-time, the lowly Otoku dares to tell Kikunosuke that his acting is not quite as good as the flatterers who surround him claim it to be. A single travelling shot photographed upwards from a very low angle takes in this midnight colloquy. While the dialogue itself is marvellously delicate, what makes the scene memor-able is the subliminal richness of the 'noises off': the gurglings of the little baby that Otoku is nursing in her arms, the tinkling of festival lanterns on the cart of a passing peddler, the gentle creaking of the carriage wheels as Kikunosuke descends from his rickshaw, finally (as a background to *this* background) the perpetual soft wail of song and samisen through open windows in the distance.[6]

The Kabuki Milieu

I hope I am succeeding in evoking something melancholy, as well as beautiful. Psychologically speaking, a mood of frustration, setback, *blockage* is the key that the film is conceived in. Kikugoro Onoe VI, whose early life the film fictionalises, rose in due course to be one of the greatest of all kabuki players, but his first years in the profession were fraught with conflict and self-doubt. He had a peculiar personality: obstinate and imperious on the one hand; tender, feminine and some-what 'spoiled' on the other. We have to bear in mind that, while it guaranteed the continuity of the art form, the tradition in Japanese theatre whereby leading kabuki players adopt their succes-sors and bring them into the family, carried with it, sometimes, a heavy price; the expectations placed on the shoulders of the chosen youth often proved to be a difficult burden to bear. The his-tory of kabuki is studded with instances of players whose rise to the top of their profession was marked, initially, by stormy and extended apprenticeships. Laurence Kominz, in his fascinating essay 'Ichikawa Danjuro V and Kabuki's Golden Age', shows how three successive holders of one of the greatest of all kabuki acting dynasties each in turn rebelled against their adoptive father before set-tling down to find a style (and an audience) that suited them.[7] So, 'late bloomers' (late chrysan-themums) were common in the profession: Danjuro V (1740–1806), according to Kominz, perhaps the single greatest kabuki player who ever lived, was one; so was his predecessor Danjuro IV (1711–78). Something of this waywardness is the background against which the audience is asked to view the oddly diffident and tentative behaviour of Kikunosuke, and to observe his fatal flaws: his shyness, his awkwardness, his propensity to make the 'wrong move'.[8] Kikunosuke's role was

---

6   Kurosawa too was fascinated by these lost sounds from the Meiji and Taisho epochs: 'The sounds I listened to as a boy are completely different from those of today,' he remarks in his memoirs. 'First of all, there was no electricity in those days. Even phonographs were not electric phonographs. Everything was natural.' In the same passage he goes on to recall some of the most memorable sounds of his childhood:

> The resounding 'boom' of the cannon at the Kudan Ushi-ga-fuchi army barracks, which fired a blank each day precisely at noon. The fire alarm bell. The sound of the fire-watchman's wooden clappers. The tofu seller's bugle. The whistle of the tobacco-pipe repairman. The sound of the lock on the candy-vendor's chest of drawers. The tinkle of the wind-chime sellers's wares. The drumbeats of the man who repaired the thongs of wooden clogs. The bells of itinerant monks chanting sutras. The big drum for the lion dance. The monkey trainer's drum. The cry of the freshwater-clam vendor. The humming of kite strings. The click of battledore and shuttlecock . . .

Kurosawa concludes: 'These lost sounds are impossible to separate from my childhood memories. I note that they are all related to the seasons.' (*Something Like an Autobiography*, 1982, pp. 32–3).

7   Donald Jenkins (ed.), *The Floating World Revisited* (1993).

8   Mizoguchi made a film about this dynasty of actors that hasn't survivied: *Danjuro Sandai/Three Generations of Danjuro* (1944). Kimitoshi Sato tells me that there is actually a Danjuro connection in Kikugoro's case: the young man had two mentors: his father, Kikugoro V, and Danjuro IX, whom for various reasons his father put in charge of his artistic education. Thus in Rokudaime (the name Kikugoro VI is usually known by) are united the two greatest historical kabuki streams.

played by an actor not trained in the kabuki but in the *shimpa* tradition. During the 1920s and 30s, he had been one of the last and greatest *onnagata* specialists (i.e. men who take women's roles). Shotaro Hanayagi – born in 1894, thus four years older than Mizoguchi – was on the old side to be playing the part of a young man. (According to Yoda, this may have been yet another reason why, after tests, Mizoguchi opted for the shooting style incorporating so much long shot and depth of field: he did not want the lines of Hanayagi's face to be visible.) The compensation, however, lies in the beautiful gravity and refinement that he brings to the part of Kikunosuke. There was a fine balance to be found here, even at the script stage: as the twistings and turnings of Kikunosuke's career take him further and further away from the presence of Otoku – the one person who clearly sees his predicament, and can offer the solace he needs – there is a danger that the audience will lose sympathy with his indecisiveness. (How absurd and perverse his prevarications seem at times, starting with his flight to the provinces.) Yet in the end this does not bother the viewer. Hanayagi anchors the film. Behind his sensitive features, the viewer detects a manly inner core that is appropriate for the character, and there is never any doubt about his ultimate faithfulness.[9]

Cinema and Theatre: the Mizoguchian Synthesis

The Story of Late Chrysanthemums is punctuated by long sequences of kabuki; the extended length of these extracts (there are three in all, accounting for some twenty minutes of screen time) serves to give the idea of performance itself an almost documentary weight and prominence. It is as if the proof of Kikunosuke's step-by-step entrance into mastery of his art form cannot be taken on trust, as something that is 'given' by the narrative, but needs to be shown (and experienced by the audience) actually happening. In these full-dress, extended sequences, the Western viewer is exposed as never before to that radical 'Otherness' of Japanese gesture that I opened this chapter contemplating. Kabuki theatre is above all an art of the actor: it is the actor's genius, not the genius of the playwright, that most defines its ontological status. Clamorous and noisy in one sense, the art form dramatises at its centre a moment of preternatural stillness. Here the actor, having completed his astonishing arabesques, strikes the stationary pose know as a *mie* which contains (as if in a snapshot) the essence of all that has gone before. The concentrated energy inherent in this gesture produces a thrill in the audience that is impossible to describe if you have not experienced it yourself: it is what theatre *is* – it is what art is, and therefore (by extension) what life is. In his memoir, *Childhood Years*, which I have occasionally cited in these pages, the famous novelist Junichiro Tanizaki looks back on certain kabuki performances he attended as a boy. The actor he most admired was Kikugoro's predecessor and father figure, Kikugoro Onoe V.

---

9   It is an interesting thought that Mizoguchi might have approached the 'real' Kikugoro to play his youthful self – the actor was still alive and not too much past his prime to make such a daring casting a possibility. Only a couple of years previously, in fact, Kikugoro had had his first taste of the movies when he appeared in a documentary called *Kagajimishi*, made by Yasujiro Ozu to introduce Western audiences to the artistry of kabuki dance. It is a fascinating performance and intriguing (even to the untrained eye) to compare to the extracts danced by Hanayagi in *The Story of Late Chrysanthemums*. Mizoguchi returned to Kikugoro in 1949 concerning another project he was planning about kabuki theatre – aborted, however, by the actor's death in July of that year. Rokudaime/Kikugoro is still worshipped by aficionados as an avatar of the classic kabuki dance: no one in living memory, it is said, was able to combine such grace with such vehemence. Hanayagi was 'only' a *shimpa* actor: but what a good shot he makes of bringing Kikugoro to life in these theatre sequences!

The refined world of Kabuki: players from behind a screen watching Kikunosuke's performance in *The Story of Late Chrysanthemums* (1939)

> How clearly I remember him running along the palace balustrade to the tumultuous applause of the audience. Carrying a drum, he stops for a moment at the edge of the set and executes a fixed pose (*mie*) before disappearing. What a divine art kabuki is! Can there ever be anything to equal it?[10]

About the best of kabuki may be said what Ferdinando Taviani says about Indian performance art:

> Indian theatre and dance present us with an opportunity to see the physical equivalent of words like *god*, *goddess*, *divine*; the eyes can suddenly become an image of the sun, the actor or dancer can be both the archer and the bow, the flying arrow and the wounded doe.[11]

Viewed in this light, of course, there is nothing to beat the sublimity of theatre, and cinema itself (mere 'mechanical reproduction' in Walter Benjamin's famous phrase; wedded moreover to an ethic of unsophisticated naturalism) can only bow its head and admit inferiority. 'Alive or dead?' was the question asked at the beginning of this chapter. But the theatre is *always* alive! Any film

---

10 Junichiro Tanizaki, *Childhood Years: A Memoir* (1988), p. 152.

11 Quoted in Eugenio Barba and Nicola Savarese, *The Secret Life of the Performer: A Dictionary of Theatre Anthropology* (1991), p. 98.

director who loved the stage as much as Mizoguchi did must have had moments when he wondered if he had followed the right branch of the profession. But at the same time, the sceptic inside him will have whispered: I can *say* this, but do I believe it? For might not the truth be rather the opposite, that theatre only becomes beautiful and meaningful when it is refracted through the medium of film? It is a strange and true reflection that directors such as Mizoguchi and Renoir (or Bergman and Welles, or Hitchcock and Rivette; or Cocteau and Carné) in some sense *teach us what theatre really is*. By juxtaposing, in their movies, extracts from staged performances with the counter-dramas that take place 'in the wings', they give us, so to speak, the best of both worlds. So, in *The Story of Late Chrysanthemums*, we have the stupendous artifice of the kabuki scenes. But we also have a truth that can only be called non-theatrical, even anti-theatrical, the truth of the private, tender, intimate scenes that take up the majority of the movie's running time: scenes in which nothing is 'staged' and everything simply is as it is in life itself. Kikunosuke, in the kitchen with Otoku, carves a melon and expertly de-pips it. He offers her a slice. She accepts it. An epiphany? The gesture has no need of interpretation; its casualness, its limpidity, its plangency are the essence of Mizoguchi's living art.

APPENDIX 1 | Mizoguchi and French Film Criticism[1]

Japan emerged in the West as a national cinema to be reckoned with at more or less the same time that the famous French film magazine *Cahiers du Cinéma* was getting under way – in other words, during the early to mid-1950s. There was a reciprocal interaction between the two phenomena. The longstanding debate carried on in *Cahiers'* pages (and in the pages of sister reviews such as the weekly periodical *Arts*) concerning the respective merits of Mizoguchi and Kurosawa was one of the key encounters that helped to put Japanese cinema 'on the map' for a whole generation of French, and subsequently European and American, cinephiles. Leading the discussion were André Bazin himself (the editor of the magazine) and among others, future film-makers Jean-Luc Godard, Jacques Rivette and Eric Rohmer: these latter three, Mizoguchians to a man.

Bazin's position was always more nuanced and unpolemical than that of his disciples: it appears he loved equally the dynamic, public, 'masculine' Kurosawa, and the director whom he calls the 'tender and musical' Mizoguchi. If the latter's cinema was (perhaps) more authentically native than Kurosawa's, this did not necessarily make it *ipso facto* better, in Bazin's eyes: they both had their fine qualities to elucidate. Defending Kurosawa against the charge sometimes levelled against him that his films are a bastard hybrid of East and West, Bazin writes (in 1957):

> [Kurosawa's] admiration for John Ford, Fritz Lang and Chaplin in particular is clear enough. But this is not a passive influence. What matters for him is not just absorbing it; his intention is to use it to trans-mit back to us an image of Japanese tradition and culture that we can assimilate visually and mentally. He succeeds in doing this so well with *Rashomon* that this film can truly be said to have opened the gates of the West to Japanese cinema. In its [*Rashomon*'s] wake came many other films – notably Mizoguchi's – which have revealed to us a production which, if not more authentic, is at any rate more characteristic and more pure.

Bazin's young protégés at *Cahiers* – critics for the meantime, but soon to become film-makers – were less reticent, and more partisan. For Rivette, Godard and Rohmer, Mizoguchi's superiority to Kurosawa was self-evident, as the extracts quoted below indicate. Here is Rivette in 1958 (the year, incidentally, of Bazin's death):

> Enough of comparisons: the little Kurosawa–Mizoguchi game has had its day. Let the champions of Kurosawa withdraw from the match; one can only compare what is comparable and equal in ambi-tion. Mizoguchi alone imposes the sense of a specific language and world answerable only to him.

---

1   See also 'Further Reading', under the entries *Cahiers du Cinéma* and *Positif*.

The extravagance of the partisanship perhaps makes the contemporary reader smile (it is so evidently wrong-headed, in one way: how, in retrospect, could anyone deny the idiosyncratic Kurosawa his own specific 'language'?); but in the course of his vigorous advocacy Rivette makes at least one crucial point that modern compartmentalised scholarship is in danger of forgetting:

> These films – which tell us, in an alien tongue, stories that are completely foreign to our customs and ways of life – talk to us in a familiar language. What language? The only one to which a film-maker should lay claim when all is said and done: the language of *mise en scène*. For modern artists did not discover African fetishes through a conversion to idols, but because those unusual objects moved them as sculptures. If music is a universal idiom, so too is *mise en scène*: It is this language, and not Japanese, that has to be learned to understand 'Mizoguchi'. A language held in common, but here brought to a degree of purity that our Western cinema has known only rarely.[2]

The specific detailed historical saga of France's discovery of Mizoguchi is a topic for another study. Only a few (a very few) key staging-points are outlined here. Bazin's introduction to Mizoguchi was through a viewing of *Ugetsu Monogatari* which he noticed briefly from the Venice Film Festival in the October 1953 issue of *Cahiers du Cinéma*, returning to the movie with further appreciative remarks the following year in a book-format summary of world current film production (*Cinéma 53 à travers le monde*: Editions du Cerf. The *Cahiers* review, together with this summary, form items 136 and 155 of the Andrew brothers' *Kenji Mizoguchi: A Guide to References and Resources*). Interestingly, in view of what I am calling Bazin's fine impartiality, the Venice review's judgment is that Mizoguchi's 'refusal to philosophise' makes *Ugetsu* in the end a superior work of art to *Rashomon*. Be that as it may, Bazin during the mid-1950s began to explore in a systematic way the whole range of Japanese cinema that was becoming available in France. From this period dates his magisterial essay 'The Lesson of Japanese Cinema Style', extracts of which I quote below, published in the magazine *Arts* – the source also of two appreciations of *Ugetsu*, by Godard and Rohmer, which appeared a year apart, in February 1958 and March 1959 respectively. It is fascinating to re-read these essays. The force, enthusiasm, and broad general culture of the writers – discernible even in extracts – belong to a golden age of film criticism.

BAZIN: 'The Lesson of Japanese Cinema Style' (Extract)

> Distance and perilous ways of distribution play a similar role as do the abuses of time. It is clear that we are hard pressed to discriminate in our admiration for such and such Japanese film between its specific merits and those it shares with Japanese art in general. Must we renounce our pleasure and doubt its value because of this? Not at all. On the contrary, I see this as a confirmation of the exemplary merits of Japanese film. There are no other productions in the world that give us the feeling of being more perfectly homogenous with the artistic spirit of a civilization. I've already seen some twenty to twenty-five Japanese films, diverse in genre and quite unequal in result. Between the sensitive and

---

2   Quoted in Jim Hillier (ed.), *Cahiers du Cinéma: The 1950s – Neo-Realism, Hollywood, New Wave* (1985), p. 264. The whole section in this book on the impact of Japanese cinema (pp. 248–68), including Hillier's introductory note, is illuminating.

intimist neo-realism of *Okasan* (Mikio Naruse), the baroque and sensual romanticism of *Beauty and the Bandits* (Keigo Kimura), the sumptuous and tragic ritual of *Gate of Hell* (Teinosuke Kinugasa), by way of the naturalistic melodrama of *The Golden Demon* (Eizo Tanaka), the Parisian public itself already has some idea of this truth. But what I have not seen, even when the performance was boring, naïve, or, in my Western eyes, worthless, is a Japanese film that is vulgar or in just bad taste.

The evolution of Western art, its divorce from the people and its exacerbated individualism have combined to mean that the quality of anonymity has progressively disappeared from our society since the eighteenth century. The style is that of the man; it is no longer that of a civilization. We have great painters, great writers and even great filmmakers. But we really have no great literature and, even less, great cinema. By this I mean no common style, no minimum language of which the most mediocre artist can blunderingly make use. The most admirable aspect of classical literature is not Racine or Madame de Sévigné but the fact that so many of their contemporaries wrote like them. It is the modern prejudice of our authors that hides from us in Racine the tremendous rhetorical groundwork from which his genius benefited. Perhaps the cinema has gone through a primitive stage (or should we say 'classical'?) in every country, the high point of its High Middle Ages. At that time, works were often anonymous. In any case, film existed as an entity in spite of the talents of its craftsmen. Today, perhaps only Hollywood still offers us – up to a certain point – the example of a cinema that is valuable not just in its individual works but also for the language of its 'commercial' productions. There, the cinema is homogenous to the civilization that it satisfies and expresses. But in Europe, the cinema no longer exists. There are only good and bad films, like books or paintings.

To elaborate further: in the most favourable cases our cinema endeavours to equal the traditional arts, usually novels or the theatre. It manages to do so from time to time, but with difficulty. *The Diary of a Country Priest* by Bresson is not inferior to Bernanos' book, but what about *Le Rouge et le Noir* (Claude Autant-Lara, 1954) or *The Pastoral Symphony*? We see that what is known as an 'average film' implies the mobilisation of less talent, taste, skill, culture and creative will than, say, an average novel.

Yet it seems that Japanese films differ both from ours as well as from those of Hollywood. A country with an old culture and strong traditions, Japan seems to have assimilated film with the same ease that it used to assimilate all other Western technology. This technology did not destroy their culture but was immediately integrated into it, and cinema effortlessly moved over to the level of Japanese art in general. Whereas when Castellani and Renoir use colour more tastefully and intelligently than their contemporaries, it is the result of their talent and culture, in Japan the opposite is the case. It would be difficult to find a director so uncouth and unpolished that he would not spontaneously compose his shots according to the best plastic traditions of Oriental art. In the same vein, there is not one Japanese who could drop a cup of tea on a straw mat, nor, in the whole archipelago, is there a badly pruned cherry tree. And what I say about cherry trees and *mise en scène* is true, quite naturally, of their dramatic expressions. I see the true revelation of Japanese film in this amazing and unique lesson of style, not of the creative artist but of an entire civilization, which, to the last man, would not know how to violate the ritual of pain.

(*Arts*, 9–15 March 1955, trans. Sabine d'Estrée)

GODARD: *Ugetsu Monogatari* (Extract)

Admired at the time of the Venice Film Festival, *Ugetsu Monogatari* is Kenji Mizoguchi's masterpiece, and one which ranks him on equal terms with Griffith, Eisenstein and Renoir.

Efficacity and sobriety are the characteristics of great film-makers, and Kenji Mizoguchi does not belie this rule. As Philippe Demonsablon pointed out in a pertinent article on *The Life of Oharu*, his art is to abstain from any solicitation irrelevant to its object, to leave things to present themselves without intervention from the mind except to efface its traces, thus increasing a thousandfold the efficacity of the objects it presents for our admiration. It is, therefore, a realist art, and the *mise en scène* will be realist.

This simplicity is not without paradox, for it must achieve its austerity through an accumulation of matter. The compositions are guided initially by the laws of movement. But there is no baroque embellishment, no purpose other than to allow the substance itself to reach us. No image is comic, tragic, fanciful, erotic in itself, and yet it is all these things at once. Mizoguchi's art is the most complex because it is the simplest. Camera effects and tracking shots are rare, but when they do suddenly burst into a scene, the effect is one of dazzling beauty. Each crane shot (here Preminger is easily outstripped) has the clean and limpid line of a brush-stroke by Hokusai.

The action takes place at the end of the sixteenth century, during the time of the civil wars. It tells the story of Genjuro, a humble potter who is bewitched by the beautiful Lady Wakasa, and of his brother, a vainglorious brute who dreams of military prowess. After many disappointments in the city, they both return home to spend the rest of their lives in the fields.

Everything which made the power and magnificence of *Chikamatsu Monogatari*, the cool cruelty of *A Picture of Madam Yuki*, the jovial bawdry of *Street of Shame*, the tenderness of *Osaka Elegy*, is here combined, and the effect increased a thousandfold. It is *Don Quixote*, *The Odyssey* and *Jude the Obscure* rolled into one: an hour and a half of film which seems to last an eternity. Subtlety of *mise en scène* is here carried to its highest degree. Mizoguchi is probably the only director in the world who dares to make systematic use of 180-degree shots and reaction shots. But what in another director would be striving for effect, with him is simply a natural movement arising out of the importance he accords to the decor and the position the actors occupy within it.

Let me quote two examples of technical conjuring tricks which are the acme of art. Genjuro is bathing with the fatal enchantress who has caught him in her net; the camera leaves the rock pool where they are disporting themselves, pans along the overflow which becomes a stream disappearing into the fields; at this point there is a swift dissolve to the furrows, other furrows seem to take their place, the camera continues tranquilly on its way, rises, and discovers a vast plain, then a garden in which we discover the two lovers again, a few months later, enjoying a picnic. Only masters of the cinema can make use of a dissolve to create a feeling which is here the very Proustian one of pleasure and regret.

A 'Proustian' pleasure: the picnic interlude in *Ugetsu Monogatari*

Another example: Having killed the enchantress, Genjuro returns home. He does not know that his loving wife is dead. He enters, looks in all the rooms, the camera panning with him. He moves from one room to the next, still followed by the camera. He goes out, the camera leaves him, returns to the room and frames his wife, in flesh and blood, just at the moment when Genjuro comes in again and sees her, believing (as we do) that he didn't look properly, and that his gentle wife is really alive.

The art of Kenji Mizoguchi is to prove that real life is at one and the same time elsewhere and yet here, in its strange and radiant beauty.

(*Arts*, 5–12 February 1958, trans. Tom Milne)

ROHMER: *Ugetsu Monogatari*

This week, a new masterpiece. I do not use the term lightly. If you have just seen *Ivan the Terrible*, run right over to see *Ugetsu*. As luck would have it, two of the 'twelve best films of all time' (if you subscribe to the list recently published by *Cahiers du cinéma*) have come out in Paris almost simultaneously.

All of Paris should run to see this film. People who love the movies and people who don't care anything about them. Those who are interested in Japan and those who aren't. Like all great works, *Ugetsu* shatters the bounds between genres and the frontiers between nations. There could be no better ambassador for Japanese civilization than this story drawn from medieval legends. A world in appearance very different from ours will be revealed to you. You will perceive clearly the common source of our humanity, the crucible from which emerged both *The Odyssey* and the *Round Table* cycle, works with which *Ugetsu Monogatari* has troubling analogies.

If you love Japanese films, go and see this one. It's the most beautiful. If those that have been shown on our screens in the past have disappointed you, here is the opportunity to change your opinion. Kenji Mizoguchi, who died three years ago, was undoubtedly his country's greatest film-maker. He was able to bend to his purpose an art form born in another part of the world, one whose potential his countrymen have not always been able to exploit fully. You won't find in him any servile desire to copy the West. His conceptions of the frame, of acting, of rhythm, of composition, of time and space, are entirely homegrown. But he touches us in the same way Murnau, Ophuls and Rossellini have touched us.

For the film-maker as for the poet there is only one great subject: the idea of Unity hidden beneath the diversity of appearances or, translated into dramatic terms, the exalting and deceptive quest for paradise. And here this motif constitutes the very heart of the fable, since it shows us the mirages to which two peasants fall victim. One is tempted, like Don Quixote, by the demon of war; the other, like Lancelot, by the demon of the senses. But when this idea is translated into images, there is nothing abstract about it, and in this instance demonstrates the superiority of the Japanese film-makers over the likes of us, products of the West, incapable of projecting the enchantment of fairy tales onto the screen. Our period films smack of masquerade, our fantastic films of trickery: neither thing is true of this one.

The elegant style of this film and the refinement of all its details hold infinitely rich lessons for us. But don't be alarmed. Seeing it is not like going to school. *Ugetsu* possesses, on top of everything else, a quality that you might have doubts about if you only went by my emphatic praise. For the film is lively, engrossing, playful, easy, alternately moving and full of humour. It has nothing of the official masterpiece's solemn, abstruse character. No hieratic snobbery, no Far Eastern slowness. On the contrary, you will be surprised, almost disappointed, to see the word 'The End' appear so quickly on the screen.

(*Arts*, 25 March–2 April 1959, trans. Charles and Mirella Affron)

APPENDIX 2 | Mizoguchi's Attitude Towards Geisha

In 1936, following the release of *Osaka Elegy* and *Sisters of the Gion*, Mizoguchi took part in a 'table ronde' in the offices of the film magazine *Kinema Jumpo*. Six film critics were present besides Mizoguchi himself and the conversation ranged widely over all aspects of his work up until that date. The extract printed here deals with Mizoguchi's background research in the geisha quarters of Kyoto. Plainly, as the extract reveals, he had known brothels and geisha houses at first hand in his youth and young manhood; now, ten years later, in 1936, at the age of thirty-eight, he revisits them, he says, as an outsider and 'non-user', powered by a strong sociological interest in the changes that have taken place under Japan's growing militarism.

(Participants in the conversation: Shinbi Iida, Fuyuhiko Kitagawa, Kotaro Yamamoto, Matsuo Kishi, Jun'ichiro Tomoda, Tatsihiko Shigeno.)

KISHI: If one really wants to amuse oneself in Kyoto, is Gion the best place to do it in?

MIZOGUCHI: Certainly, it's the most traditional of the quarters. I visited it several times to find out about the lives of the geisha: I went to see the houses where they lived. I got the impression that economic conditions for them were really harsh at the moment. It's rare to find a geisha who earns more than 150 yen per appointment. (It's slightly different if one's talking about the ones who offer 'extra services' of a sexual nature.) I did a lot of research on the type of people who are these geishas' clients. I soon saw that the average age of such men is about forty. You very rarely find anyone younger.

YAMAMOTO: So that's why the people in your film look as old as they do!

MIZOGUCHI: The oldest man I heard about was sixty-eight, and I can tell you he wasn't going to these places merely as an onlooker. Good for him, anyway!

IIDA: That's interesting.

KISHI: And what about the profession of these guys?

MIZOGUCHI: A lot of them are businessmen or employees of small firms. One has to write one's name and address in the visitors' book, and quite a few of them didn't know how to do this properly. I carried out a fair amount of research. Recently these houses have come under much stricter government surveillance. The people who work there are obliged to write down any identifying characteristics of the clientele on the back of their registration papers. So you'll find a card saying things like: 'Dresses occidental-style, has a long face, sports such and such a type of footwear' and so on. None of the clients know about this. In short, everything is pretty well organised; if anything happens, the police are able to track down the persons involved thanks to these useful pieces of paper.

KISHI: So the chambermaids carry out this work every day?

MIZOGUCHI: I believe so.

YAMAMOTO: Usually people who go out to amuse themselves in Kyoto prefer Kobu or Miyakawa-cho – rather few go to Gion Otsu itself?

MIZOGUCHI: I heard that in the old days there were a lot of students, but since they've been prohibited from entering this quarter, the place is like a desert.

YAMAMOTO: But placing *Sisters of the Gion* in Kobu seems to me an excellent idea, given that you wanted to give a sense of the 'typical' atmosphere of Kyoto.

KISHI: One couldn't shoot such a film in Miyagawa-cho, I suppose?

MIZOGUCHI: I believe it would be possible to do it, even there.

KISHI: Doesn't the law forbid filming in these kinds of places?

MIZOGUCHI: I don't know how the law stands at the moment. In my film I planned to have a scene in which an *oiran* [high-class prostitute] is seen walking in these neighbourhoods, but it was cut by the censors. Maybe one of the reasons for this cut was because of the precise location where I shot this scene. I had her crossing the Temple of Gion at Benkei and walking along one of the lateral streets around there. If one enters these Kyoto neighbourhoods by driving off the principal highways, one quickly finds oneself in spots like these, full of geisha houses. The censorship didn't appreciate how 'visible' this was, so they cut the scene.

IIDA: In other words, it was simply too clear where it was shot?[1]

MIZOGUCHI: Exactly.

TOMODA: Could you clarify a bit the role that *yatona* [girls who pay house visits] play in this world?

MIZOGUCHI: That's difficult to be precise about. I did some research into the subject, and one thing to say is that the *yatona* of Kyoto are a bit different from their cousins in Osaka.

YAMAMOTO: I think it would be an interesting phenomenon for a film to explore. There is great variety in this profession: some *yatona* are rather rich, others not. Even when they hail from the same milieu, they can be very different.

KISHI: As far as the protagonist of *Sisters of the Gion* is concerned, did you a have real-life model in mind?

MIZOGUCHI: No, I don't believe so . . .

KITAGAWA: So she [Omocha, the character played by Yamada] is purely the fruit of your imagination?

---

1   The location of this particular shot may be clear enough, but there is an ambiguity about the 'general location' of the film. Yamamoto (above) says Kobu; Yoda says Otsu. Yoda tells us in his memoirs: 'Gion was divided in two: Kobu (upper Gion) and Otsubu (Lower Gion). Kobu was the quarter of the geisha *de luxe* and Otsubu of the prostitutes. We chose Otsubu as our background – the district of desire.' *Souvenirs de Kenji Mizoguchi* (1997), p. 49 [Author's translation]. Shindo's documentary on Mizoguchi, which introduces us to some of the geisha who knew the director at this time, seems to support Yoda's view: i.e. that the majority of the film was shot in Otsubu. It is interesting that Yoda's description of the making of *Sisters of the Gion* paints a rather more raffish and less 'scientific' picture of Mizoguchi's relationship to the Gion than the one projected here – he calls him an habitué, not merely an observer, and claims that the director often (even in the mid-1930s) visited the quarter for the purposes of seeking pleasure, along with a small band of intimate companions: Seikichi Terekado (his first assistant from Shinko), Hiroshi Mizutani (Mizoguchi's production designer, whom he met at this time, through Terekado) and finally the assistant director Koichi Takagi (*Souvenirs*, pp. 47–50).

MIZOGUCHI: The way it happened was this: I created both characters myself, then I looked around to see if there was anybody in real life who resembled them.

KITAGAWA: Do such people exist in reality?

MIZOGUCHI: Certainly they do! And people who live, sometimes, even more tragically! You wouldn't believe how dramatic some of these lives are!

KISHI: Do you yourself like this kind of woman?

MIZOGUCHI: It's perhaps a bit embarrassing to say whether such women please me or not . . .

KISHI: But you do like the 'edokko' type of woman, don't you? [Woman of the people, hailing from Tokyo]

MIZOGUCHI: I'll tell you: what I like are slightly plump women. I believe this can be put down to the fact that my beloved mother was a bit fat. She died when I was young [in 1915] – so, perhaps out of some kind of nostalgia, I'm fond of women with her figure. I know it might sound a bit ridiculous to say so, but I prefer fat women – they're the ones that really attract me.

KISHI: Perhaps because they allow you to feel again the heat of maternal warmth!

MIZOGUCHI: Well, as you know, as the years go by, people's tastes sometimes change.

IIDA: In the majority of films you seem to like to describe women with strong characters.

MIZOGUCHI: What I like to dramatise, within the limits that the censorship allows me, is a basic underlying conflict played out between men and women.

IIDA: Concerning *Sisters of the Gion*, do you see yourself as spiritually close to the younger sister [Yamada], and would you say that you paint her portrait with a certain detachment?

MIZOGUCHI: No to both questions.

TOMODA: Perhaps what I'm going to say may strike you as a bit impertinent, but looking at these two films [*Sisters of the Gion* and *Osaka Elegy*], I get the impression that they're a bit auto-biographical; certainly, one can find in them traces of your profound knowledge of women . . .

MIZOGUCHI: Ah no! Remember please that these last ten years I've remained completely outside this milieu. I'm a happily married man.

TOMODA: Perhaps, then, they're about experiences you had when you were younger?

SHIGENO: Perhaps it's just because you're no longer 'troubled with women' that you're able to describe their feelings so well. At the time that you made *Taki no Shiraito* (*The Water Magician*, 1933) and *The Jinpu Group* (1934), I believe you were tormented. You were in love with women . . . with all women. But recently, with *Osaka Elegy*, you seem to have moved beyond that point . . .

(*Kinema Jumpo* no. 597, 1 January 1937. Text reproduced in *Positif* no. 237, December 1980, and translated from French by the author)

APPENDIX 3 | Mizoguchi, *The Loyal 47 Ronin* and the War Years

Mizoguchi's thoughts on *The Loyal 47 Ronin* may be examined in a short document he published in the magazine *Jidai Eiga* in September 1941, two months before Part 1 of the film was released. In it, he states that different epochs require different responses from their artists, and that Japan has now moved into a stage where the *Weltanschaung* (he uses the German word) is 'superindividualist and nationalist' rather than what it used to be, 'personal and romantic'. The situation is not something he either approves of or disapproves of: it is simply a fact to be recorded that the artist, in the present juncture, has new responsibilities. Nonetheless, as he understands it, these responsibilities are essentially artistic rather than propagandistic, and for him this means continuing to explore, as seriously and soberly as possible, the cultural heritage of his country. He says at the end of the article:

> I have absolutely no particular ambition for this film . . . For me, it is the culmination of a hobby of mine: a lifelong effort to open up a channel of Japanese cinema in which history is treated broadly and humanely.

The modern reader is struck by how explicit Mizoguchi is in his insistence that cinema should not be politicised:

> Artists understand well enough what changes the nation, in the face of historical realities, demands of them. It does not require of them that they mouth slogans, or repeat clichés of propaganda . . . Towards its artists, the nation asks only that they continue to operate artistically: nothing more.[1]

This is bravely said. (He says other things too, but this is the essence of the argument.) In general, Japanese war films, taken as a whole, were far less bellicose than might be supposed. In his analysis of twenty-seven films made between 1937 and 1947, the American historian John Dower finds a consistent reluctance (which he contrasts favourably to Allied wartime propaganda) to demonise the enemy, or even to identify it beyond some shadowy abstraction; many of these films, especially those made in the early stages of the conflict, continue to surprise the viewer with their realism, dignity and restraint. 'Almost none of the Japanese war films can be seen as a glorification of war,' Dower writes (1993: 'Japanese Cinema Goes to War', Chapter 2), 'and some are transparently at war with themselves.' He goes on:

---

1   Quotations from '*Genroku Chusingura no Konpon Taido*', *Jidai Eiga*, September 1941, text reproduced in *Positif* no. 236, November 1980, and translated from French by the author.

This is especially apparent in the films of the China War period made prior to Pearl Harbor, such as *Chocolate and Soldiers* [Také Sado, 1941] and *Five Scouts* [Tomotaka Tasaka, 1939], where humanistic and antiwar sentiments frequently threatened to override the propagandistic message.

But later films were equally ambiguous. He cites as typical the film *Army* (Keisuke Kinoshita, 1944), where

> The suffering breaks through with startling and unexpected intensity – almost as if unplanned by the film-makers – as we encounter a mother who in the end finds it impossible to 'bear the unbearable' and send her son off to war with stoic pride. When the young man finally marches off to war, as his mother has repeatedly encouraged him to do, she literally claws her way through the crowd of bystanders cheering off the departing troops, desperate to prolong the sight of her doomed offspring. War may be a duty for every mother and mother's son, but it is also the final, ultimate enemy.

This is obviously a complicated subject and only so much can be said in a short note such as this. Anderson and Richie (1959) note that, while a number of film-makers such as Kunio Watanabe and Kajiro Yamamoto (Kurosawa's mentor) did indeed lend their skills to the construction of large-scale, wartime propaganda exercises, other directors – including some of the most famous – managed to keep a low profile during the war years. Mansaku Itami, for example, made no films at all, pleading illness; nor do the wartime films of Gosho, or Kinoshita, or Toyoda or Ozu display many recognisable 'national policy' overtones. This ought to be seen for the rather remarkable phenomenon that it is. It was not that Japanese culture, in other respects, was immune to the lure of propaganda. Dower cites lurid instances of the newspaper coverage of the war in China in which victims of Japanese aggression were routinely referred to with extraordinary cruelty and callousness. (In one notorious instance, in 1937, a Tokyo newspaper ran a competition to find out which Japanese soldier would be the first to cut down 150 Chinese with his samurai sword: prizes were offered.)[2] At the other end of the scale, Japanese novelists and intellectuals were not noted, either, for any very robust opposition to the war. Donald Keene (in a typically cogent essay on the subject: 'The Great East Asian War', *Landscapes and Portraits* [Tokyo, 1971]) says that, among well-known authors, only Nagai and Tanizaki remained unaffected by the wave of enthusiasm that swept up their contemporaries at the outbreak of Pacific hostilities. Thus the fact that, among the film-making community, there was any scepticism at all (let alone outright opposition) is itself interesting and noteworthy.

How thorough-going was Mizoguchi's own scepticism? What were his *real* feelings about the conflict? Commenting later on the years in question, Mizoguchi stressed their moral horror for him: 'It was a horrible time. There's really nothing more to say about it,' he remarks in an interview he gave in 1954, in which he goes through his career film by film. In so far as he offered any resistance at all to the authorities, he is self-deprecating and unheroic: 'At that time [he is speaking about 1945] everyone was mobilised. As for me – I hid.' Linking such evasive measures to the

---

2   John Dower (1986) 'War Hates and War Crimes', p. 42. But Iris Chang, who provides a photocopy illustration of the relevant newspaper in her book *The Rape of Nanking* (1997), also records instances where Japanese journalists showed proper shock at such excesses (pp. 47–8).

'Official' Mizoguchi: photograph taken during ceremonies in November 1940 to mark the 2,600th anniversary of the birth of Japan

greatest of his contemporaries, he remarks in the same interview: 'Ozu and I successfully avoided nuisances from the military authorities.'[3]

Yet against this self-portrait of exemplary low-keyed prudence, one has to take into consideration Mizoguchi's official prominence, in the early part of the war as president, of the Association of Japanese Film Directors. Tadao Sato gives us a brief glimpse of him, dressed in a tall hat and swathed in decorations, at the ceremony that took place in November 1940 to mark the 2,600th anniversary of the foundation of Japan, an event which, Sato says, moved him greatly. Yoda, too, in his memoirs, has a fascinating passage about the trip that he and Mizoguchi made to China in the summer of 1943 to scout a film that Shochiku was preparing at the time. During this journey, Mizoguchi demanded to be treated as a general (he had originally intended to go to China wearing a sword), and flew into a petulant rage when the company liaison officers in Shanghai accorded him less respect than he felt was his due. Commenting on this strange behaviour, Yoda writes blandly:

---

3 *Kinema Jumpo* no. 80, January 1954. I quote from the French version of this interview which appeared in *Cahiers du Cinéma* no. 95, May 1959.

I thought at first that this was simply an instance of puerile behaviour [on Mizoguchi's part] but thinking about it, I now realise it was dictated by the courage of a man who was above all anxious to defend
the proper dignity due to his profession.

On the surface it is hard to know quite what to make of this statement.[4]

    The facts of the war years may be resumed thus: between 1940 and 1945 Mizoguchi made
seven films altogether (included here as a single film is the two-part *The Loyal 47 Ronin*). Four of
these films – *The Woman of Osaka* (1940), *The Life of an Actor* (1941), *Three Generations of Danjuro* (1944) and *The Song of Victory* (1945) – are now lost. That leaves, in addition to *The Loyal 47
Ronin*, two surviving films: *Musashi Miyamoto* (1944) and *The Famous Sword Bijomaru/Meito
Bijomaru* (1945), both of them made for Shochiku, and both written not by Yoda but by
Mizoguchi's boyhood friend Matsutaro Kawaguchi. They are usually spoken about disparagingly
(Mizoguchi himself giving the lead here), as if they were self-evidently unworthy of comment. I
would not want to dwell overmuch on their aesthetic qualities, but they are certainly 'interesting';
and maybe not as dire, from an artistic point of view, as is sometimes suggested.[5] The two films
share with *The Loyal 47 Ronin* the theme of vengeance, and its deferral; both films – one
implicitly (since it belongs to the *chambara* genre), the other explicitly, through its title – meditat-
ing on the sword as an instrument of justice. In *The Famous Sword Bijomaru* (a period drama set
in the 1860s, at the time of the Imperial Restoration), there is an extended sequence that shows
the eponymous blade being manufactured. As the hero hammers the molten steel tube from
which the *katana* is going to be shaped, the ghostly presence of the film's heroine joins him at the
anvil to instil into his labours courage and perseverance. The sword, then, is mystical and holy:
because it has been made with the right spirit, it will not break or crack when the heroine eventually comes to use it to defend the imperial cause. Similar considerations of purity apply to the idea
of the sword in *Musashi Miyamoto* (set in the sixteenth century). Here the premise is that the heroine's parents and brother have been killed by a group of outlaws, leading her to plan vengeance
upon them. The legendary samurai Musashi, to whom Shino-o (Kinuyo Tanaka) turns for spiritual
guidance and for instruction in the arts of swordplay is initially reluctant to encourage her. The
code that he follows insists that swords should only be used against worthy opponents; if a sword
is going to be unsheathed, it should only be unsheathed as a last resort, and never in anger or cold
vengeance. Complicated twists of events lead to Musashi (Chojuro Kawarazaki) taking over the
quest from the heroine, but significantly, when he does eventually face his (or her) foe, he casts
aside his own combat sword in favour of a wooden paddle – he will not test his own blade on
human flesh.

    Like *The Loyal 47 Ronin*, then, these two war films may be read 'against genre' –
simultaneously for and against vengeance, depending upon what light you look at them under.
The problem is that the image of the sword is liable to make the modern viewer uneasy, for we
cannot help bearing in mind the terrible uses that both sword and bayonet *were* put to by the

---

4   Yoda quotation from p. 89 of *Souveinirs de Kenji Mizoguchi*, (1997 [author's translation]). Sato citation taken from the
    chronology section of *The World of Kenji Mizoguchi* (1982).

5   Keiko McDonald, among others, has no time for them (*Mizoguchi*, 1984, pp. 67–9). Indeed, I have not come across a critic
    prepared to put in a good word for them.

Japanese military machine during this time. It is difficult, surely, to exaggerate the cruelty of the crimes committed by both Japanese officers and conscripts in the pursuit of military dominance over a long period of time. Iris Chang reminds us that, while one in twenty-five allied prisoners-of-war died in German captivity, the corresponding figure for prisoners in Japanese hands was one in three. And many of these deaths were executions, with the emphasis on beheadings. They were the preferred or 'sporting' way of dispatching prisoners (shooting them was considered the lazy option). We are left asking ourselves: What is it appropriate to think about swords and their idealisation in these movies? Kyoko Hirano tells us that the American authorities, planning the occupation of Japan during the war, concocted a propaganda argument purporting to show the greater humanity of firearms (i.e. the preferred American weapon) over sword and blade in popular representations of violence in cinema; yet the reasoning behind such a preference seems, in the cold light of day, evidently specious and self-serving.[6] According to Yoda, Mizoguchi, on the aforementioned trip to China, first wore a sword and then abandoned it, as part of his fantasy of being a general. (Note that if he really *had* been commissioned, the sword would have gone with the uniform: a ceremonial appurtenance – the same as in all armies everywhere.) Yet he did abandon the weapon, and that itself is noteworthy. At this distance, definitive judgments (which aren't sanctimonious) are difficult to reach – there is probably no verdict that will satisfy everyone.

---

6   Kyoko Hirano (1992), p. 67. See also for a recent, unforgiving look at Japanese sword culture in the Pacific War: Brian MacArthur, *Surviving the Sword* (2005).

Filmography

The Song of Home (*Furusato no Uta*, 1925)
Director: Kenji Mizoguchi
Script: Ryunosuke Shimizu, based on a story by Choji Matsui
Photography: Tatsuyuki Yokota
Cast: Shigeru Kido/Kifugi (Naotaro), Masujiro Takagi (Naotaro's father), Sueko Ito (Naotaro's mother), Mineko Tsuji (Okinu), Kentaro Kawamata (Junichi), Shiro Kato (Junichi's father), Shizue Matsumoto (Junichi's mother), Michiko Tachibana (Taro Maesake), Hiromichi Kawata (school principal), Yutaka Mimau (American professor)
Running time: 45 minutes
Filmed at: Nikkatsu Taishogun Studios, Kyoto
Release date: 3 December 1925

Tokyo March (*Tokyo Koshinkyoku*, 1929) [fragment]
Director: Kenji Mizoguchi
Script: Chiio Kimura and Shuichi Hatamoto, based on Kan Kikuchi's novel of the same name, serialised in the magazine *Kingu*
Photography: Tatsuyuki Yokota
Cast: Shizue Natsukawa (Orie), Koji Shima (Yoshiki Fujimoto), Isamu Kosigi (Yukichi Sakuma, his friend), Eiji Takagi (Yoshiki's father), Takao Irie (Yoshiki's sister [not shown in the surviving fragment])
Original running time: 80 or 102 minutes according to different sources. (Surviving fragment is 20 minutes)
Filmed at: Nikkatsu Uzumasa Studios, Kyoto
Release date: 31 May 1929
Nikkatsu had planned to make this their first sound film, but the technology was not quite there. Instead, a (silent) version was released in tandem with a record of the same title, written by Yaso Saijo (words) and Shinpei Nakayama (melody). The record enjoyed a great success (250,000 copies sold) and helped to bolster the movie's fortunes.

Home Town (*Furusato*, 1930)
Director: Kenji Mizoguchi
Script: Satoshi Kisaragi, Shuichi Hatamoto and Masashi Kobayashi, from an original idea by Iwao Mori

Photography: Tatsuyuki Yokota and Yoshio Mineo
Sound: Toshio Naryu and Yoshikatsu Urashima
Music: Toyoaki Tanaka, Tamaki Maeda, Mr and Mrs Constantine Shapiro
Cast: Yoshie Fujiwara (Fujimura), Shizue Natsukawa (Ayako, his girlfriend), Fujiko Hamaguchi (Natsue Omura, Ayako's rival), Kunio Tamora (Sankichi), Heitaro Doi (Hattori)
Running time: 107 minutes
Filmed at: Nikkatsu Uzumasa Studios, Kyoto
Release date: 14 March 1930
Mizoguchi's first sound film. His next eight films (only one of which survives) were silent.

The Water Magician (Taki no Shiraito, 1933)

Director: Kenji Mizoguchi
Producer: Takako Irie
Production supervisors: Yoshizo Mogi and Takejiro Tsunoda
Script: Yasunaga Higashibojo, Shinji Masuda and Kennosuke Tateoka, based on the novel *Giketsu Kyoketsu* (*Ripe Virility*) by Kyoka Izumi
Photography: Shigeru Miki
Cast: Takako Irie (Taki no Shiraito), Tokihiko Okada (Kin-san), Suzuko Taki (Nadeshiko), Bontaro Miake (Shinzo), Ichiro Sugai (Iwabuchi), Koju Murata (Minami, knife thrower), Kumeko Urabe (Ogin), Minoru Oharu (Tanjiro), Nobuo Kosaka (Inspector Takamura), Etsuzo Oki (judge)
Running time: 110 minutes
Filmed at: Shinko Kinema Uzumasa Studios, Kyoto.
Production Company: Irie Production
Release date: 1 June 1933
A commercial success: Irie and Okada were two popular stars of the time. But in the same year Mizoguchi fell out with Irie (apparently he didn't agree with women running their own production companies).

The Downfall of Osen (Orizuru Osen, 1935)

Director: Kenji Mizoguchi
Producer: Masaichi Nagata
Script: Tatsunosuke Takashima, based on the short story 'Baishoku Kamonanban' by Kyoka Izumi
Photography: Minoru [Shigeto] Miki
Lights: Masuichi Nakanishi
Special effects: Hichiro Nishi
Costumes: Sajiro Ogasa
Sound: Tsuneo Sayato, Yunichi Murota and Eiichi Mikura
Music: Akitada Matsui
Narrator: Akitada Matsui

Cast: Isuzu Yamada (Osen), Daijiro Natsukawa (Sokichi), Shin Shibata (Kumazawa), Genichi Fujii (Matsuda), Mitsuru Tojo (Amadani), Jinishi Kitamura (Sakazujki no Heishiro), Shizuko Takizawa (Osode), Sue Ito (Sokichi's grandmother)
Running time: 78 minutes
Filmed at: Daiichi Sagano Studios, Kyoto
Production company: Daiichi Eiga
Release date: 20 January 1935

Oyuki Madonna (*Maria no Oyuki*, 1935)
Director: Kenji Mizoguchi
Producer: Masaichi Nagata
Script: Matsutaro Kawaguchi and Tatsunosuke Takashima, from Guy de Maupassant's story 'Boule de suif'
Photography: Minoru Miki
Sound: Junichi Murota
Music chosen by: Koichi Takagi, played by Chuotoki Ongaku Kyokai, directed by Ryuho Sakai and Kanema Yusaku
Editor: Junkichi Ishigi
Cast: Isuzu Yamada (Oyuki), Komako Hara (Okin), Daijiro Natsukawa (Shingo Asakura), Eiji Nakano (so-called priest), Keiji Oizumi (rice merchant), Kinue Utagawa (merchant's daughter), Shin Shibata (Keishiro Yokoi), Yoko Umemura (Michiko, his wife), Toichiro Nagishi (Gonda Hyoe), Shizuko Takizawa (Oise, his wife), Kasuke Koizumi (Gisuke, the driver), Tadashi Torii (army colonel)
Running time: 78 minutes
Filmed at: Daiichi Sagano Studios, Kyoto
Production company: Daiichi Eiga
Release date: 30 May 1935

Mizoguchi considered the script to be sub-par. The scenarist, Kawaguchi, Mizoguchi's friend and collaborator from boyhood, was an important shimpa *playwright in his own right. Among other writers (such as Eiichi Seto and Ryuichiro Yagi) he was responsible, at around this time, for modernising and revivifying the theatrical repertory. Plays like* Tsuruhachi and Tsurujiro *(1934),* The Story of the Elegant Fukagawa *(1935) and* The Life of a Meiji Woman *(1935) gave* shimpa *drama a new lease of life during the 1930s.*

Poppy (*Gubijinso*, 1935)
Director: Kenji Mizoguchi
Producer: Masaichi Nagata
Script: Haruo Takayagi and Daisuke Ito, from the novel by Soseki Natsume
Photography: Minoru Miki
Sound: Yasumi Mizoguchi, Tatsuki Murita, with six assistants
Music chosen by: Ryuho Sakai and Koichi Takagi
Costumes: Shojiro Kosoza, with advice from Daizaburo Nakamura

Editor: Tatsuko Sakane
Cast: Kuniko Miyake (Fujio Kono, pupil and would-be lover of Seizo Ono), Chiyoko Okura (Sayoko Inoue), Yukichi Iwata (Sayoko's father), Ichiro Tsukida (Seizo Ono, Sayoko's fiancé), Daijiro Natsukawa (Munechika, Fujio's fiancé), Kazuyoshie Takeda (Kingo, Fujio's half-brother), Toichiro Negishi (Asai, Seizo Ono's friend)
Running time: 72 minutes
Filmed at: Daiichi Sagano Studios, Kyoto
Production company: Daiichi Eiga
Release date: 31 October 1935

Osaka Elegy (Naniwa Erejii, 1936)
Director: Kenji Mizoguchi
Producer: Masaichi Nagata
Script: Yoshikata Yoda, from the serial 'Mieko' by Saburo Okada, in the magazine *Shincho*
Photography: Minoru Miki
Sound: Kase Hisashi and Yasumi Mizoguchi
Music: Koichi Takagi
Cast: Isuzu Yamada (Ayako Murai), Seichi Takegawa (Junzo, her father), Chiyoko Okura (Sachiko, Ayako's sister), Shinpachiro Asaka (Hiroshi, Ayako's brother), Benkei Shiganoya (Asai, company owner), Yoko Umemura (Sumiko, his wife), Eitaro Shindo (Fujino, Ayako's boss, friend of Asai), Kensaku Hara (Nishimura, Ayako's fiancé), Kuneo Tamura (doctor), Takasi Shimura (police inspector)
Running time: 66 minutes
Filmed at: Daiichi Sagano Studios, Kyoto
Production company: Daiichi Eiga
Release date: 28 May 1936
Mizoguchi's first collaboration with Yoda. This film and Sisters of the Gion *were shot quickly: the production period in each case was under a month.*

Sisters of the Gion (Gion no Shimai, 1936)
Director: Kenji Mizoguchi
Producer: Masaichi Nagata
Script: Yoshikata Yoda
Photography: Minoru Miki
Sound: Kase Hisashi
Cast: Isuzu Yamada (Omocha), Yoko Umemura (Umekichi, her sister), Benkei Shiganoya (Furusawa, Umekichi's patron), Kazuko Hisano (Furusawa's wife), Fumio Okura (antique shop proprietor), Taizo Fukami (Kimura, the drapery clerk), Eitaro Shindo (Kudo, his boss)
Running time: 69 minutes
Filmed at: Daiichi Sagano Studios, Kyoto
Production company: Daiichi Eiga
Release date: 15 October 1936

The Straits of Love and Hate (*Aien Kyo*, 1937)

Director: Kenji Mizoguchi
Producer: Masaichi Nagata
Script: Yoshikata Yoda, from an idea by Matsutaro Kawaguchi
Photography: Minoru Miki
Production design: Hiroshi Mizutani
Sound: Akira Ando, Kentaro Nada, with effects by Shohachiro Kineya
Music: Mizuo Ukagami
Editors: Tazuko Sakane and Mitsuo Kondo
Cast: Fumiko Yamaji (Ofumi), Masao Shimizu (Kenkichi, Ofumi's lover), Seizaburo Kawazu (Yoshitaro, Ofumi's new lover), Yutaka Mimasu (Kenkichi's father), Kiyoe Aki (Kenkichi's mother), Seiichi Kato (Ofumi's uncle), Haruo Tanaka (Hirose, Kenkichi's Tokyo friend and landlord), Kaoru Nobe (Hirose's wife), Kumeko Urabe (adoptive mother of Ofumi's child), Keiji Ozumi (her husband)
Running time: 88 minutes
Filmed at: Shinko Kinema Oizumi Studios, Tokyo
Production company: Shinko
Release date: 17 June 1937
First officially credited collaboration with production designer Hiroshi Mizutani. (Unofficially, he had worked with Mizoguchi since 1934.)

The Story of Late Chrysanthemums (*Zangiku Monogatari*, 1939)

Director: Kenji Mizoguchi
Producer: Nobutaro Shirai
Production planner: Matsutaro Kawaguchi
Script: Yoshikata Yoda and Matsutaro Kawaguchi, after a story by Shofu Muramatsu and a theatrical adaptation of that story by Sanichi Iwaya
Photography: Minoru Miki
Production design: Hiroshi Mizutani
Décors: Tsunetaro Kikukawa and Dai Arawaka
Costume: Seizo Yamaguchi and Yoshizaburo Okumura
Artistic research: Sohachi Kimura, Nanboku Kema
Historical research: Seikichi Terekado
Sound: Ryuichi Shikita and Fumizo Sugimoto, with three assistants
Music: Senji Ito and Shiro Fukai
Players of instruments: Katsukjuro Kineya and Tamezo Mochizuki
Singers and chanters: Bunshi Tokiwazu, Bunnosuke Tokiwazu, Sempachi Sakata and Enjiro Toyosawa
Choreography: Kikuzo Otowa
Editor: Koshi Kawahigashi

Cast: Shotaro Hanayagi (Kikunosuke Onoe [Kikugoro Onoe VI]), Kakuko Mori (Otoku), Kokichi Takada (Fukusuke Nakamura), Gonjuro Kawararaki (Kikugoro Onoe V), Yoko Umemura (Osato, his wife), Ryotaro Kawanami (Eiju Dayu), Nobuko Fushimi (Onaka, a geisha)

Running time: 142 minutes

Production company: Shochiku

Filmed at: Shochiku Shimokamo Studios, Kyoto

Release date: 13 October 1939

Filmed under ideal conditions, according to Mizoguchi. Mizoguchi knew Kikugoro personally, and after the war invited him to take the main role in a film dealing with Kakiemon, a master potter of the Edo period. The project was aborted by the kabuki master's sudden death in July 1949.

The Loyal 47 Ronin (Genroku Chushingura, 1941–2)

Director: Kenji Mizoguchi

Producer: Nobutaro Shirai

Script: Kenichiro Hara and Yoshikata Yoda, from Seika Mayama's modern kabuki play cycle based on a well-known incident that took place in 1701

Photography: Kohei Sugiyama, with three lighting assistants

Production design: Hiroshi Mizutani and Kaneto Shindo

Set decoration: Matsuji Ono, Shun Rokugo, Nobutaro Ogura, Sumao Matsuoka, Dai Arakawa and Hisakichi Osawa

Set paintings on sliding doors: Harunobu Numai and Eigo Ito

Costumes: Ryuzo Kawada and Kisaburo Okamura

Hairstyles: Ishitaro Takagi

Sound: Hidekata Sasaki, Fumizo Sugimoto and Koichi Tashiro, with four assistants

Musical supervision: Shiro Fukai

Music played by: Kokyokugaku-dan Shin, directed by Kazuo Yamada

Architectural advisers: Yoshikuni Okuma and Motoharu Fujita

Historical advisers: Kusune Kainoso, Tsutomu Ema and Sadajiro Utumi

Garden design: Harubei Ogawa

Weapons adviser: Sumio Kubo

Linguistic adviser: Taizo Ehara

Cast: Chojuro Kawarazaki (chamberlain Oishi), Yoshizaburo Arashi (Lord Asano, his master), Mantoyo Mimasu (Lord Kira), Shizue Yamagichi (Oriku, Oishi's wife), Sensho Ichikawa (his elder son), Umenosuke Nakamura (his younger son), Yasuko Mitsui (his daughter), Mitsuko Muira (Yosenin, Lady Asano), Kunitaro Kawarazaki (Jurozaemon), Mieko Takamine (Omino), Kanemon Nakamura (Sukeemon), Utaemon Ichikawa (Tsunatoyo Tokugawa), Keichi Shimada (Arai Hakusaki), plus forty-seven other named parts

Running time: 222 minutes [Part I: 110 minutes; Part II: 112 minutes]

Production company: Koa Eiga (division of Shochiku)

Filmed at: Koa Uzumasa Studios, Kyoto (Part I); Shochiku Studios, Kyoto (Part II)

Release date: Part I: 1 December 1941; Part II: 11 February 1942

The film cost ¥105 million and all but bankrupted Shochiku. (According to the Andrew brothers, the cost of a major film at this time rarely exceeded ¥100,000.) Though the public didn't like the film, the government was pleased, awarding it a special artistic prize through the Ministry of Education.

Musashi Miyamoto (*Miyamoto Musashi*, 1944)

Director: Kenji Mizoguchi
Script: Matsutaro Kawaguchi, adapted from Kan Kikuchi's serial of the same name appearing in the newspaper *Mainichi Shinbun*
Photography: Minoru Miki
Martial arts adviser: Hiromasa Kono
Cast: Chojuro Kawarazaki (Musashi Miyamoto), Kinuyo Tanaka (Shinobu Nonomiya), Kigoro Ikushima (Genichiro Nonomiya, her brother), Kanemon Nakamura (Kojiro Sasaki, rival swordsman)
Running time: 53 minutes
Filmed at: Shochiku Studios, Kyoto
Release date: 28 December 1944

The Famous Sword Bijomaru (*Meito Bijomaru*, 1945)

Director: Kenji Mizoguchi
Script: Matsutaro Kawaguchi
Photography: Minoru Miki and Haruo Takeno
Artistic adviser: Kusune Kainosho
Cast: Shotaro Hanayagi (Kiyone Sakurai), Isuzu Yamada (Sasae Onoda), Ichijiro Oya (Kozaemon Onoda), Eijiro Yanagi (Kiyohide Yamatomori), Kan Ishii (Kiyotsugu)
Running time: 65 minutes
Filmed at: Shochiku Studios, Kyoto
Release date: 8 February 1945

Victory of Women (*Josei no Shori*, 1946)

Director: Kenji Mizoguchi
Producers: Sennosuke Tsukimori (planning) and Kenichiro Yasuda (head of production)
Script: Kogo Noda and Kaneto Shindo
Photography: Toshio Ubukata
Production design: Isamu Motogi, with Kazuma Kaoda and Jiro Nakamura
Sound: Hisao Ono, with Rokusaburo Saito
Music: Kozoaki Asai
Editor: Yoshiko Sugihara
Cast: Kinuyo Tanaka (Hiroko), Michiko Kuwano (Michiko, her elder sister), Eiko Uchimura (Yukiko, her younger sister), Toyoko Takahashi (Setsu, Hiroko's mother), Mitsuko Miura (Moto Asakura, Hiroko's client), Shin Tokudaira (Yamaoka), Akiko Kazami (Hiroko's legal colleague), Shinyo Nara (judge), Katsuhira Matsumoto (Kono, Advocate General)
Running time: 84 minutes

Filmed at: Shochiku Ofuna Studios, Tokyo
Release date: 18 April 1946
Michiko Kuwano, a great personal friend of Mizoguchi, died shortly after the completion of this production.

Five Women Round Utamaro (*Utamaro o Meguru Gonin no Onna*, 1946)

Director: Kenji Mizoguchi
Producer: Toyokazu Murata
Script: Yoshikata Yoda, adapted from a novel by Kanji Kunieda
Photography: Minoru Miki
Production designer: Isamu Motoki
Historical and artistic adviser: Kusune Kainosho
Sound: Hisashi Kase
Music: Hisato Osawa and Tamezo Mochizuke
Editor: Shintaro Miyamoto
Cast: Minosuke Bando (Utamaro), Kinuyo Tanaka (Okita), Kotaro Bando (Seinosuke), Eiko Ohara (Yukie), Hiroko Kawasaki (Oran), Shotaro Nakamura (Shozaburo), Toshiko Izuka (Takasodé), Kyoko Kusojima (Oman), Kiniko Shiratao (Oshin), Minpei Tomimoto (Takemaro)
Running time: 106 minutes
Filmed at: Shochiku Studios, Kyoto
Release date: 17 December 1946
Kanji Kunieda, the author of the original novel, attacked Mizoguchi in the press on the film's release for betraying the book's eroticism. Mizoguchi answered these charges in a radio interview, broadcast on 25 January 1947.

The Love of Sumako the Actress (*Joyu Sumako no Koi*, 1947)

Director: Kenji Mizoguchi
Producers: Hisao Itoya and Tazuko Sakane
Script: Yoshikata Yoda, from the novel *Karumen Yukinu* (*Carmen Is Dead*) by Hideo Osada
Photography: Minoru Miki
Production design: Isamu Motoki
Sound: Kaname Hashimoto, assisted by Tatsuo Sakai and Mitsuo Okada
Music: Hisato Osawa
Theatrical consultants: Eitaro Ozawa and Koreya Senda
Historical adviser: Seiichi Kato
Costume adviser: Kusune Kainosho
Costumes: Kotaro Kato
Editor: Shintaro Miyamoto
Cast: Kinuyo Tanaka (Sumako Matsui), So Yamamura (Hogetsu Shimamura), Eijiro Tono (Shoyo Tsubouchi), Eitaro Ozawa (Kichizo Nakamura), Kikue Mori (Ichiko Shimamura), Hisao Kokubota (Shimpei Nakayama), Zeya Chida, Teruko Kishi, Shin Tokudaiji, Tomoo Nagai, Sugisaku Aoyama
Running time: 96 minutes

Filmed at: Shochiku Studios, Kyoto
Release date: 16 August 1947
Sumako's life was the subject of another film in the same year as this, The Actress (Joyo), directed by Teinosuke Kinugasa for Toho, and starring Isuzu Yamada. (Tadao Sato prefers the Kinugasa version.) Thematically, Mizoguchi's film bears interesting comparison with other, more recent films about women artists struggling in a man's world such as Camille Claudel *(Bruno Nuytten, 1988) and* Frida *(Julie Taymor, 2002).*

Women of the Night (*Yoru no Onnatachi*, 1948)
Director: Kenji Mizoguchi
Producers: Mitsushio Shimizu and Hisao Itoya
Script: Yoshikata Yoda, from the novel *Joseimatsuri* (*Feast of Women*) by Eijiro Hisaita
Photography: Kohei Sugiyama
Production design: Hiroshi Mizutani
Sound: Taro Takahashi
Assistants: Tatsuo Sakai and Mitsuo Okada
Music: Hisato Osawa, played by Hisashi Nakazawa and the MSC Orchestra
Editor: Tazuko Sakane
Cast: Kinuyo Tanaka (Fusako Owada), Sanae Takasugi (Natsuko, her sister), Tomie Tsunoda (Kumiko, Fusako's sister-in-law), Mitsuo Nagata (Kuriyama), Minpei Tomomoto (Koki Owada, Fusako's brother-in-law), Kumeko Urabe (female pimp)
Running time: 73 minutes [105 minutes]
Filmed at: Shochiku Studios and on location in the Kansai area
Release date: 28 May 1948
For the second year in succession, Kinuyo Tanaka's performance in a Mizoguchi film won her the award for Best Actress at the Mainichi Film Festival.

My Love Has Been Burning (*Waga Koi Wa Moenu*, 1949)
Director: Kenji Mizoguchi
Producers: Hisao Itoya, Kiyoshi Shimazu and Tomoji Kubo
Script: Yoshikata Yoda and Kaneto Shindo, from a novel by Kogo Noda itself drawing on Hideko Kageyama's memoir *Mekake no Hanshogai* (*Half a Lifetime as a Mistress*)
Photography: Kohei Sugiyama and Tomotara Nashiki
Production design: Hiroshi Mizutani
Art department: Daia Arakawa, Junichiro Osumi, Kiyoharu Matsuno and Sueyoshi Kimura
Costumes: Tsuma Nakamura
Sound: Taro Takahashi and Takeo Kawakita
Assistants: Tatsuo Sakai and Mitsuo Okada
Music: Senji Ito, played by the Shochiku Kyoto Orchestra
Historical research: Sunao Kai

Cast: Kinuyo Tanaka (Eiko Hirayama), Shinobu Araki (Eiko's father), Ikuko Hirano (Eiko's mother), Eitaro Ozawa (Hayase), Ichiro Sugai (Kentaro Oe), Mitsuko Mito (Chiyo), Kuniko Miyake (Mrs Kishida), Eijiro Tono (Ito), Hiroshi Murata (Chiyo's husband), Sadako Sawamura (Omasa, female prisoner)
Running time: 96 minutes
Filmed at: Shochiku Studios, Kyoto
Release date: 13 February 1949

The Andrew brothers (in Kenji Mizoguchi: A Guide to References and Resources, *p. 85) provide this useful historical note: 'A depression in 1881 caused silk farmers in the Chichibu district of Saitama-ken to fall prey to usurers. In 1883 they banded together and asked the government to help them out of this bottomless pit, but were completely ignored. The [extragovernmental] Liberal Party (Jiyu-to) became established there in 1884 as a result of an election campaign, and through it the silk farmers increased the pressure of their demands. On 2 November of that year, with the help of Liberal Party members from other regions, the Chichibu Liberal party raided the government office, police headquarters, and usurers' houses. They controlled the Chichibu area for two days before being driven out by government forces. On 11 November government troops caught up this retreating contingent. Seven rebels were executed, 289 were given heavy sentences, 448 lighter sentences, and 2642 were fined in what came to be known as the Chichibu Incident.' It is worth noting that Mizoguchi had already broached the incident in an earlier (now lost) film* Aizo Toge/The Mountain Pass of Love and Hate *(1934).*

A Picture of Madame Yuki (Yuki Fujin Ezu, 1950)
Director: Kenji Mizoguchi
Producers: Kazuo Takimura, Ryohei Arai and Saiya Kashima
Script: Yoshikata Yoda and Kazuro Funabashi, based on a novel by Kazuro's brother Seiichi Funabashi that was serialised in the magazine *Shosetsu Shincho*
Photography: Joji Ohara
Production design: Hiroshi Mizutani
Artistic adviser: Kusune Kainosho
Sound: Masakazu Kamiya
Assistants: Haku Komori and Seiichiro Uchikawa
Music: Fumio Hayasaka
Editors: Toshio Goto and Shiro Timba
Cast: Michiyo Kogure (Madame Yuki), Eijaro Yanagi (Naoyuki, her husband), Ken Uehara (Masaya, Yuki's friend), Yuriko Hamada (Ayako, Naoyuki's mistress), Yoshiko Kuga (Hamako, Madame Yuki's servant), Haruya Kato (Seitaro, house servant)
Running time: 88 minutes
Filmed at: Shintoho Studios, Kyoto
Release date: 14 October 1950

Miss Oyu (Oyu-sama, 1951)

Director: Kenji Mizoguchi
Producers: Masaichi Nagata and Matsutaro Kawaguchi
Script: Yoshikata Yoda, adapted from Junichiro Tanizaki's novel *Ashikari* (*Harvest of Reeds*)
Photography: Kazuo Miyagawa and Kenichi Okamoto
Production design: Hiroshi Mizutani
Art department: Yonematsu Hayashi and Kosaburo Nakajima
Paintings: Tazaburo Ota
Costumes: Shima Yoshizane
Artistic adviser: Kusune Kainosho
Sound: Iwao Otani
Music: Fumio Hayasaka
Tea ceremony adviser: Kaisen Iguchi
Noh advisers: Shogin Hagiwara, Kanahichi Koharu
Choreography: Mutsumei Shigeto
Editor: Mitsuzo Miyata
Cast: Kinuyo Tanaka (Miss Oyu), Nobuko Otowa (Oshizu, her sister), Yuji Hori (Shinnosuke, the 'stranger'), Kiyoko Hirai (Osumi), Reiko Kongo (Otsugi), Eijaro Yanagi (Eitaro), Eitaro Shindo (Kusaemon), Kanae Kobayashi (wet-nurse), Fumiko Yokoyama (clerk), Jun Fujikawa (clerk), Soji Shibata (clerk), Inosuke Kahara (shop-boy), Ayuko Fijishiro (maid), Shozu Nanbu (physician), Midori Komatsu (hostess), Sachiko Aima (teacher of flower arrangement), Sumao Ishihara (priest)
Running time: 96 minutes
Filmed at: Daiei Studios, Kyoto
Release date: 22 June 1951

The Lady from Musashino (Musashino Fujin, 1951)

Director: Kenji Mizoguchi
Producers: Hideo Koi and Teruo Maki
Script: Yoshikata Yoda, from the novel by Shohei Ooka, adapted by Tsuneari Fukuda
Photography: Masao Tamai
Production design: Takashi Matsuyama
Sound: Shoji Kageyama
Music: Fumio Hayasaka
Editor: Ryoji Bando
Cast: Kinuyo Tanaka (Michiko Akiyama), Masayuki Mori (Tadao, her husband), So Yamamura (Eiji Ono, next-door neighbour), Yukiko Todoroki (Tomiko, his wife), Minako Nakamura (Yukiko, their daughter), Akihiko Katayama (Tsutomo Miyaji, Michiko's lover), Eitaro Shindo (Shinzaburo Miyaji), Kiyoko Hirai (Tamiko Miyaji), Satoshi Nishida (Narita), Toyoji Shiosawa (Harue Narita), Reiko Otani, Yasuzo Fukami, Noriko Sengoku
Running time: 88 minutes
Filmed at: Toho Studios, Kyoto

Release date: 14 September 1951

The Andrew brothers' summary of this film, in which they state that Tsutomo unequivocally 'rejects [Michiko's] inheritance' by walking off to make a new start in the city, seems unduly one-sided. Certainly, Tsutomo walks away from the house, but on the soundtrack we hear Michiko's letter of bequest being read out as a voice-over. The music, the rhythm, the very way the scene is shot all seem to entertain the possibility that Tsutomo will use his inheritance, as Michiko urges him to do, to pursue useful works such as setting up schools and hospitals. Mizoguchi: 'I wanted to describe the same kind of woman that I portrayed in Madame Yuki but something about the character didn't work out properly.'

The Life of Oharu (*Saikaku Ichidai Onna*, 1952)

Director: Kenji Mizoguchi

Producers: Hideo Koi

Script: Yoshikata Yoda, adapted from Ihara Saikaku's novel *Koshoku Ichidai Onna* (*The Life of an Amorous Woman*)

Photography: Yoshimi Hirano

Production design: Hiroshi Mizutani

Sound: Miwa Kamiya, assisted by Rychei Arai and Seiichiro Uchikawa

Music: Ichiro Saito

Koto played by: Masakoe Hagiwara

Samisen played by: Enjiro Toyosawa

Joruri accompaniment: Gendayu Takemoto

Choreography: Yachiyo Inoue

Puppets: Monjiro Kiritake

Artistic/historical adviser: Isamu Yoshii

Editor: Toshio Goto

Cast: Kinuyo Tanaka (Oharu), Toshiro Mifune (Katsunosuke), Masao Shimizu (Kikuoji), Tsukie Matsura (Tomo, Oharu's mother), Ichiro Sugai (Shinzaemon, her father), Kiyoko Tsuji (landlady of an inn), Toshiaki Konoe (Lord Matsudaira), Hisako Yamane (Lady Matsudaira), Yuriko Hamada (Otsubone Yoshioka), Noriko Sengoku (lady-in-waiting Sakurai), Haruyo Ichikawa (lady-in-waiting Iwabashi), Kyoko Kusajima (lady-in-waiting Sodegaki), Eitaro Shindo (Kahei Sasaya), Sadako Sawamura (Owasa, his wife), Hiroshi Oizumi (Bunkichi, Sasaya's employee), Eijiro Yanagi (counterfeiter), Jikichi Ono (Yakichi Ogiya, Oharu's husband, a merchant of fans), Chieko Higashiyama (the old nun Myokai), Tozen Hidari (owner of the clothes rental store), Takashi Shimura (old pilgrim), Benkei Shiganoya (Jihei, Sasaya's chief clerk)

Running time: 148 minutes [133 minutes]

Filmed at: Shintoho Studios, Kyoto

Release date: 3 April 1952

Mizoguchi: 'I had been thinking of the film for five or six years before I made it. It is good to ponder long before commencing a project.'

Tales of the Watery Moon (Ugetsu Monogatari, 1953)

Director: Kenji Mizoguchi
Producers: Masaichi Nagata and Hisakazu Tsuji (planning)
Script: Yoshikata Yoda and Matsutaro Kawaguchi, from two stories from Akinari Ueda's collection *Ugetsu Monogatari* ('The House Amid the Thickets' and 'The Lust of the White Serpent') and two tales by Guy de Maupassant ('Decoré!' and 'Lit 29')
Photography: Kazuo Miyagawa, assisted by Shozo Tanaka
Production design: Kisaku Ito, assisted by Yusuo Iwaki
Lighting: Kenichi Okamoto
Scenery and setting: Tasaburo Ota and Uichiro Yamamoto
Costumes: Shima Yoshimi
Make-up and hairstyles: Zenya Fukuyama and Ritsu Hanai
Artistic/historical adviser: Kusune Kainosho
Dialogue adviser: Isamu Yoshii
Pottery adviser: Zengoro Eiraku
Choreography: Kinsichi Kodera
Sound: Iwao Otani, assisted by Teru Suzuki
Music: Fumio Hayasaka, assisted by Ichiro Saito
Editor: Mitsuzo Miyata
Cast: Masayuki Mori (Genjuro), Kinuyo Tanaka (Miyagi), Ichisaburo Sawamura (Genichi, their son), Sakae Ozawa (Tobei), Mitsuko Mito (Ohama), Machiko Kyo (Lady Wakasa), Kikue Mori (Ukon, her attendant), Tokiko Mito, Tokuko Ueda (ladies-in-waiting to Lady Wakasa), Ryosuke Kagawa (headman of village), Eigoro Onoe (defeated general), Saburo Date (his retainer), Kozabuno Ramon (Lord Niwa), Ichiro Amano (boatman), Kichijiro Ueda (shopkeeper), Sugisaku Aoyama (Buddhist priest), Shozu Nanbu (Shinto priest), Reiko Kondo (proprietress of brothel), Teruko Omi, Keiko Koyanagi, Masako Tomura (prostitutes), Jun Fujikawa, Ryuji Fukui, Eiji Ishiguro, Koji Fukuda (soldiers)
Running time: 97 minutes
Filmed at: Daiei Studios, Kyoto, and on location near Lake Biwa
Release date: 23 March 1953
The film won the Silver Lion at the 1953 Venice Film Festival in addition to the Italian Critics' Prize. Art direction, sound work and camera all received special recognition at different festivals. Originally, Mizoguchi was in favour of a harsher ending: according to his first thoughts, Tobei shouldn't have been allowed to 'see the light', but should continue to pursue his misguided social ambitions. Daiei demurred, citing commercial reasons, and imposed the present ending in which both the main characters are made to see the error of their ways.

Gion Festival Music (Gion Bayashi, 1953)

Director: Kenji Mizoguchi
Producer: Masaichi Nagata, Hisakazu Tsuji (planning) and Masatsugu Hashimoto (production)
Script: Yoshikata Yoda, from a magazine story by Matsutaro Kawaguchi
Photography: Kazuo Miyagawa

Production design: Kazume Koike, assisted by Ichizo Kajitani
Lighting: Kenichi Okamoto
Backgrounds and sets: Seizaburo Ogura, Takejiro Nakajima.
Costumes: Yoshiko Kurosawa
Costume adviser: Yoshio Ueno
Hair: Tsuru Nakai
Sound: Iwao Otani
Music: Ichiro Saito and Takemichi Mochizuki
Editor: Mitsuzo Miyata
Cast: Michiyo Kogure (Miyoharu), Ayako Wakao (Eiko), Seizaburo Kawazu (Kusuda), Kanji Koshiba (Kanzaki), Eitaro Shindo (Sawamoto, Eiko's father), Ichiro Sugai (Saeki), Chieko Naniwa (Okimi), Saburo Date (Imanishi), Haruo Tanaka (Ogawa), Kikue Mori (geisha instructor)
Running time: 85 minutes
Filmed at: Daiei Studios, Kyoto
Release date: 12 August 1953
Mizoguchi: 'I wanted to make the Ayako Wakao character tougher and more ambitious, but once again the producers interfered for purely commercial reasons.'

Sansho the Bailiff (Sansho Dayu, 1954)

Director: Kenji Mizoguchi
Producers: Masaichi Nagata, Hisakazu Tsuji (planning) and Masatsugu Hashimoto (production)
Script: Yoshikata Yoda and Fuji Yahiro, from the tale by Ogai Mori first published in the magazine *Chuo Koron*
Photography: Kazuo Miyagawa
Production design: Hiromoto Ito and Shozaburo Nakajima, with Uichiro Yamamoto
Lighting: Kenichi Okamoto
Costumes: Yoshio Ueno and Shima Yoshimi
Sound: Iwao Otani
Music: Fumio Hayasaka
Traditional music: Kanehichi Odera and Tamezo Mochizuki
Combat adviser: Shohei Miyauchi
Architectural adviser: Giichi Fujiwara
Editor: Mitsuzo Miyata
Cast: Kinuyo Tanaka (Tamaki), Yoshiaki Hanayaki (Zushio, her son), Kyoko Kagawa (Anju, his sister), Masao Shimizu (Masauji Taira, their father), Eitaro Shindo (Sansho the bailiff), Akitake Kawano (Taro, Sansho's son), Ryosuke Kagawa (Donmo, his other son), Ken Mitsuda (Fujiwara no Mitsuzane, prime minister), Chieko Naniwa (old lady), Kimiko Tachibana (Namiji), Yoko Kosono (Kohagi), Ichiro Sugai (minister of justice), Masahiko Kato (Zushio as boy), Naoki Fujima (Zushio as infant), Keiko Enami (Anju as child), Bontaro Akemi (Kichiji), Kikue Mori (pirate procuress), Ryonosuke Higashi (brothel owner), Ichiro Amano (gatekeeper), Sumao Ishihara (old graveyard keeper)
Running time: 123 minutes

Filmed at: Daiei Studios, Kyoto
Release date: 31 March 1954
Awarded the Silver Lion at the 1954 Venice Film Festival.

The Woman of Rumour (Uwasa no Onna, 1954)

Director: Kenji Mizoguchi
Producers: Masaichi Nagata, Hisakazu Tsuji (planning) and Masatsugu Hashimoto (production)
Script: Yoshikata Yoda and Masashige Narusawa
Photography: Kazuo Miyagawa
Production design: Hiroshi Mizutani
Sound: Iwao Otani
Music: Toshiro Mayuzumi
Noh music: Kurozaemon Katayama
Lighting: Kenichi Okamoto
Paintings: Tazaburo Ota
Set decorator: Takejiro Nakajima
Special effects: Kyochiro Yamamoto
Costumes: Yoshie Ueno and Ayako Hasegawa
Make-up: Masanori Kobayashi
Hair: Ritsu Hanai
Kyogen (Noh mime): Chuzaburo Shigeyama
Choreography: Yukihime Harusame and the Kyoto Sento Machi Geisha Group
Noh and Kyogen adviser: Kanehichi Odera
Editor: Kanji Sugawara
Cast: Kinuyo Tanaka (Hatsuko Mabuchi), Yoshiko Kuga (Yukiko, her daughter), Eitaro Shindo (Yasuichi Harada, her protector), Tomoemon Otani (Kenji Matoba, the young doctor), Bontaro Miyake (Kobayashi), Chieko Naniwa (Osaki), Haruo Tanaka (Kawamoto), Hisao Toake (Yamada), Michiko Ai (Aioi Dayu), Sachiki Mine (Chiyo), Teruko Daimi (Onoue Dayu), Teruko Kusugi (Tamakoto Dayu), Kimiko Tachibana (Usugumo Dayu), Midori Komatsu (Okane), Kanae Kobayashi (Oharu), Sayako Nakagimi (Oteru), Setsuko Kunieda (Oyasu), Teruku Fuji (Osono)
Running time: 83 minutes
Filmed at: Daiei Studios, Kyoto
Release date: 20 June 1954

A Story from Chikamatsu, aka Crucified Lovers (Chikamatsu Monogatari, 1954)

Director: Kenji Mizoguchi
Producers: Masaichi Nagata, Hisakazu Tsuji (planning) and Masatsugu Hashimoto (production)
Script: Yoshikata Yoda, from Matsutaro Kawaguchi's adaptation of Chikamatsu Monzaemon's puppet play *Koi Hakke Hashiragoyomi* (*The Almanac of Love*), and from Iharu Saikaku's novel *Five Women Who Loved Love*
Photography: Kazuo Miyagawa
Production design: Hiroshi Mizutani, assisted by Uichiro Yamamoto and Yaichi Ebise

Lighting: Kenichi Okamoto
Costumes: Natsu Ito
Make-up: Masanori Kobayashi
Hair: Ritsu Hanai
Sound: Iwao Otani
Music: Fumio Hayasaka
Traditional music: Tamezo Mochizuki and Eijiro Toyosawa
Editor: Kanji Sugawara
Historical research: Hosei Ueno
Cast: Kazuo Hasegawa (Mohei), Kyoko Kagawa (Osan), Eitaro Shindo (Ishun), Yoko Minamida (Otama), Sakae Ozawa (Sukeyemon), Haruo Tanaka (Doki), Chieko Naniwa (Oko), Ichiro Sugai (Genbei), Hisao Toake (chamberlain Marionkoji), Shinobu Araki (majordomo), Ryonosuke Azuma (Bairyu Akamatsu), Hiroshi Mizuno (Councillor Kuroki), Ichiro Amano (blind music teacher), Kimiko Tachibana (Ocho), Reiko Kongo (maid at inn), Midori Komatsu (old woman), Keiko Koyanagi (Okaya), Kanae Kobayashi (Otatsu), Sayoko Nakagami (Osono), Koichi Katsuragi (priest), Shoji Shibata, Satoshi Mikami, Takashi Shinohara (workers)
Running time: 102 minutes
Filmed at: Daei Studios, Kyoto
Release date: 23 November 1954

The Empress Yang Kwei Fei (Yokihi, 1955)
Director: Kenji Mizoguchi
Producers: Masaichi Nagata and Run-run Shaw (Shao I-Fu), with Hisakazu Tsuji (planning)
Script: Yoshikata Yoda, Matsutaro Kawaguchi, Masashige Narusawa and Ch'in Tao from an eighth-century poem 'The Song of Unending Sorrow' by Po Chü-I
Assistant director: Yasuzo Masumura
Photography (Daieicolor): Kohei Sugiyama
Production design: Hiroshi Mizutani
Colour consultant: Tatsuyuki Yokota
Lighting: Yukikazu Kubota
Period authenticity: Lu Shih-hou
Historical research: Seko Ro
Sound: Kunio Hashimoto
Cast: Machiko Kyo (Yang Kwei Fei), Masayuki Mori (Emperor Hsüan Tsung), So Yamamura (An Lu Shan), Sakae Ozawa (Chao, later Yang Kuo-chung), Eitaro Shindo (Kao Li-hsi), Tatsuya Ishiguro (Premier Li), Isao Yamagata (Yang Hsien), Haruko Sugimura (princess Yen Ch'un), Yoko Minamida (T'ao Hung), Bontaro Akemi (Hsuan-Li Ch'en), Chieko Murata (Hua Lu), Michine Ai (Hua Hung), Noboru Kiritachi (Hua Tsui), Yukiko Murasae (Fei Ch'eng)
Running time: 98 minutes
Filmed at: Daei Studios, Kyoto
Release date: 3 May 1955

Tales of the Taira Clan (*Shinheike Monogatari*, 1955)

Director: Kenji Mizoguchi
Producers: Masaichi Nagata, Matsutaro Kawaguchi and Hideo Matsuyama (planning)
Script: Yoshikata Yoda, Masashige Narusawa and Hisakazu Tsuji, from the novel of the same name by Eiji Yoshikawa, serialised in the weekly magazine *Shukan Asahi*
Photography (Eastmancolor): Kazuo Miyagawa
Production design: Hiroshi Mizutani
Colour consultant: Mitsuzo Wada
Music: Fumio Hayasaka and Masaru Sato
Cast: Raizo Ichikawa (Taira no Kiyomori), Michiyo Kogure (Yasuko, Kiyomori's mother), Eijaro Yanagi (ex-Emperor Shirakawa), Ichijiro Oya (Tadamori, Kiyomori's father), Yoshiko Kuga (Tokiko, his fiancée), Narutoshi Hayashi (her brother), Eitaro Shindo (Banboku), Tatsuya Ishiguro (Fujiwara no Tokinobu, Tokiko's father), Shunji Natsumi (Emperor Toba), Koreya Senda (Yorinaga), Mitsusaburo Ramon (Ryokan), Ichiro Sugai (carpenter)
Running time: 108 minutes
Filmed at: Daiei Studios, Kyoto
Release date: 21 September 1955

Street of Shame (*Akasen Chitai*, 1956)

Director: Kenji Mizoguchi
Producers: Masaichi Nagata, Hisao Ichikawa (planning) and Keiichi Sakane (production)
Script: Masashige Narusawa, based on Yoshiko Shibaki's short story 'Susaki no Onna' ('The Women of Susaki')
Photography (black-and-white): Kazuo Miyagawa
Production design: Hiroshi Mizutani
Lighting: Yukio Ito
Set decoration: Kiichi Ishizaki and Shigeharu Onda
Paintings: Taro Kawahara
Special effects: Ichiro Kanda
Neon effects: Shogo Kanaya
Credits design: Outei Kaneko
Sound: Mitsuo Hasegawa, with Shojiro Hanaoka
Music: Toshiro Mayuzumi
Editor: Kanji Sugawara
Cast: Machiko Kyo (Mickey), Ayako Wakao (Yasumi), Michiyo Kogure (Hanae), Aiko Mimasu (Yumeko), Kumeko Urabe (Otane), Kenji Sugawara (Eiko), Yasuko Kawakami (Shizuko), Hiroko Machida (Yorie), Eitaro Shindo (Kurazo Taya), Sadako Sawamura (Tatsuko Taya, his wife), Toranosuke Ogawa (Mickey's father), Bontaro Miake (night guard), Daisuke Kato (policeman), Jun Tatara (Yumeko's client), Yosuke Irie (Shuichi, Yumeko's son), Kuninori Takado (Keisaku Kadowaki), Eiko Miyoshi (Saku, his wife)
Running time: 94 minutes
Filmed at: Daiei Studios, Tokyo
Release date: 18 March 1956

Lost Films

The Resurrection of Love (*Ai ni Yomigaeru Hi*, 1923)

Home Town (*Kyoko*, aka *Furusato*, 1923)

Dreams of Youth (*Seishun no Yumeji*, 1923)

City of Desire (*Joen no Chimata*, 1923)

Sad Song of Failure (*Haizan no Uta wa Kanashi*, 1923)

813: Adventures of Arsène Lupin (*813: Rupimono*, 1923)

Foggy Harbour (*Kiri no Minato*, 1923)

Blood and Soul (*Chi to Rei*, 1923)

The Night (*Yoru*, 1923)

Among the Ruins (*Haikyo no Naka*, 1923)

Song of the Mountain Pass (*Toge no Uta*, 1923)

The Sad Idiot (*Kanashiki Hakuchi*, 1924)

Death at Dawn (*Akatsuki no Shi*, 1924)

The Queen of Modern Times (*Gendai no Jo-o*, 1924)

Women Are Strong (*Josei Wa Tsuyoshi*, 1924)

This Dusty World (*Jin Kyo*, 1924)

Turkeys in a Row (*Shichimencho no Yukue*, 1924)

A Chronicle of May Rain (*Samidare Zoshi*, 1924)

A Woman of Pleasure (*Kanraku no Onna*, 1924)

The Death of Police Officer Ito (*Ito Junsa no Shi*, 1924)

Queen of the Circus (*Kyokubadan no Jo-o*, 1924)

Out of College (*Gakuso o Idete*, 1925)

No Money, No Fight (*Musen Fusen*, 1925)

The Earth Smiles (*Daichi wa Hohoemu*, 1925)

Lament of the White Lily (*Shirayuri wa Nageku*, 1925)

Shining in the Red Sunset (*Akai Yuhi ni Terasarete*, 1925)

Street Sketches (*Gaijo no Suketchi*, 1925)

The Human Being (*Ningen*, 1925)

General Nogi and Kumasan (*Nogi Taisho to Kumasan*, 1926)

The Copper Coin King (*Doka-O*, 1926)

A Paper Doll's Whisper of Spring (*Kaminingyo Haru no Sasayaki*, 1926)

My Fault, New Version (*Shin Ono ga Tsumi*, 1926)

The Passion of a Woman Teacher (*Kyoren no Onna Shisho*, 1926)

The Boy of the Sea (*Kaikoku Danji*, 1926)

Money (*Kane*, 1926)

Imperial Favour (*Ko-On*, 1927)

The Cuckoo (aka *A Loving Heart*) (*Jihi Shincho*, 1927)

A Man's Life (*Hito no Issho*, 1928)

My Lovely Daughter (aka *What a Charming Girl*) (*Musume Kawaiya*, 1928)

The Bridge of Nihon (*Nihonbashi*, 1929)

The Morning Sun Shines (*Asahi wa Kagayaku*, 1929)

Metropolitan Symphony (*Tokai Kokyogaku*, 1929)
Mistress of a Foreigner (*Tojin Okichi*, 1930)
And Yet They Go (*Shikamo Karera Wa Yuku*, 1931)
Man of the Moment (aka *The Gods of Our Time*) (*Toki no Ujigami*, 1932)
The Dawn of Manchuria and Mongolia (*Manmo Kenkoku no Reimei*, 1932)
Gion Festival (*Gion Matsuri*, 1933)
The Jinpu Group (*Jinpuren*, 1934)
The Mountain Pass of Love and Hate (*Aizo Toge*, 1934)
Ah, My Home Town (*Aa Kokyo*, 1938)
The Song of the Camp (*Roei no Uta*, 1938)
The Woman of Osaka (*Naniwa Onna*, 1940)
The Life of an Actor (*Geido Ichidai Otoko*, 1941)
Three Generations of Danjuro (*Danjuro Sandai*, 1944)
Victory Song (*Hisshoka*, 1945)

Further Reading

The reader who is interested in Japan's culture but does not speak Japanese is lucky, because there is a fine tradition of writers on Japan in the English language who express themselves with scholarship, clarity and elegance. The tradition in question goes back to the re-discovery of Japan by the West in the 1860s. Scholar–diplomats like Ernest Satow, Sir Rutherford Alcock and Lord Redesdale, who first gave the world their impressions of the newly opened country, are still readable today (a taste that is shared, in fact, by the Japanese themselves, or at least some of them – Alcock was one of Kafu Nagai's favourite writers). Sir George Sansom is another fine pillar of this tradition: everything he writes about the country is lucid and interesting – traits shared, closer to the present day, by his American 'equivalent', ex-ambassador Edwin O. Reischauer. Brilliant interpreters of Japan in English abound, in fact: a short list of authorities would include: (from the past) Lafcadio Hearn and Sir Arthur Waley, along with Waley's pupil Ivan Morris; (from the present) Donald Keene, John Dower (that fine modern historian), and the polymathic cultural critic, Ian Buruma.

These are the writers on Japan whom anyone should read for an essential grounding in the country's manners, customs and history. Another kind of knowledge is literary. A number of novels and memoirs have made a strong mark on me: Tanizaki's *The Makioka Sisters* (1957) read many years ago in the translation by Edward G. Seidensticker; also another extraordinary twentieth-century novel, this time in English, *The Ginger Tree*, by Oswald Wynd; and two absorbing memoirs, *The Railway Man* (1995) by Eric Lomax (a magnificent tale of Anglo-Japanese reconciliation set against the background of the construction of the Burma–Siam railway) and *Yet Being Someone Other* (1982) by Laurens Van der Post (a wonderfully Conradian account of a friendship with a Japanese sea captain during the course of a voyage to Japan that Van der Post made with William Plomer in 1926). In my opinion, these four works have great spiritual power and really tell you something true about the Japanese mentality. Less 'exalted', but in their own way thought-provoking, and even profound, are two memoirs by younger authors whose subtitles bespeak a complementary perspective: *Pictures from the Water Trade: An Englishman in Japan* (1985) by John David Morley and *The Old Sow in the Back Room: An Englishwoman in Japan* (1994) by Harriet Sargeant.

Sargeant's witty, self-deprecating and astute book reminds me how finely Japanese culture and history has been served by women writers. There was Ruth Benedict in the 1940s (*The Chrysanthemum and the Sword: Patterns of Japanese Culture* – a key text), and more recently a host of scholars whose works will inevitably figure on the reading list of any student of the subject: Keiko McDonald (doyenne of writers about Mizoguchi in English), Joan Mellen, Audie Bock, Kyoko Hirano, Joanne Bernardi, Chika Kinoshita etc. Many of the best writers about geisha are women: sections of the present work rely heavily on the scholarship of women who have really got into this world such as Lesley Downer, Liza Dalby and Cecilia Segawa Seigle. As with any writer worthy of the name, it is not only what is said, but the way it is said. How liberal these writers seem in their judgments, how unembattled politically (so to speak) and how sophisticated. Perhaps it is not really so remarkable: Japanese prose literature, after all, began a thousand years ago with the twin lightning bolts of Lady Murasaki and Sei Shonagon. Marvellous women novelists have continued this tradition into the twentieth century (a favourite of mine being Fumiko Enchi).

When it comes to film criticism itself, my reader may be aware, and perhaps disappointed, that I have gone out of my way to resist being 'controversial'. *Mizoguchi and Japan* is an introductory essay: I have been less interested in engaging with the positions of previous scholars and critics than I have been in attempting to find out (and put down clearly in writing) what I myself think about Mizoguchi. Attested authorities on the Japanese film such as Noël Burch, David Bordwell and David Desser have not been closed with – deliberately. In so far as my book does place itself in the orbit of a critical tradition, it looks towards the lively Japanophile journalism provided by such magazines as *Positif* and *Cahiers du Cinéma* in France, and by the film columns (extensive and generous) of literary magazines such as *The New Yorker* and *The New York Review of Books*. Many of the critics I admire most are journalists, or at least part-time journalists: André Bazin (naturally), David Thomson, Andrew Sarris, Michel Ciment, Hubert Niogret, Jean-Loup Bourget are some of them.

Four books in particular have been indispensable during the months of writing this study. Anderson and Richie's pioneer research effort, *The Japanese Film: Art and Industry* (1959, new edition 1982) provides all the background necessary. It is written moreover in clear approachable prose. Next, Yoshikata Yoda: readers who have got as far as this will know how much I owe to the Japanese screenwriter's memoirs, accessed through the French edition brought out a few years ago by *Cahiers du Cinéma*. His is truly a close-up portrait, 'warts and all' as was said of Carlyle's Cromwell. Living in Mizoguchi's company day in day out for over twenty-five years, Yoda brings the director to life as no one else is capable of doing.

A third book that has never left my desk came out as long ago as 1981: this is Dudley and Paul Andrew's *Kenji Mizoguchi: A Guide to References and Resources*, a fine work of scholarship, and *really* indispensable (the word can be overused, but not in this case). I have frequently consulted it, in tandem with James Quandt and Gerald O'Grady's *Mizoguchi the Master* (1996), a thick newspaper-format catalogue produced to accompany the centenary retrospectives of Mizoguchi's films that took place from the middle to late 1990s. This catalogue may not be the most beautiful thing in the world to look at, but it is packed full of facts, opinions and readings, from a variety of sources. In addition, it contains the fullest bibliography of writings on Mizoguchi currently available (including the key Japanese sources).

Books and Articles Consulted

Adair, Gilbert. *Flickers: An Illustrated Celebration of 100 Years of Cinema*. London: Faber & Faber, 1995.

Akinari, Ueda. *Ugetsu Monogatari: Tales of Moonlight and Rain*. Ed. and trans. Leon M. Zolbrod. New York, 1977.

Alcock, Rutherford. *The Capital of the Tycoon: A Narrative of a Three-Year Residence in Japan*. 2 vols, New York: Greenwood Press, n.d. [1863].

Anderson, Joseph and Donald Richie. *The Japanese Film: Art and Industry* [1959]. Princeton, NJ: Princeton University Press, 1982.

Anderson J[oseph] L. 'Spoken Silents in the Japanese Cinema; or, Talking to Pictures', in A. Nolletti Jnr and D. Desser (eds). *Reframing Japanese Cinema: Authorship, Genre, History*. Bloomington and Indianapolis: Indiana University Press, 1992.

Andrew, Dudley. *Film in the Aura of Art*. Princeton, NJ: Princeton University Press, 1984.

Andrew, Dudley and Carole Cavanaugh. *Sansho Dayu*. London: BFI, 2000.

Andrew, Dudley and Paul Andrew. *Kenji Mizoguchi: A Guide to References and Resources*. Boston: G. K. Hall, 1981.

Barba, Eugenio and Nicola Savarese (eds). *The Secret Life of the Performer: A Dictionary of Theatre Anthropology*. London: Routledge, 1991.

Bazin, André. *Orson Welles: A Critical View*. New York: Harper Colophon, 1978.

Bazin, André. *What Is Cinema?* 2 vols. Ed. and trans. Hugh Gray. Berkeley: University of California Press, 1967.

Bazin, André. *The Cinema of Cruelty from Buñuel to Hitchcock*. Ed. and intr. by François Truffaut, trans. Sabine d'Estrée. New York: Seaver Books, 1982.

Beasley, W. G. 'Modern Japan: A Historian's View', in *Modern Japan: Aspects of History, Literature and Society*. Berkeley: University of California Press, 1975.

Benedict, Ruth. *The Chrysanthemum and the Sword: Patterns of Japanese Culture* [1946]. New York, 1974.

Benfey, Christopher. *The Great Wave: Gilded Age Misfits, Japanese Eccentrics and the Opening of Old Japan*. New York: Random House, 2003.

Bernardi, Joanne. '*Ugetsu Monogatari*: The Screenplay', in J. Quandt and G. O'Grady (eds). *Mizoguchi the Master* (see below).

Bock, Audie. *Japanese Film Directors*. Tokyo: Kodansha International, 1978.

Bordwell, David. *Ozu and the Poetics of Cinema*. London and Princeton: BFI, 1988.

Bordwell, David. 'Mizoguchi and the Evolution of Film Language', in S. Heath and P. Mellencamp (eds), *Cinema and Language*. Frederick: University Publications of America, 1983.

Bordwell, David. 'Visual Style in Japanese Cinema, 1925–1945', *Film History* vol. 7 no. 1, 1995.

Bourget, Jean-Loup. *L'Histoire au cinéma: le passé retrouvé*. Paris: Gallimard, 1992.

Bremmer, Jan and Herman Roodenburg (eds). *A Cultural History of Gesture*. Cambridge: Cambridge University Press, 1991.

Burch, Noël. *To the Distant Observer: Form and Meaning in the Japanese Cinema*. London: Scolar Press, 1979.

Burch, Noël. 'Approaching Japanese Cinema', in S. Heath and P. Mellencamp (eds). *Cinema and Language*. Frederick: University Publications of America, 1983.

Buruma, Ian. *A Japanese Mirror: Heroes and Villains of Japanese Culture*. London: Cape, 1984.

Buruma, Ian. 'MacArthur's Children', in *The New York Review of Books*, 21 October 1999.

Buruma, Ian. *Inventing Japan: From Empire to Economic Miracle 1853–1964*. New York: The Modern Library, 2003.

Cahiers du Cinéma. Paris, 1951– [Monthly film magazine founded by André Bazin and Jacques Daniel-Volcroze over fifty years ago, and still publishing. For *Cahiers* early encounters with Mizoguchi, see Appendix 1 of the present work: 'Mizoguchi and French Film Criticism'. Later issues keep up the interest:

No. 95 (May 1959) contains a translated text by Mizoguchi entitled 'Mes Films' in which the director delivers himself of precious, if laconic, comments on each of his films up till *Gion Festival Music* (1953). I have used this frequently in the present study.

During the 1960s, *Cahiers* published an important issue containing interviews by Ariane Mnouchkine with Mizoguchi collaborators Yoshikata Yoda, Kazuo Miyagawa, Matsutaro Kawaguchi, Eiji Takagi, Hiroshi Mizutani, Kinuyo Tanaka, and Kyuichi Tsuji (no. 158, August–September 1964).

Later in the same decade, the magazine brought out Yoda's memoirs across eight separate issues of the magazine (nos 166–7, 169, 172, 174, 181, 186, 192 and 206).

An 'hors série' dossier on Mizoguchi in September 1978 reunited all these essays and interviews, publishing them together with a new filmography devised by Tony Rayns. *Cahiers*' championship of Mizoguchi is long-standing and consistent: Jean Douchet, who contributed two essays on the director in no. 114 (December 1960) was/is still on hand to edit an important Mizoguchi dossier thirty-two years later (no. 463, December 1992: interviews with soundman Iwao Otani, Daiei producer Akinari Suzuki and Mizoguchi himself, all dating from 1951, plus a long essay by Douchet himself: 'La Réflexion du désir'). *Cahiers* returned to the subject once again in its July–August 1996 issue, in a dossier prepared by Emmanuel Burdeau and Thierry Lounas ('Mizoguchi encore': no. 504 – contemporary *Cahiers* critics deliver their opinions on a wide selection of Mizoguchi movies). More recently, the cinema of the 'long take', under the aegis of Mizoguchi, has been intelligently examined by Jean-Marc Lalanne and Olivier Joyard in two special Cannes editions (nos 569 [June 2002] and 580 [June 2003]: 'C'est quoi ce plan?')]

Carrière, Jean-Claude. *The Secret Language of Film*. London: Faber & Faber, 1995.

Chang, Iris. *The Rape of Nanking*. New York: Penguin, 1997.

Chikamatsu Monzaemon. 'The Almanac of Love'/Koi Hakké Hashiragoyomi [1715], in *Masterpieces of Chikamatsu*. Trans. Asataro Miyamori. London: Kegan Paul, 1926.

Clark, Timothy and A. N. Morse. *The Dawn of the Floating World*. London: Royal Academy of Arts, 2001.

Cortazzi, Hugh (ed.). *Mitford's Japan: The Memoirs and Recollections of the First Lord Redesdale*. London: Athlone Press, 1985.

Dalby, Liza Crihfield. *Geisha* [1983]. Berkeley: University of California Press, new edition, 1998.

De Bary, William Theodore (ed. and trans.) *Saikaku's Five Women Who Loved Love*. Rutland: Tuttle Publishing, 1956.

Dower, John W. *War without Mercy: Race and Power in the Pacific War*. New York: Pantheon Books, 1986.

Dower, John W. *Japan in War and Peace: Selected Essays*. New York: New Press, 1993.

Dower, John. *Embracing Defeat: Japan in the Aftermath of World War II*. New York: W. W. Norton & Co., 1999.

Downer, Lesley. *Women of the Pleasure Quarters: The Secret History of the Geisha*. New York: Broadway Books, 2001.

Downer, Lesley. *Madame Sadayakko: The Geisha Who Bewitched the West*. New York: Gotham Books, 2003.

Enchi, Fumiko. *Masks* (a novel) [1959]. Trans. J. W. Carpenter. London: Random House, 1985.

Encyclopedia of Japan [Indispensable English-language work in nine volumes]. Tokyo: Kodansha, 1983.

Fong, Wen C. *Beyond Representation: Chinese Painting and Calligraphy 8th–14th Century*. New York, New Haven and London: Metropolitan Museum of Art, Yale University Press, 1992.

Freiberg, Freda. *Women in Mizoguchi Films*. Melbourne: Japanese Film Studies Centre, 1981.

Golden, Arthur. *Memoirs of a Geisha* (novel). London: Chatto & Windus, 1997.

Goossen, Theodore W. (ed.). *The Oxford Book of Japanese Short Stories*. Oxford: Oxford University Press, 1997.

Hibbert, Hugh. *The Floating World in Japanese Fiction*. New York: Oxford University Press, 1959.

High, Peter B. *The Imperial Screen: Japanese Film Culture in the Fifteen Years War of 1931–1945*. Madison: University of Wisconsin Press, 2003.

Hillier, Jim (ed.). *Cahiers du Cinéma: The 1950s – Neo-Realism, Hollywood, New Wave*. Cambridge, MA: Harvard University Press, 1985.

Hirano, Kyoko. *Mr Smith Goes to Tokyo: Japanese Cinema under the American Occupation 1945–1952*. Washington and London: Smithsonian Institute, 1992.

Hollander, Anne. *Moving Pictures*. New York: Knopf, 1989.

Horie-Webber, A. 'Modernisation of the Japanese Theatre: The Shingeki Movement', in W. G. Beasley (ed.). *Modern Japan: Aspects of History, Literature and Society*. Berkeley: University of California Press, 1975.

Ikeda, Daisuku and Makoto Nemoto. *On the Japanese Classics: A Conversation*. New York and Tokyo: Weatherhill, 1979.

Iwamoto, Kenji. 'Sound in the Early Japanese Talkies', in A. Nolletti Jnr and D. Desser (eds). *Reframing Japanese Cinema*. Bloomington and Indiana: Indiana University Press, 1992.

Jansen, Marius B. *The Making of Modern Japan*. Cambridge and London: Harvard University Press, 2000.

Jenkins, Donald (ed.). *The Floating World Revisited*. Portland and Honolulu: Portland Museum and University of Hawaii Press, 1993.

Kano, Ayako. *Acting Like a Woman in Modern Japan: Theatre, Gender and Nationalism*. New York: Palgrave, 2001.

Keene, Donald. *Major Plays of Chikamatsu*. New York: Columbia University Press, 1961.

Keene, Donald. 'Realism and Unreality in Japanese Drama', in *Landscapes and Portraits: Appreciations of Japanese Culture*. Tokyo: Kodansha International, 1971.

Keene, Donald. *The Pleasures of Japanese Literature*. New York: Columbia University Press, 1988.

Keene, Donald. *On Familiar Terms. A Journey across Cultures*. New York: Kodansha International, 1994.

Keene, Donald. *Dawn to the West: A History of Japanese Literature*. 4 vols. New York: Columbia University Press, 1998.

Keene, Donald. *Emperor of Japan: Meiji and His World 1852–1912*. New York: Columbia University Press, 2002.

King, Francis (ed. and intr.) *Lafcadio Hearn: Writings from Japan – an Anthology*. London: Penguin, 1984.

Kinoshita, Chika. 'Floating Sound: Sound and Image in *The Story of the Last Chrysanthemum*', in J. Quandt and G. O'Grady (eds). *Mizoguchi the Master* [q.v.].

Kirihara, Donald. 'Kabuki, Cinema and Mizoguchi Kenji', in S. Heath and P. Mellencamp (eds). *Cinema and Language*. Los Angeles, 1983.

Kirihara, Donald. *Patterns of Time: Mizoguchi in the 1930s*. Madison: University of Wisconsin Press, 1992.

Kishi, Matsuo. 'Mizoguchi Kenji', in *Jinbutsu: Nihon Eiga Shi [Personages: A History of Japanese Film]*, vol. 1. Tokyo, 1970. [An essential biographical source in Japanese from which many of the shorter English-language sketches, such as that in Andrew and Andrew (1981), draw their material.]

Kiyosawa, Kiyoshi. *Diary of Darkness: The Wartime Diary of Kiyosawa Kiyoshi*. Trans. Eugene Soviak and Kamiyama Tamie. Princeton: Princeton University Press, 1998.

Komatsu, Hiroshi. 'The Fundamental Change: Japanese Cinema Before and After the Earthquake of 1923', in *Griffithiana* no. 38/39, Gemona, 1990.

Kurosawa, Akira. *Something Like an Autobiography*. Trans. Audie Bock. New York: Knopf, 1982.

Lameris, Bregtje. 'Writing the Lost Films', in *The Collegium Papers* (III). Pordenone, Le Giornate del Cinema Muto, 2001.

Lane, Richard. *Images from the Floating World*. Fribourg: Alpine Fine Arts Collection, 1978.

Le Fanu, Mark. 'To Love is to Suffer: Reflections on the Later Cinema of Heinosuke Gosho', *Sight and Sound* vol. 55 no. 3, 1986.

Le Fanu, Mark. 'Metaphysics of the Long Take: Some Post-Bazinian Reflections', in *P.O.V.: A Danish Journal of Film Studies* no. 4, December 1997.

Le Fanu, Mark. 'On Editing', in *P.O.V.* no. 6, December 1998 <imv.au.dk/publikationer/pov/POV.html>.

Liddell, Jill. *The Story of the Kimono*. New York: E. P. Dutton, 1989.

Lomax, Eric. *The Railway Man*. London: Jonathan Cape, 1995.

Maruyama, Masao. *Thought and Behaviour in Modern Japanese Politics*. Trans. and ed. Ivan Morris. Oxford: Oxford University Press, 1963.

Masuda, Sayo. *Autobiography of a Geisha* [1957]. Trans. G. G. Rowley. New York: Columbia University Press, 2003.

Maupassant, Guy de. 'Décoré!', in *Les Soeurs Rondoli*. Paris: P. Ollendorff, 1884.

MacArthur, Brian. *Surviving the Sword*. London: Time Warner, 2005.

McCullough, Helen Craig (trans. and ed.). *Genji and Heike: Selections from* The Tale of Genji *and* The Tale of the Heike. Stanford: Stanford University Press, 1994.

McDonald, Keiko. *Mizoguchi*. Boston: Twayne Publishers, 1984.

McDonald, Keiko I. *Japanese Classical Theatre in Films*. London and Toronto: Associated University Press, 1994.

McDonald, Keiko (ed. and intr.). *Ugetsu: Kenji Mizoguchi, Director* [English translation of the film's shooting script, with contextual materials by various hands]. New Brunswick: Rutgers University Press, 1993.

Mellen, Joan. *The Waves at Genji's Door: Japan through Its Cinema*. New York: Pantheon, 1976.

Mesnil, Michel (ed.). *Kenji Mizoguchi*. Paris: Éditions Seghers, 1965.

Milne, Tom (ed. and trans.). *Godard on Godard*. London: Secker and Warburg, 1972.

Miyagawa, Kazuo. *The Life of a Cameraman*. Tokyo: PHP Kenkyujo, 1985.

Morley, John David. *Pictures from the Water Trade: An Englishman in Japan*. London: André Deutsch, 1985.

Morris, Ivan. *The World of the Shining Prince: Court Life in Ancient Japan*. Oxford: Oxford University Press, 1964.

Morris, Ivan. *The Nobility of Failure*. London: Secker and Warburg, 1975.

Morris, Ivan (trans. and ed.). *The Life of an Amorous Woman, by Iharu Saikaku*. New York: New Directions, 1963.

Morris, Ivan (trans. and ed.). *The Pillow Book of Sei Shonagon*. New York: Columbia University Press, 1991.

Nagai, Kafu. *During the Rains and Flowers in the Shade: Two Novellas*. Trans. Lane Dunlop. Stanford: Stanford University Press, 1994.

Nolletti, Arthur, Jnr. *The Cinema of Gosho Heinosuke: Laughter Through Tears*. Bloomington: University of Indiana Press, 2004.

Ohnuki-Tierney, Emiko. *Kamikaze, Cherry Blossoms and Nationalisms: The Militarization of Aesthetics in Japanese History*. Chicago and London: University of Chicago Press, 2002.

Positif. Paris, 1952– [The 'other' French film magazine, along with *Cahiers du Cinéma*, its great rival. *Positif*'s earliest issues espoused a poetics of revolt: it was left-wing and atheist (whereas *Cahiers* – in those days – was liberal and Catholic). The magazine's attachment to surrealism made it unfriendly towards the spirituality of certain directors of the period – Mizoguchi included, but also Bresson, Bergman and Dreyer – whose works hint, in places, at religious transcendence. Times change, however: *Positif* has always been a essentially inclusive rather than an exclusive magazine, and many of its contributors have written incisively on Japanese cinema.

Four issues in particular contain outstanding dossiers on Mizoguchi: no. 212, November 1978 (essays by Gérard Legrand, Alain Masson and Hubert Niogret), and nos 236–8 inclusive (November and December 1980; January 1981).

No. 236 has Mizoguchi's text on *The Loyal 47 Ronin*, along with essays by Alain Masson and Yann Tobin, and an important interview with Yoda by Hubert Niogret and Dudley Andrew.

The following issue (237) contains a transcript in translation of the first part of a 'table ronde' that Mizoguchi took part in, in 1936, in the offices of the Tokyo film magazine *Kinema Jumpo*. No. 238 concludes the 'table ronde', and winds up the three-part enquiry with a long (translated) essay by Dudley Andrew: 'Kenji Mizoguchi: La passion de l'identification'.

Subsequently, the magazine has carried several excellent dossiers on Japanese cinema classical and contemporary, for example no. 388 (June 1993: essays by Agnès Peck, Gérard Legrand, Max Tessier, Hubert Niogret and Michel Ciment).]

Powell, Brian. 'Matsui Sumako: Actress and Woman', in W. G. Beasley (ed.). *Modern Japan: Aspects of History, Literature and Society*. Berkeley: University of California Press, 1975.

Powell, Brian. *Kabuki in Modern Japan: Mayama Seika and His Plays*. London, 1990.

Quandt, James and Gerald O'Grady (eds). *Mizoguchi the Master*. Toronto: Ontario Cinemathèque, 1996.

[Collector's item: a newspaper-format catalogue prepared for the Mizoguchi centenary retrospective by James Quandt of the Ontario Cinemathèque, the dossier contains transcripts of historical interviews with the director conducted by Matsuo Kishi, Tsuneo Hazumi and Hajime Takizawa, along with interesting first-hand reminiscences by Mizoguchi's colleagues, Yoshikata Yoda, Masashige Narusawa, Isuzu Yamada, Hiroshi Mizutani, Koji Asaka and Shin Okada. In addition, there are separate essays by twenty-six modern critics on different aspects of the Mizoguchi oeuvre and an extensive bibliography prepared by Gerald O'Grady].

Quennell, Peter. *The Marble Foot: An Autobiography 1905–1938*. New York: Viking Press, 1976.

Quennell, Peter. *A Superficial Journey through Tokyo and Peking*. London: Faber & Faber, 1932. Reprinted New York: Oxford University Press, 1986.

Reischauer, Edwin O. *Japan Past and Present* [1946]. New York: Knopf, 1964.

Reischauer, Edwin and John Fairbank. *East Asia: The Great Tradition*. Boston: Houghton Mifflin, 1958.

Reischauer, Edwin, John Fairbank and Albert Craig. *East Asia: The Modern Transformation*. Boston: Houghton Mifflin, 1965.

Richards, Jeffrey. *Visions of Yesterday*. London: Routledge and Kegan Paul, 1973.

Richie, Donald, *Japanese Cinema: Film Style and National Character*. London: Doubleday, 1972.

Richie, Donald [with additional material by Joan Mellen]. *The Films of Akira Kurosawa*. Berkeley, Los Angeles and London: University of California Press, 1984.

Richie, Donald. *A Lateral View: Essays on Culture and Style in Contemporary Japan*. Berkeley: Stone Bridge Press, 1992.

Richie, Donald. *A Hundred Years of Japanese Film: A Concise History with a Selective Guide to Videos and DVDs*. Tokyo, New York, London: Kodansha International, 2001.

Said, Edward. *Orientalism: Western Conceptions of the Orient*. New York: Pantheon Books, 1978.

Sansom, George. *The Western World and Japan: A Study in the Interaction of European and Asiatic Cultures*. New York: Knopf, 1950.

Sansom, George. *A History of Japan*. 3 vols. London: Dawson, 1958–63.

Sansom, George. *Japan: A Short Cultural History* [1931]. London: The Cresset Library, 1987.

Sargeant, Harriet. *The Old Sow in the Back Room: An Englishwoman in Japan*. London: John Murray, 1994.

Sarris, Andrew. 'Ugetsu: A Meditation on Mizoguchi', in Philip Nobile (ed.). Favorite Movies: Critics' Choice. New York: Macmillan, 1973.

Sato, Tadao. Currents in Japanese Cinema. Trans. Gregory Barrett. Tokyo: Kodansha International, 1982.

Sato, Tadao. Mizoguchi Kenji no Sekai/The World of Kenji Mizoguchi. Tokyo: Chikuma Shobo, 1982 [written in Japanese: I possess a manuscript copy of this in French, trans. Jean-Paul Le Pape].

Sato, Tadao. 'Théâtre et cinéma au Japon', in Max Tessier (ed.). Cinéma et littérature de l'ère Meiji à nos jours, Paris: Centre Georges Pompidou, 1986.

Sato, Tadao. Le Cinéma Japonais. 2 vols. Paris: Centre Georges Pompidou, 1997.

Satow, Ernest. A Diplomat in Japan. London: Seeley, Service & Co. Ltd, 1921.

Screech, Timon. The Lens within the Heart: The Western Scientific Gaze and Popular Imagery in Later Edo Japan. Cambridge: Cambridge University Press, 1996.

Screech, Timon. Sex and the Floating World: Erotic Images in Japan 1700–1820. London: Reaktion, 1999.

Scruton, Roger. Death-devoted Heart: Sex and the Sacred in Wagner's 'Tristan and Isolde'. New York: Oxford University Press, 2004.

Seidensticker, Edward. Kafu the Scribbler: The Life and Writings of Nagai Kafu 1879–1959. Stanford: Stanford University Press, 1965.

Seidensticker, Edward (trans.) The Tale of Genji. 2 vols. New York: Knopf, 1976.

Seidensticker, Edward. Tokyo Rising: The City since the Great Earthquake. New York: Knopf, 1990.

Seidensticker, Edward. Tokyo Central: A Memoir. Seattle: University of Washington Press, 2002.

Shindo, Kaneto and Yoshikazu Hayashi (eds). Creativity in Hiroshi Mizutani's Cinematic Art. Tokyo, 1973 [In Japanese: extracts trans. for the author by Kimitoshi Sato].

Shively, Donald, James Brandon and William Malm. Studies in Kabuki: Its Acting, Music and Historical Context. Honolulu: University of Hawaii, 1978.

Shively, Donald H. and Albert M. Craig (eds). Personality in Japanese History. Ann Arbor: Centre for Japanese Studies, University of Michigan, 1995.

Silva, Arturo (ed. and intr.). The Donald Richie Reader: 50 Years of Writing on Japan. Berkeley: Stone Bridge Press, 2001.

Takashina, Shuji, J. Thomas Rimer and Gerald D. Bolas (eds). Paris in Japan: The Japanese Encounter with European Painting. Tokyo and St Louis: The Japan Foundation, 1987.

Tanizaki, Junichiro. The Makioka Sisters. Trans. Edward G. Seidensticker. New York: Knopf, 1957.

Tanizaki, Junichiro. Childhood Years: A Memoir. Trans. Paul McCarthy. Tokyo: Collins, 1988.

Tessier, Max. Images du cinéma japonais. Paris: H. Veyrier, 1981.

Tessier, Max (ed.) Cinéma et littérature de l'ère Meiji à nos jours. Paris: Centre Georges Pompidou, 1986.

Thomson, David. Entry on Mizoguchi in A Biographical Dictionary of Film [1975]. London: André Deutsch, 1994.

Truffaut, François. Les Films de ma vie [1975]. London: Allen Lane, 1980.

Tsumura, Hideo. *Mizoguchi Kenji to Iu Onoko [A Man Called Mizoguchi Kenji]*. Tokyo: Film Art Center, 1977. [In Japanese: selected translations made for the author by Kimitoshi Sato].

Van der Post, Laurens. *Yet Being Someone Other*. London: Hogarth Press, 1982.

Ve-Ho [Ho-Xich-Ve]. *Kenji Mizoguchi*. Paris: Éditions Universitaires, 1963.

Waley, Arthur. *An Introduction to the Study of Chinese Poetry* [1923]. New York, 1958.

Waley, Arthur. *The Secret History of the Mongols and Other Essays*. London: Allen & Unwin, 1963.

Wichmann, Siegfried. *Japonisme: The Japanese Influence on Western Art since 1858*. London: Thames and Hudson, 1981.

Wood, Robin. 'The Ghost Princess and the Seaweed Gatherer', in *Personal Views: Explorations in Film*. London: G. Fraser, 1976.

Wood, Robin. 'On *Sisters of the Gion*', in J. Quandt and G. O'Grady (eds). *Mizoguchi the Master*. Toronto: Ontario Cinemathèque, 1996.

Wynd, Oswald. *The Ginger Tree* (novel). London: Collins, 1977.

Yamaguchi, Takeshi (ed.). *Mizoguchi Kenji*. Tokyo: Heibonsha, 1998 [Comprehensive centennial album in Japanese, with photographs: selected translations made for the author by Kimitoshi Sato and Shuko Noguchi].

Yoda, Yoshikata. *Mizoguchi Kenji no Hito to Geijutsu*. [Tokyo, 1964]. Translated into French as *Souvenirs de Kenji Mizoguchi* by Koichi Yamada, Bernard Béraud and André Moulin. Paris: Petite Bibliothèque des Cahiers du Cinéma, 1997.

Young, Louise. *Japan's Total Empire: Manchuria and the Culture of Wartime Imperialism*. Berkeley: University of California Press, 1998.

List of Illustrations

Sansho the Bailiff, Daiei; *Victory of Women*, Shochiku Ofuna; *Five Women Round Utamaro*, Shochiku Co. Ltd; *Miss Oyu*, Daiei; *Tales of the Taira Clan*, Daiei; *Street of Shame*, Daiei; *Ugetsu Monogatari*, Daiei; *The Life of Oharu*, Shintoho Eiga/Koi; *Gion Festival Music*, Daiei; *Sisters of the Gion*, Daiichi Eiga; *The Woman of Rumour*, Daiei; *Chikamatsu Monogatari*, Daiei; *The Loyal 47 Ronin*, Koa Eiga/Shochiku Co. Ltd; *The Empress Yang Kwei Fei*, Daiei/Shaw Brothers; *The Love of Sumako the Actress*, Shochiku Co. Ltd; *My Love Has Been Burning*, Shochiku Co. Ltd; *The Downfall of Osen*, Daiichi Eiga; *The Story of Late Chrysanthemum*s, Shochiku Co. Ltd.

Index

Page numbers in *italics* indicate illustrations; those in **bold** indicate entries in the filmography; n = endnote.